Middle Grounds

studies in contemporary American fiction

Middle

studies
American

University of Pennsylvania Press · Philadelphia

Grounds

in contemporary fiction

Alan Wilde

Penn Studies in Contemporary American Fiction
a series edited by Emory Elliott, Princeton University

Copyright © 1987 by the University of Pennsylvania Press
All rights reserved
Printed in the United States of America

Library of Congress Cataloging-in-Publication Data
Wilde, Alan.
   Middle grounds.

   (Penn studies in contemporary American fiction)
   Bibliography: p.
   Includes index.
   1. American fiction—20th century—History and
criticism.   I. Title.
PS379.W497   1987   813'.54'09   87-13877
ISBN 0-8122-8069-5

Designed by Adrianne Onderdonk Dudden

for Daniel O'Hara

contents

acknowledgments

However many months, even years, one spends in what seems to be unbroken, solitary labor, one is always engaged in a conversation of sorts. There are, written covertly into the pages that follow, the suggestions, challenges, questions, and encouragement—or simply the very welcome voices—of the following friends and colleagues whom I would here like to thank overtly: Zack Bowen, Charles Caramello, Timothy Corrigan, L. S. Dembo, Ellen Kimbel, Susan Lanser, Joan Lindquist, Larry McCaffery, Marjorie Perloff, Margaret Rowe, Robert Storey, and Jane Tompkins. I am also particularly grateful to my students in two graduate seminars on contemporary American fiction both for allowing me to try out my theories on them and for entering themselves, with unfailing intelligence and enthusiasm, into what were for me the most profitable of dialogues.

Three special debts require a separate paragraph. David Kennedy, whose knowledge of even the most neglected byroads of contemporary fiction continues to startle me, has steered me again and again onto the right path. Jack Undank, thanks to his painstaking and unsparing reading of the entire manuscript and to his always illuminating suggestions, made each chapter far better than it would otherwise have been. The book is dedicated to Daniel O'Hara, once my student, now the best of colleagues and friends. To his critical intelligence, his genuine concern with the life of the mind, his humane attitude to so many of the problems I canvass in the pages that follow, and, most especially, to his friendship, I owe more than it is possible to indicate here.

This work was written with the generous help of a fellowship from the John

Simon Guggenheim Memorial Foundation and with the equally generous aid of a study-leave from Temple University. I want to acknowledge with gratitude the support of both, and of my Dean, Lois Cronholm.

Thanks to the various editors at the University of Pennsylvania Press, the transformation of manuscript into book has been both pleasant and expeditious. Zachary W. Simpson has been especially helpful and encouraging, and I am happy to record my debt to him.

I am grateful to three journals and to their editors, L. S. Dembo, Albert Frank Gegenheimer, and William V. Spanos, for having published earlier versions of some chapters and for permission to reprint them. The essays are: "'Strange Displacements of the Ordinary': Apple, Elkin, Barthelme, and the Problem of the Excluded Middle," *boundary* 2, 10 (Winter 1982), 177–99; "Shooting for Smallness: Limits and Values in Some Recent American Fiction," *boundary* 2, 13 (Winter/Spring 1985), 343–69 (copyright *boundary* 2, 1982, 1985 respectively); "Dayanu: Max Apple and the Ethics of Sufficiency," *Contemporary Literature*, 26 (Fall 1985), 254–85 (copyright 1985 by the Board of Regents of the University of Wisconsin System); "Acts of Definition, or Who Is Thomas Berger?," *The Arizona Quarterly*, 39 (Winter 1983), 312–50 (copyright 1984 by Arizona Board of Regents).

The index for this book was prepared by Robin Nilon with admirable skill and care. My final thanks and gratitude go to her.

It is among the miseries of the present age that it recognizes no medium between literal and metaphorical.
S. T. *Coleridge*, The Statesman's Manual

So all the time objects are calling to me, whether I answer them or not.
E. M. *Forster*, Commonplace Book

Alas: for where Fancy's springs are unlevee'd by hard Experience they run too free, flooding every situation with possibilities until Prudence and even Common Sense are drowned.
John Barth, "Anonymiad"

introduction

chances for diversity

Perhaps humanism cannot be radically denied or disavowed—at least not by a human voice.

Fred R. Dallmayr, *"Is Critical Theory a Humanism?"*

Probably the first thing that needs to be said about this book is that the middles or middle grounds to which its title refers are both varied and interrelated. When I began, it was with the hope of explaining to myself (and others) why the work of several impressive contemporary American writers has been, as I continue to see it, either relatively overlooked (Max Apple, Ted Mooney, Thomas Berger) or misconstrued (Donald Barthelme, Thomas Pynchon). I soon came to realize that these writers and others had fallen victim to an easy but inadequate habit of categorizing the fiction of the last few decades as *either* realistic *or* experimental—experimentalism being equated in this scheme simply and exclusively with metafiction (or with one of its several and more extreme incarnations). The result of such assumptions, which are as widespread in criticism as they are in journalism,[1] is that readers have been regularly invited to view the novels and stories of the last twenty years in rigidly binary terms: to recognize and respond either to traditional mimetic representations of a fixed, if increasingly constraining, reality or to summary rejections of any and all possibilities of engaging the world in the dynamics of an ongoing dialogue.

My own quite different sense of the literary landscape has gradually shaped itself into the belief that by accepting these mutually exclusive categories—according to which the world is either taken for granted (realism) or declared epistemologically off-limits (metafiction)—we have been led to what one of Pynchon's characters calls "an intolerable double vision."[2] Or, to put it the other way round, we have been conditioned to ignore or to misapprehend a good deal of writing that refuses this double vision and that, even as it interrogates our traditional beliefs, continues to claim for literature, however tentatively or obliquely, a referential function. This, then, is the first of my middle grounds: specifically, the kind of fiction that rejects equally the oppositional extremes of realism on the one hand and a world-denying reflexivity on the other, and that invites us instead to perceive the moral, as well as the epistemological, perplexities of inhabiting and coming to terms with a world that is itself ontologically contingent and problematic. And I want to propose further, recognizing the inflammatory nature of the argument, that the best hope of American fiction lies precisely with the writers I'm considering. Traditional realism, however impressive in the hands of writers like Bellow and Updike, has dwindled among more recent practitioners (Joan Didion, Ann Beattie, Mary Robison, Raymond Carver) into a pinched and meager resignation, a resentfully cynical acquiescence to things "as they are" and, so it is implied, must be. As for the reflexive left-wing of experimentalism, for all its often boisterous deconstructions of the traditional relations between literature and life, it has left us with emblems of a world hardly less narrow and restricted. Between these two groups exist the writers I mean to examine (and praise), and the opening section of the book will be devoted to establishing a context for them. The first chapter sets forth the theory I have sketched here, arguing in the process with such exponents of metafictional, or surfictional, writing as Raymond Federman and Ronald Sukenick and, equally, with Gerald Graff as the leading defender of contemporary realism. The second attempts to illustrate and substantiate the theory in a discussion of works by Stanley Elkin, Apple, and Barthelme, the last of whom, I want to suggest, is a far more morally concerned writer than those who celebrate the ludic and self-referential elements in his work take him to be.

I have introduced the word "moral" deliberately, since it speaks not only to an overlooked aspect of Barthelme's fiction but to my own methodological assumptions and, as will become clear shortly, to my ideological concerns. Having adopted a phenomenological approach in my last book, I have tried in this one to assess more directly and self-consciously its potential strengths and limitations—to take account, that is, of the renewed interest in phenomenology that has followed in the wake of Reader-Response Criticism and the resurgence of hermeneutical studies. The virtue of such an approach (to contemporary fiction in particular) lies, it seems to me, in its ability to acknowledge the variousness, the deliberate "incoherence," that postmodern writers frequently claim for their work, without denying the distinctive configuration that necessarily embraces—embraces, not resolves—the discrete parts of any author's work. On the other hand, the desire to respond to such work with self-effacing empathy, which is the cornerstone of most phenomenological studies, runs the danger of an un-seemly neutrality in so patently an ideological age. My effort, therefore, has been to understand as fully as possible the fundamental structures that inform the fictions I deal with but also to do justice to the moral concerns that accompany the acts of writing and reading alike. This combination of ethical and phenomenological criticism stakes out another of the book's middle grounds, which, although it will be in evidence throughout, is explored most directly in its second section. (If postponing a detailed statement of methodology strikes the reader as quirky, I can only say that the decision was deliberate—that it represents an attempt to focus attention not on yet another critical approach, however enabling that may prove to be, but on the writers who are the object of the "grid" it supplies.) There, at any rate, a theoretical discussion of phenomenology finds its application in the fiction of Thomas Berger, whose insistently parodic, self-concealing enterprises and equivocally normative positions present a particular challenge to a criticism that claims to find in a writer's career a consistency beneath the surface evidence of discontinuity and change.

The third section of the book is devoted to a number of authors whose fiction represents not only a formal or structural middle ground but, more directly, a conscious and deliberate thematizing of the problem of middles. These writers are, in other words, intent on exploring ways and means of breaking out of traditional either/or modes of thinking and perceiving. For most of them, as they seek to redefine the world around them, this exploration entails an attempt to set against the temptations of the absolute and the extreme the more modest and tentative claims of "the ordinary." Or, rather, their effort is to reveal *its* extraordinariness—to make manifest, in Stanley Elkin's phrase, those "strange displacements of the ordinary"[3] that testify to the world's potential significance without denying its complexity or, indeed, its stubborn dailiness. Paradoxically, however, such writers traffic in limit situations, testing their own allegiance to the ordinary by a variety of strategic and thematic transgressions intended, ultimately, to reassert the problematical middle ground that they for the most part occupy. I say "for the most part" because in the first of these chapters I propose that the novels of Thomas Pynchon at times confirm but at others test, even dramatically undermine, the notion of what I shall call the literature of interrogation or "midfiction." Since the discussion of Pynchon is central to the book, it is probably worth saying a few words about it here, in anticipation of later elaboration. Briefly, my argument runs as follows: whereas all of his books posit an ideal of a middle (the "domain *between* zero and one," as *Gravity's Rainbow* puts it[4]), only *The Crying of Lot 49* effectively realizes that ideal. In *V.* and *Gravity's Rainbow* the postulated middles reveal themselves, upon examination, to be no more than so many markers of desire and intention, which the novels' deeper impulses (in phenomenological terms, their intentional structures) parody or subvert.

V. and *Gravity's Rainbow* provide, then, for reasons that have to do with the characteristic extremity of Pynchon's own fundamental grasp of the world, examples of the failure to acknowledge limits. *Lot 49*, which at once acknowledges and transgresses them, may be seen as paradigmatic of the other works that will be discussed hereafter. And of something else besides. If that most self-questioning and suspensive of Pynchon's novels achieves a thematic middle ground, it also suggests an ideological alternative to the stances assumed by realism and metafiction. That alternative is the subject of the next chapter, which deals with Barthelme and Mooney and (as realist counterexamples) with Didion, Beattie, Robison, and Carver. The question to be posed here has to do with the chances for a revitalized humanism in our postmodern age: for some tertium quid that avoids equally the moribund humanism that continues to inform the works of those writers I have chosen to call "catatonic realists" and the rabid antihumanism that allies so much of postmodern writing with poststructuralist theory. My aim here is twofold. I want, first of all, to explore the charges leveled, often persuasively, by writers such as Barthes, Foucault, and, in particular, Derrida against the fundamental assumptions of humanism. But I want also to advance the belief that in modified form (that is, as a less imperial and more existential set of beliefs) humanism can and does persist in the work of writers who are as attuned as their more self-consciously experimental contemporaries to the passing of modernism and its values—and also to currently widespread assumptions about our questionable relations to language.

The persistence of humanism is the burden of another chapter as well, this one concerned with Max Apple's novel and stories, the stories especially. Modest in their scope, they speak of chance and contingency and, increasingly, of loss, but in them, the ordinary becomes extraordinary, becomes nothing less than the generative site of a new humanistic and existential ethic and of the form or forms that articulate it. For this reason, the Apple chapter is the last in this section, a summation of its position and, on Apple's part, an exemplary response to the unshaded oppositional positions endorsed by so much of the fiction and criticism of our time.

The final section makes explicit a concern that haunts the entire book and that underlies so much of postmodern and poststructuralist controversy, namely, the question or questions of whether and to what degree contemporary fiction can be said to retain, despite persuasive arguments to the contrary, a referential function. For the novelists and short-story writers I have dealt with, the answer to the first question is in all cases yes, though the affirmation involves a belief, not in the possibility of a naive mimesis that seeks to re-present the world, but, rather, in a cooperative enterprise that matches the constraining force of that world with the powers of consciousness to "invent" it into being. My test cases in exploring the specifically midfictional notion of invention, which contrasts, as will be seen, with metafiction's apparently more spacious conception of imaginative freedom, are Barthelme and Grace Paley, represented in one case by a single, in the other by a handful of stories. (Other works by Barthelme are discussed in chapters two and five.) I raise this point in order to say something about the principles of selection that govern the discussions that follow. To begin with, this study is in some ways an outgrowth of, if not a sequel to, an earlier book, *Horizons of Assent*, which devoted the third and last of its sections to a consideration of postmodernism.[5] Inevitably, its choices have to some degree conditioned my decisions about which writers to consider here, and at what length. For example, because one of the chapters in *Horizons of Assent* is devoted to Barthelme, I've felt free to deal more sparingly and selectively with his fiction this time around. On the other hand, Berger and Pynchon, who go unmentioned or all but unmentioned in that book, and Apple, who receives less attention there than he deserves, are treated at length in what follows. In addition, it has seemed wiser on the whole to devote more space to lesser known writers. (Pynchon, whose mysterious presence dominates American letters at the moment, is, as in so much else, the exception.)

But something more fundamental than either of these explanations is at issue: despite the fact that several of the novelists or short-story writers I've chosen to deal with are examined extensively and despite the fact that a phenomenological approach might be thought to demand such treatment for all of them, my primary concern has been not with a survey of all these authors' writings, but with the kind of fiction they, individually and collectively, in single stories and in bodies of novels, represent. That admission leads, in turn, to the acknowledgment that here and elsewhere in the book other writers might have been considered as well—among them (in some of their works at least), Jerome Charyn, Don DeLillo, Russell Banks, Toni Morrison, Robert Coover, and John Irving. If I have omitted them, it is, again, because I conceive of *Middle Grounds* less as a comprehensive overview of all those who might be thought of as "midfictional" than as an argument on behalf of this kind of literature: an argument first about its existence and then about its value. It is, in short, the general implications of the following study that most interest me; and these have to do with how, exactly, we choose to read the map of contemporary American fiction—whether as simply a matter of binary oppositions or as something richer and more complex. More complex, it should be said and admitted, than whatever is implied by adding to the now standard categories of realism and metafiction a third that seeks to carve out a space for its own procedures and beliefs. Obviously, as the differences among even the writers I will be dealing with indicate, what we confront when we survey the fiction of our own time are not so many discrete blocks of like-minded novelists and short-story tellers but a spectrum of markedly individual talents. On the other hand, one must begin somewhere, and given the moral and formal impasse that literature, not to say criticism, seems to have reached at this moment,[6] it may be best to keep matters relatively uncluttered. Consequently, it is by way of attending to some of the more paradigmatic (but always singular) of those midfictional writers who escape our current classifications that the following chapters attempt to lodge a claim for just that "diversity" that Pynchon's Oedipa Maas regrets as she waits "for a symmetry of choices to break down, to go skew."[7]

The claim involves, as I've already suggested, a belief in the continuing legitimacy and vitality of humanism; and since, as Tzvetan Todorov has recently written, "the dominant tendency of American criticism is anti-humanism,"[8] it is probably wise to stipulate briefly, in a book devoted to writers who contravene this tendency, the nature of the attack and the grounds for a possible defense. The case against humanism has been made most recently in the first of two issues devoted to the subject by the journal *boundary 2*,[9] and one could hardly hope to find anywhere else so comprehensive or so spirited an indictment of what becomes in its pages the all-purpose enemy of a good that is variously and too often vaguely specified. Connected with such pejoratively conceived notions as identity, representation, decorum, culture, metaphysics, and, of course, the always anathematized center, humanism becomes, on this collective reading, an elitist and repressive enterprise, masking under a show of disinterestedness its disciplinary, regulative, and exclusionist motives and interests. Ethno-, logo-, and phallocentric, it is seen as coercing free play and suppressing differences in order to confirm its own (and the dominant culture's) hidden, hegemonic power, in—so the argument runs—the hypostatically and transcendentally imagined name of Man.

Foucault lurks, as does Derrida, but by now it is hardly necessary to specify particular sources for what has solidified into a climate of opinion, according to which humanism is seen not only as reprehensible but as hypocritical, or at least self-deluding. "Thus," as William V. Spanos writes,

despite its pluralism, its alleged tolerance of the play of difference, humanism, in giving privileged status to Man, privileges the panoptic, assimilative imagination that assumes that the texts which are natural and good—proper—are those which have "discovered" the identity inhering in difference, and those which are bad, i.e., contribute to anarchy, the texts that do not or refuse to resolve the conflict of difference in the name of the humanistic *Logos*, i.e., that resist encirclement, cultivation, and colonization. Blinded to self-inquiry by its assumption of natural right, the humanistic problematic thus tacitly limits what is permissible to those writers and texts that confirm (Western) Man's centrality.[10]

I'm less certain than Spanos that the ability to uncover identity in difference marks what, following Foucault, he calls the "panoptic" imagination. (My choice of the word "uncover" in place of "discover" is deliberate and is meant to allow for the possibility of a continuity that, within the flow of historical contingency, is adaptively sought rather than imposed.) But my purpose is not to quarrel with his suggestive analysis, nor with those of other critics who have found in "the humanistic problematic" the dark underside of much Western thought and action.[11]

On the other hand, Spanos' remarks do raise a number of related questions about the propriety and justice of equating humanism with certain of its practitioners and with a selective accounting of its consequences and effects. If, as Gerald Graff writes (correctly, I believe), "it is not the ideals of Enlightenment liberalism that need to be attacked but rather the failure to put them into practice,"[12] it follows that the conception of humanism to be found in a good deal of current criticism is far too unhistorical, unshaded, monolithic, and too inattentive—in spite of an insistence on difference and particularity—to times, places, and mentalities incommensurate with our own. It also follows that, particularly in the frequent absence of clear countervalues, the critique of humanism risks destroying the most effective weapons at its disposal in the battle it is so intent on waging. At the same time, the restrictiveness of the antihumanists' arguments is matched by a sometimes startling inclusiveness in their assignment of writers to either of two opposing camps. Spanos' list of humanists, for example, includes "not only . . . Matthew Arnold and his lineage (Babbitt and More on the 'right,' F. R. Leavis, Lionel Trilling, M. H. Abrams, Walter Jackson Bate, at the 'center,' and Eugene Goodheart and Gerald Graff, on the 'left'), but also . . . I. A. Richards, T. S. Eliot, and their heirs, the New Critics"[13]; while in *Intellectuals in Power*, Paul Bové offers as his exemplary figures, in addition to Richards, Auerbach, Marshall Hodgson, Said, and Foucault.[14]

The list could easily enough be extended by dipping into other contemporary indictments of humanism. My concern, however, is not with the placing of this or that particular critic, or indeed with critics at all, but with the principles that dictate the strict division of literary figures, theorists and others, into the rival configurations of "us" and "them." In fact, the problem becomes more dramatic and puzzling as one turns from the critical wars to the contemporary novelists and short-story writers who are at times called upon to substantiate the claims of theory. Both Spanos and Thomas Docherty, for example, invoke Pynchon in aid of their antihumanist arguments, and it is easy enough to concede that the objects of Pynchon's own attacks are often the ones these theorists aim at as well. I would argue, however, that the coincidence in no sense entails the inclusion of Pynchon himself in the ranks of antihumanists. As I've already stated and as I'll be maintaining throughout this book, the need to categorize writers, according to the current fashion, in binary terms, to see them as neces-sarily one thing or another, deprives them of precisely the uniqueness that Pynchon argues for in *The Crying of Lot 49*. To be sure, poststructuralists and antihumanists alike have taken as their own project the defense of difference and *différance*. So, for Spanos, humanism attempts "to assimilate or homogenize (i.e., de-differentiate) and pacify what it takes to be errant, deviant, eccentric, i.e., 'monstrous'"; and for Bové, "humanism excludes 'irrationalisms' as inessen-tial to the progress of the species."[15]

No doubt, some humanisms do (it makes more sense, surely, to think of the term and what it represents as plural), but it is also the case that alternative genealogies make available quite different notions of what "the humanistic prob-lematic" values and entails. Pynchon's affirmation of diversity, for example—or, rather, Oedipa's plaintive question: "How had it ever happened here, with the chances once so good for diversity?"[16]—recalls nothing so much as Margaret Schlegel's central speech in the last chapter of Forster's *Howards End*[17]:

"It is only that people are far more different than is pretended. All over the world men and women are worrying because they cannot develop as they are supposed to develop. Here and there they have the matter out, and it comforts them. . . . Don't you see that all this leads to comfort in the end? It is part of the battle against sameness. Differences—eternal differences, planted by God in a single family, so that there may always be colour; sorrow perhaps, but colour in the daily gray."[18]

There is no need to emphasize the contrasts in tone and mood between Oedipa's words and Margaret's (or between Pynchon's novel and Forster's). My point is simply, or perhaps not so simply, to suggest that across the span of the century humanism, or one version of it, can be seen to reveal itself in both writers not as a belief that Man is the measure (if that phrase implies Man's imperial control of all he surveys), nor yet as an "elitist" defense of individualism—though, cer-tainly, the kind of humanism I'm describing speaks everywhere and always to the worth of the individual, to the individual's need and capacity to realize his or her own potential for being. What this other strain of humanism rests on, what enables and sustains its resistance, in the words of Barthelme's Mad Moll, to "the sickliness of same"[19] is, precisely, Pynchon's diversity and Forster's eternal differences: the recognition and respect that both, whatever their manifest differ-ences, demonstrate for the variousness of human beings and the messy unclas-sifiability of their experiences.

Does it matter that one try in this way, always adaptively, to salvage or recuperate part, at least, of the humanist heritage? Obviously, it is the informing belief of this book that it does, that it matters a good deal. What, after all, do we find as we look around us today? Poststructuralists and metafictionists who have adopted as their foundational premise an inviolable and self-confirming skepticism; antihumanists who have proved readier to analyze than to correct the ills of a society they deplore; post-Freudians and others who, having sought to liberate desire in the name of free play and *jouissance*, have done so, as much as the most collectivist-minded of critics, by denying the claims and titles of the individual. Given all this, it becomes crucial to recognize that humanism, at its best, continues to withstand the many dogmas and determinisms that threaten, at the expense of everything marginal or "other," to supplement nature's entropic, leveling tendencies with their own. Indeed, as I write, the Supreme Court has affirmed Georgia's sodomy law, the Pope has declared against Liberation Theology (while affirming the reality of angels), and fundamentalists in Tennessee have mounted yet another attack on textbooks that teach evolution and present the "wrong" view of gender roles. Diderot and Voltaire, one imagines, turn in their graves.

It would be easy enough to multiply instances of actual or attempted coercion (the report of the Attorney General's commission on pornography, the Justice Department's ruling on the treatment of victims of AIDS, the attempts of the President and the Pro-Lifers to undo abortion rights) and just as easy to extend the analysis to the international scene, instancing Afghanistan, Nicaragua, and South Africa. Or to academe itself, where the oppositional discourses of Marxism and deconstruction, even as they assert their own specific rights and privileges, join together to shovel the last handful of dirt on humanism's unregretted corpse. But the ceremony, I've been trying to suggest, is as unwise as it is premature. To judge from the writers I discuss in this book, humanism offers, or may offer, an alternative and perhaps more effective way of achieving many of the goals that critics like Spanos and Bové set for themselves in their efforts to dismantle the post-Arnoldian (or, in Docherty's case, the post-Cartesian) "tradition." Less oppositional than interrogative, humanism of this kind bypasses the ideological wars of our times—especially "the opposition between Marxism and 'post-structuralism'" that, according to Todorov's shrewd analysis, "is not as radical as all that"[20]—and makes its contribution in a spirit, not of compromise, disinterestedness, or objectivity, but of active and passionate doubt.

As committed as the antihumanists or the deconstructionists to the defense of difference, the writers I've described as midfictional are less systematic than either, more intent on discovering the separate and distinct ways in which the self creates, in time and through its acts, its existential definition. At issue is an anti-ideological stress on the individual, on *parole* over *langue*, on the self creating rather than created, on the inevitability for human beings of a human—an anthropic, if not anthropomorphic—definition.[21] In short, the emphasis on the individual's priority over, and dialogic response to, whatever collectivity he or she is inevitably part of, intimates, in its rejection of all received opinions, the unsettled ground where the humanistic values of these writers locate themselves. Predictably, the temper of such fiction and of such belief, based as it is on a more modest, if no less urgent, conception of what humanism is capable of, calls for different tactics; and, as I'll argue in a later chapter, the advice with which Barthelme's "Manual for Sons" ends ("'small' is one of the concepts that you should shoot for"[22]) provides the key to the spirit of much midfictional writing. In any case, it is clear by now that, strategically and axiologically, the writers I plan to discuss break ranks with the critical and literary theories that currently dominate the American academic world, which no doubt helps to explain the neglect or misconstruction of their novels and stories. The dangers of self-definition at a time when "collectives" abound are apparent enough and there is no need to rehearse the fate of those who attempt it. As Max Apple said in a recent interview: "With all ideologies, it's always the guy in the middle—that's all of us—who's getting screwed."[23] The guy in the middle will serve, appropriately, as an emblem for humanism besieged and, more importantly, for what it nevertheless empowers: the diversity that Apple and his companions in this study illustrate and enact.

Notes

1. To offer one example at this point, Thomas Docherty's provocative *Reading (Absent) Character: Towards A Theory of Characterization in Fiction* (London: Clarendon-Oxford University Press, 1983) subsumes under the category of experimental literature writers as different, according to the argument set forth in this book, as Ronald Sukenick on the one hand and Barthelme and Pynchon on the other. See too the comment from the *New York Times Book Review*, quoted below in chapter one.

I don't mean to suggest that all critics of contemporary literature share the assumptions I'm speaking about. For several intelligent, thoughtful, and nuanced treatments of recent fiction, see Charles Caramello, *Silverless Mirrors: Book, Self & Postmodern American Fiction* (Tallahassee: Florida State University Press, 1983); Larry McCaffery, *The Metafictional Muse: The Works of Robert Coover, Donald Barthelme, and William H. Gass* (Pittsburgh: University of Pittsburgh Press, 1982); Patrick O'Donnell, *Passionate Doubts: Designs of Interpretation in Contemporary American Fiction* (Iowa City: University of Iowa Press, 1986); and Philip Stevick, *Alternative Pleasures: Postrealist Fiction and the Tradition* (Urbana: University of Illinois Press, 1981). O'Donnell's indispensable book appeared after I had completed my manuscript, although I had read a few chapters before its publication. It addresses, in a different context, some of the same problems I concern myself with below (see *Passionate Doubts*, pp. 132–36 and chapter seven). Although the words that make up the title of his book appear later on in this introduction, the borrowing was, I believe, unconscious; but it indicates fellow-feeling at the least.

2. Thomas Pynchon, *V.* (1963; rpt. New York: Bantam Books, 1979), p. 440.

3. Stanley Elkin, *The Dick Gibson Show* (1971; rpt. New York: Warner Books, 1980), p. 274.

4. Thomas Pynchon, *Gravity's Rainbow* (New York: The Viking Press, 1973), p. 55.

5. See Alan Wilde, "The Recovery of Depth," *Horizons of Assent: Modernism,*

Postmodernism, and the Ironic Imagination (1981; pbk. ed. Philadelphia: University of Pennsylvania Press, 1987), pp. 127–88.

6. The most cogent, discriminating, and persuasive study of modern criticism that I'm aware of is Daniel T. O'Hara's *The Romance of Interpretation: Visionary Criticism from Pater to de Man* (New York: Columbia University Press, 1985).

7. Thomas Pynchon, *The Crying of Lot 49* (1966; rpt. New York: Bantam Books, 1972), p. 136.

8. Tzvetan Todorov, "All Against Humanity," *Times Literary Supplement*, 4 October 1985, p. 194. See also the book that Todorov is reviewing: Robert Scholes's *Textual Power: Literary Theory and the Teaching of English* (New Haven and London: Yale University Press, 1985). In fairness, it should be noted that not all critics see antihumanism as a "dominant tendency." Marc Chénetier, for example, in his introduction to *Critical Angles: European Views of Contemporary American Literature* (Carbondale and Edwardsville: Southern Illinois University Press, 1986) complains about "trudg[ing] through endless series of humanistically inclined commentaries that hardly allow us to seize the novelty of the many authors who have emerged over the last thirty years" (p. xvii). It may be that antihumanism describes the attitude only of America's (and Europe's) currently most visible criticism, but even if that is the case, it is hardly possible to ignore what has become an ever more strident series of attacks on humanism in life and letters.

9. See "On Humanism and the University I: The Discourse of Humanism," ed. William V. Spanos, *boundary 2*, 12–13 (Spring/Fall 1984). I want to make it clear, as I generalize about this issue of *boundary 2*, that not all of its contributions endorse what may be thought of as the spirit and thrust of the volume. The exceptions include the essays by Charles Altieri, Fred R. Dallmayr, Gerald Graff, and Daniel O'Hara.

10. William V. Spanos, "*boundary 2* and the Polity of Interest: Humanism, the 'Center Elsewhere,' and Power," *boundary 2*, 12–13 (Spring/Fall 1984), 181.

11. Well worth consulting on this problem is the recent book by Paul Bové, *Intellectuals in Power: A Genealogy of Critical Humanism* (New York: Columbia University Press, 1986). In a series of scrupulous and provocative analyses, Bové discriminates between traditional (hegemonic) and critical (oppositional) humanism but argues that, ultimately, both groups fail to offer "'a way out' of our historical moment" (p. 248). Even if one does not agree that "critical humanism can no longer function legitimately as the toolbox of oppositional intellectual practice" (p. xi), it is impossible to overlook the subtlety of Bové's readings of individual critics and the even-handedness with which he constructs his "genealogy." Much of Bové's analysis parallels Spanos', but at its heart is the belief that humanism offers "a highly anomic ideal, promoting the individual pursuit of sublime representative status through attempts at individual magistral achievements" (p. 110). Because even oppositional discourses are part of humanism's genealogy, the most the book offers, or can offer, is the hope that "some nonhumanistic possibility is emerging" (p. 275).

I've already mentioned (see footnote 1) Thomas Docherty's *Reading (Absent) Character*. Docherty's opposition to humanism, which he connects with Cartesianism and the valuing of depth, individuality, continuity, and explicability, leads in turn to a series of attacks on the integrity of the author, the character, and the reader. What is perhaps most fascinating about Docherty's stimulating study is the degree to which the usual poststructuralist arguments are advanced, albeit in the name of phenomenology, very much as orthodoxy. Like other critics I discuss later, Docherty sets himself, predictably, against not only realism and mimesis but the possibility of referentiality. The key concepts of the book include the decentralization, discontinuity, and dissolution of the self (not only the characters' but the reader's), as well as the corollary privileging of language (the self, as might be expected, "is that which is constituted in language" [p. 34]); and, like so many of the critics in the issue of *boundary 2* that I've been discussing, Docherty, in working these concepts out, illustrates, even as he deplores, the perils of binary thinking. See below, chapters two and six, on the question of the author.

I realize that, in focusing on critics like Docherty, Bové, and Spanos in this introduction, I run the risk of illuminating the nature of antihumanism more than that of humanism. The strategy is deliberate: I am trying here to clear the ground for a more positive discussion of humanism as I turn in subsequent chapters to writers who, it will be seen, embody its principles and values.

12. Gerald Graff, "Humanism and the Hermeneutics of Power: Reflections on the Post-Structuralist Two-Step and Other Dances," *boundary 2*, 12–13 (Spring/Fall 1984), 504.

13. Spanos, p. 174.

14. In his preface, Bové writes: "Of course, this genealogy would have looked different if other figures had been treated. Trilling, Arnold, Raymond Williams, and Louis Althusser come to mind as forming another possible configuration around similar issues. Or R. P. Blackmur, Henry Adams, and the critics of American literature suggest a third" (p. xvii).

15. Spanos, p. 178; Bové, p. 296.

16. Pynchon, *The Crying of Lot 49*, p. 136.

17. I'm not in any way suggesting that the echo is necessarily deliberate, but David Cowart in *Thomas Pynchon: The Art of Allusion* (Carbondale and Edwardsville: Southern Illinois University Press, 1980), pp. 115–19 argues, largely in terms of *The Collected Tales*, for Pynchon's knowledge and use of Forster's work.

18. E. M. Forster, *Howards End*, ed. Oliver Stallybrass (1910; rpt. London: Edward Arnold, 1973), pp. 335–36.

19. Donald Barthelme, "The Emerald," *Sixty Stories* (New York: G. P. Putnam's Sons, 1981), p. 417.

20. Todorov, p. 1094. Compare Gerald Graff's observation that "the two current groups who get most intensely worked up over the inherent evil of 'humanism' are post-structuralist philosophers and members of the Moral Majority" (p. 497).

21. See the essay from which I've chosen my epigraph, Fred R. Dallmayr's "Is Critical Theory a Humanism," *boundary 2*, 12–13 (Spring/Fall 1984), 463–93. In central figures of the Enlightenment, indeed in the very discourses of its natural and human sciences, there is the acknowledgment that "truths" are a strictly but staunchly human enterprise, a matter of conversing with and configuring reality, not a matter of absolute and objective definition. This will change in the nineteenth century, when Gradgrindian "facts" are taken to be features of reality itself. See Wilda C. Anderson, *Between the Library and the Laboratory: The Language of Chemistry in Eighteenth-Century France* (Baltimore and London: The Johns Hopkins University Press, 1984); and Jack Undank, "*Jacques le fataliste* and the Uses of Representation," *MLN*, 101 (Fall 1986), 741–64.

22. Donald Barthelme, *The Dead Father* (New York: Farrar, Straus & Giroux, 1975), p. 145.

23. Larry McCaffery and Sinda Gregory, "An Interview with Max Apple," *The Mississippi Review*, 13 (Fall 1984), 16.

one

strange displacements of the ordinary

1

the excluded middle

Of course one knew it hadn't actually died—had glimpsed it at the supermarket, observed it at the movies, was aware of it wheezing in one's living room. But it had surely seen its best days, had, as one of the specialists on the case observed, "shifted from the peaks to the deadly plains of contemporary literature."[1] On the other hand, and as later events showed, one ought to have been more observant, ought to have taken in the significance of the signs, scattered though they were: get-well cards from Gerald Graff, greetings from David Lodge, a bouquet from Linda Nochlin.[2] But then friends naturally expect the best, hoping against the evidence. Actually, it was the confirmation by the *Times* that forced a reconsideration of the whole matter, made one realize—however hard it was to believe—that after so many relapses realism was back, vital as ever. One couldn't be mistaken. The *Book Review,* despite its unassertive deference to various experts, *knew.* Listen: "As we move into the 80's, what is happening to fiction? Is it becoming more realistic and less experimental? Are writers more concerned with historical and nonfictional material and less interested in being 'self-referential,' in writing about writing? Are we really living, as one critic put it, in a Golden Age of the American Novel?"[3]

The final question, vibrant with capitals, is the giveaway, a collective sigh of relief—heartfelt for all its tentative indirection, confident for all its wide-eyed wonder—at sanity's return. Why exactly the thought of realism's renascence should induce such relief is another matter, best postponed for the moment. The more immediate problem is to isolate the major assumptions that underlie the *Book Review*'s essentially rhetorical questions and, further, to determine their source. The assumptions, which are neither especially profound nor original, but which are for that reason all the more seductive and misleading, can be formulated as follows: 1) experimental fiction of the last few decades defines itself essentially, even exclusively, by its adherence to the strategies and beliefs of reflexive writing; 2) realism and experimentalism describe mutually exclusive modes of perceiving and rendering the world that, between them, exhaust the possibilities of contemporary literature; and 3) the supposed decline of experimental fiction entails the ascendancy of its putative rival.

It's easy enough to understand the attraction of these propositions. Eminently simple and elegant, they gratify our age's need to make sense of vertiginous change and, in the seesaw model of development they imply, they make the dynamics of change itself comprehensible. But at a cost. The coherence and persuasiveness of the *Book Review*'s covert judgments depend upon our willingness to accept the unexamined terms that effectively shape those judgments and that, in their monolithic force, smooth out all the rough variousness of contemporary literature. To put the matter more directly, it is only by construing the notion of experimentalism too narrowly and the sense of realism too broadly, that it becomes possible, indeed necessary, to overlook a large body of work that eludes both categories.

That work is the subject of this book, but before coming to it directly, I want to pause briefly over those antithetical elements from which the *Times*'s symmetries are fashioned. To begin with the somewhat less perplexed of the terms: I've intimated already that the equation of reflexive with experimental writing is a case of the part swallowing the whole and arrogating to itself the claims and titles of its more versatile relation. Taken by itself, reflexivity, at least in its most recent incarnation, is in every way an altogether smaller affair than the *Book Review*'s urgently single-minded questions suggest; and one is tempted to respond to the claims made for it (and by it) with no more than an empirical shrug: a simple listing of names—Elkin, say, or Apple, Charyn, Boyle, Irving, Pynchon—of writers whose novels and stories demand to be thought of as experimental, certainly, but not primarily, or at all, as self-referential. Further, if one excludes from the ranks of reflexivists (plausibly, I think) others like Barthelme and Coover, whose allegiance is sporadic or partial, and restricts the term to those like Gass, Federman, Sukenick, and the Barth of such works as *Lost in the Funhouse*, whose concern is entirely and wholeheartedly with "writing about writing," it becomes easier still to identify self-consciously reflexive writing as no more than one component of the far larger and more heterogeneous mix that constitutes experimental fiction today.

Reflexivity is best viewed, then, as experimentalism's far-left wing (to give that phrase a strictly literary meaning), its most boisterous, theoretical, and self-congratulatory faction, and its most obvious, if not its most legitimate, claimant to the mantle of the avant-garde. That writing of this kind—or to call it by some of its more fashionable and provocative names, meta-, sur-, Super-, or post-contemporary fiction[4]—possesses any less of a following today than it has had during the last fifteen or twenty years seems to me doubtful, the *Times* notwithstanding. Probably it comes closer to the truth to say that, as such fiction has become less unfamiliar and therefore less threatening, it has increased slightly its margin of actual readers. At the same time, since postmodern reflexive writing remains a rather special, not to say exotic, taste, its status in purely quantitative terms hardly seems to matter very much. What does matter is that the attention bestowed on it by its patient and resolute followers has more to do with the prominence of poststructuralist metacriticism—in particular the Barthesian notion that literature, as one among many self-enclosed sign-systems, presents us in our search for reality with nothing more than an always receding series of semiotic copies[5]—than it does with the intrinsic worth of meta- or surfiction themselves. Or, rather, that their vitality and interest are largely a function of the theories they so self-consciously and relentlessly seek to illustrate.

How faithfully they illustrate them is a different and more complex question. Proclaiming his twin beliefs that "to create fiction is, in fact, a way to abolish reality" and that "there cannot be any truth nor any reality exterior to fiction," Raymond Federman, the most articulate and energetic of the surfictionists, celebrates the liberation of imagination and invention.[6] And, as a corollary, announces the superfluity of those formal imperatives that are the most potent emblems of modernism's response to the world: "It [the new fiction] will be deliberately illogical, irrational, unrealistic, non sequitur, and incoherent" (p. 13). Indeed, measured against the modernists, with their urgent desire for order and control, postmodernism's aesthetic radicals seem at first glance to be engaged in an altogether more robust, spontaneous, and freewheeling enterprise: a release, it would appear, of long pent-up energies. But appearances are in this case more than usually deceptive. Ostensibly welcoming the world's chaos, writers like Sukenick and Federman come close to depriving it of its substantiality, as the modernist balance of art and life or, more accurately, the overwhelming tension of constraining and resistant forces, gives way to far more reductive, abstracting forms of order, which operate in the *name* of free play but in the *service* of an imperiously transformative, idealizing consciousness. In short, at issue is a contemporary, covert aestheticism whose manifestations are ultimately to be found in structures that, for all their ostensible incoherence, in reality betray the ordering coercions of the artist's subjectivity. So much so that, reading the surfictionists or, still more, William Gass, one often experiences a shock of eerie recognition, as the mangled shadow of significant form falls raggedly across the page. But in these instances form functions neither as an avenue to "reality" nor as its counterweight but as a notably peculiar mirror, which reflects from its deliberately fragmented and randomized surface an image more controlled and controlling than any imagined by the modernists. That image, I'm suggesting, is of the self (the nonexistent self, according to these writers), which, substituting for an engagement with the world its invention, validates only its own identity: its unacknowledged status as the inheritor of the Romantic and modernist traditions—and, ultimately, their dead-end.

All of this is to say that contemporary reflexive writing generally compromises the interaction of fiction and reality, the "play of competing ontologies," that Robert Alter postulates as the basis of what he calls the "self-conscious novel."[7] As a result, one understands why considerably fewer novelists than critics are willing (except when, as so often among surfictionists, the two are the same) to subscribe to the dogmas of current reflexivist theory—in particular to the arrogant claims made for the constituting imagination, which, lacking modernism's always troubled and dialectical awareness of the imperial mind confronting a recalcitrant world, effectively deprive literature of all its referential function.

To maintain that literature is referential is not, however, to suggest, as Gerald Graff does, that it is therefore "realistic" or that writers whose work demonstrates a concern with the world are for that reason to be regarded as realists. Elaborating on Karl Popper's response to Kant ("Our knowledge of the world . . . owes as much to the resisting reality as to our self-produced ideas"), Graff argues:

It is this "resisting reality" that the current way of talking about fictions fails to respect. Certain common experiences of this resisting reality possess so high a degree of unrefusability that they have the force of givens in our everyday experience. . . . The reality of the physical world, the inevitability of death, the social nature of man, the irrevocability of historical events and changes—these are facts we cannot possibly *not* know, though we can argue infinitely about their significance and how we ought to understand them.   (*LAI*, p. 204)

Given so sane and undogmatic a defense of the facticity of our experience, it is hard to imagine anyone (other than the reflexivists I've been discussing) likely to refuse the evidence of a reality independent of our impositions and indeed at least partly determinative of our perceptions. On the other hand, so minimal a notion of what we share (note Graff's final, concessive clause) can hardly be said to provide the grounds for a new realism, even if it succeeds in refuting the extreme presuppositions of reflexivity. Elsewhere in his study Graff writes: "My assumption throughout this book has been the simple one that writing requires a convincing understanding of the world" (*LAI*, p. 207). But surely, in these vexed times at least, the assumption is anything but simple—in fact contravenes most writers' sense of the dynamics of their undertaking.

No doubt it is true (the point is central to Graff's discussion) that "even a work which asserts that truth is totally problematic, unknowable, relative, or a function of multiple perspectives makes the same kind of truth-claim as do such assertions outside of literature" (*LAI*, p. 162). Formulated more narrowly, however, the proposition inevitably becomes more questionable. Consider, for example, this statement: "The perception that reality is problematic is itself a mimetic perception, presupposing an objective distance between the observer and what he observes" (*LAI*, p. 11). If "objective distance" signals no more than the minimal detachment necessary to articulate one's sense of the world's indeterminacy, there is no need to quarrel. (One need not, after all, be very far removed from any phenomenon, nor need one see it steadily and whole, in order to react to it.) But if, as seems likely, the phrase implies some Archimedean point from which we can, without obscurity or obstruction, take the world's measure and render it back with manifest accuracy and fidelity, then something far less self-evident is at stake: namely, the possibility of a distinctively mimetic fiction.

Recent defenders of mimesis tend, on the whole, to ground their arguments in two claims. It is held, first of all, that literature is capable of representing, actually of *re*-presenting, reality. But for a good many of today's writers and thinkers the world offers itself not as a fully realized datum but as a potential to be activated by human beings situated directly in its midst. The task becomes, then, not one of re-presentation but (as Graff, whose incidental remarks are often more flexible than his central point, sometimes concedes) of re-creation. So Pierre Thévenaz writes: "Consciousness 'lives' itself immediately as the giver of sense, as the source of meaning for the world."[8] And from this phenomenological position, which does not leave consciousness stranded in its subjectivity but insists on the close interanimation of consciousness and world, of perception and creation, it follows that mimesis (unless one defines the term as broadly and pliably as Auerbach does) contravenes our experiential and aesthetic response to the world: our sense that the world, though determinative of our perceptions and of our literature as well, is not therefore their final and fully determinate cause.

Graff's call for "a *representation* of the social world" (*LAI*, p. 221) leads to the second of the claims made on behalf of mimesis: the assertion that, because of its resistance to "our self-produced ideas," reality emerges from the manipulative grip of idealism as not only personally but collectively significant. Our conjured world becomes, *sub specie rationis*, a shared world: the locus of common meanings available to any mind unclouded by the shadows of latter-day subjectivities. But this is surely to make things too simple. The "unrefusability" of certain aspects of our experience in no way guarantees the inherent purposefulness or coherence of experience as a whole; and if writers feel the need to reconstitute rather than reproduce their world, it is because that world is perceived less as the arena of the problematic than as its source. In what is probably the best book on the subject, J. P. Stern speaks of realism in terms of "a fundamental assent" (OR, p. 44) and, again, of "a rudimentary approval of the world" (OR, p. 76). This important point is modified to a degree and subtilized in a later remark: "Reality," Stern writes, "may well be nothing nobler, or more stable, or less contingent than 'the *fable convenue* of the philistines'; indeed, not much fastidiousness is needed to look askance at those who would greatly extol its virtues. But, whatever else may be said for or against them, the realists don't worship at its shrine, or at any other. They merely take reality for granted" (OR, p. 145).[9] But taking reality for granted is precisely what contemporary experimental writers do not and cannot do; and however much one may agree with Graff about the referential nature of even the most chaos-ridden literature, it remains difficult, in the absence of Stern's "shared reality" (OR, p. 145), to see such writing as, in any strict sense, mimetic or realistic.

This is not to say that realism is impossible today—only that it is not, any more than surfiction, a major option for most serious writers. (There are exceptions, naturally, and, as names like Bellow and Updike suggest, some very impressive ones.) Indicative and subjunctive, realism and reflexivity—or metafiction, as it will for the most part be convenient to call it from now on, given the general identification of the two—mark out the extremes of contemporary literature. But this leaves unaccounted for, as I suggested earlier, yet another class of works whose mood is, instead, one of interrogation: a questioning of, among other things, the validity of certainties—both those that take the world for granted and those that set it at naught (the dogmatically uncertain being no less absolute than its less self-conscious opposite).

How to define this middle ground? Stern once again provides a clue, and I want to return to a remark I've already quoted, restoring it now to its context. "In realism," he suggests, "the relation that obtains between a work of literature and the world outside is positive, expressive of a fundamental assent, whereas in idealism it is negative, expressive of a problematic attitude toward the world," which is, in turn, based upon "a radical alienation and distancing from those given realities of life" (OR, p. 44). Recalling Graff's "objective distance," we may note, to begin with, just how slippery this particular metaphor of perspective is, functioning as it does, alternatively, as the essential condition of one mode of perception and as the inevitable stigma of the other. But more to the point is the inadequacy of Stern's (and Graff's) binary categories. For the fiction I'm edging toward manages to incorporate the problematic *and* the assentive—though assent in this case is to be understood as strictly limited, qualified, and local: a gesture of affirmation against a background that remains, if not negative, at least refractory and contingent. Perceiving the world as neither objectively knowable nor as totally opaque, making reference to experience without pretending or indeed wishing to re-present it, such fiction comprises the tertium quid of current literature: experimentalism's poor relation, realism's militant and rebellious heir, but, finally, and most importantly, something independent of both—an integral, self-sufficient mode of apprehending and expressing the world, which, for want of an adequate designation, continues to languish in the outback of current criticism.

Notes

1. J. P. Stern, *On Realism* (London and Boston: Routledge & Kegan Paul, 1973), p. 158. The book will be referred to hereafter as *OR*.

2. My allusions are to Gerald Graff's *Literature Against Itself: Literary Ideas in Modern Society* (Chicago and London: University of Chicago Press, 1979); David Lodge's *The Modes of Modern Writing: Metaphor, Metonymy, and the Typology of Modern Literature* (Ithaca, N.Y.: Cornell University Press, 1977); and Linda Nochlin's "The Realist Criminal and the Abstract Law," *Art in America*, 61 (September-October 1973), 54–61 and (November-December), 97–103. Graff's study will be referred to hereafter as *LAI*.

3. *New York Times Book Review*, 14 December 1980, p. 3.

4. See, respectively, Robert Scholes, *Fabulation and Metafiction* (Urbana, Chicago, London: University of Illinois Press, 1979); Raymond Federman, ed., *Surfiction: Fiction Now . . . and Tomorrow* (Chicago: Swallow Press, 1975); Jerome Klinkowitz, *The Life of Fiction* (Urbana, Chicago, London: University of Illinois Press, 1977); and Jerome Klinkowitz, *Literary Disruptions: The Making of a Post-Contemporary American Fiction* (Urbana, Chicago, London: University of Illinois Press, 1975).

5. See, in particular, Roland Barthes's *S/Z* (Paris: Editions du Seuil, 1970).

6. Raymond Federman, "Surfiction—Four Propositions in Form of an Introduction," in *Surfiction: Fiction Now . . . and Tomorrow*, pp. 8 and 12. The quotation in the next sentence is taken from this essay as well. See below, chapters 8 and 9, for a discussion of alternative conceptions of the notion of invention.

7. Robert Alter, *Partial Magic: The Novel as a Self-Conscious Genre* (1975; rpt. Berkeley and Los Angeles: University of California Press, 1978), p. 182. For a more comprehensive discussion of reflexive fiction, see my book *Horizons of Assent: Modernism, Postmodernism, and the Ironic Imagination* (1981; pbk. ed. Philadelphia: University of Pennsylvania Press, 1987), chapter 5.

8. Pierre Thévenaz, *What is Phenomenology? and Other Essays*, ed. James M. Edie (Chicago: Quadrangle Books, 1962), p. 50.

9. Compare Lodge, *The Modes of Modern Writing*, p. 40 and Terrence Doody, "*Don Quixote, Ulysses*, and the Idea of Realism," *Novel*, 12 (Spring 1979), 201–02. For an ambitious and invaluable survey of the theories and assumptions of realism, see Marshall Brown, "The Logic of Realism: A Hegelian Approach," *PMLA*, 96 (March 1981), 224–41. It seems to me, however, that Brown's own provocative definition—"*We consider a piece of writing to be realistic . . . whenever and insofar as we perceive ordered silhouetting or embedding effects*" (p. 233)—tends to stir up still further rather than to calm the troubled waters of the debate.

2

the midfictional world: Elkin, Apple, and Barthelme

What we cannot name, runs the philosophical adage, we do not apprehend. If, therefore, the referential but nonmimetic literature I spoke about in the last chapter is to move beyond the state of virtuality and take on substance for us, the first order of business is one of naming; and since the category at issue is meant to provide an alternative to the extremes of realism and reflexivity, it seems useful and plausible to adopt, on the model of metafiction (but still more emphatically in contrast to it), the term "midfiction." Rejecting metafiction's pronounced tilt toward the reflexive (and all that implies by way of the relations among consciousness, "reality," and art itself)[1] and rejecting as well realism's belief in the possibility of simple mimesis, midfiction is intended to suggest neither compromise nor mediation, and still less an inevitable or necessary moderation in its perceptions of the world and in the strategies that variously render them. What it does instead is to stake out a variety of middle grounds on which it tests the assumptions of other fictional forms and, more importantly, defines its own in opposition to them. But before adding yet another newly minted term to our already overburdened supply of critical neologisms, I want to test briefly the usefulness of one other, more traditional classification, whose generic properties, both formal and methodological, strikingly resemble those to be found in the midfictional novels and stories that are the subject of this book.

The object of the comparison I'm proposing is parable, which, like mid-fiction (and unlike metafiction) founds itself on the interaction of generally plausible characters and more or less consequent, if often unexpected, events in a narrative whose setting is deliberately and determinedly concrete, sensuous, and ordinary—though as a rule none of these features is developed as it is in the traditional, verisimilar novel. Like midfiction again, parable, especially as defined by recent commentators, intends to render more fluid and existential our sense of the world's meaning and, equally, of our connection with it. (Unlike realism, parables are not, strictly speaking, about the world but about human beings' relations to it.) As a consequence, the strategies of parable characteristically involve the exploitation of ambiguity and indirection and a preference for open over closed form. It follows that the pressure of meaning and therefore the summons to interpretation that parable and midfiction alike impose are in excess of anything narrative (even symbolic narrative) ordinarily exacts from its readers. As Sallie McFague, probably the sanest and most comprehensive of recent theological critics, says in her remarks on parable, what we are dealing with is "a highly risky, uncertain, and open-ended enterprise—a maneuver of desperation, if you will."[2]

Though further comparisons remain to be made, it should probably be noted at this point that, like such other capacious and supple genres, parable, while retaining a core of centrally defining features, lends itself to a process of continual alteration, whether by parabolists themselves in their reworking of the form or by critics intent on redefining it. Thus the qualities I've been describing are to be seen at once as intrinsic to the tradition and as modifications of it. But it is the modifications that are most relevant to midfiction, and these are, in turn, the work of revisionary theologians whose aim it has been in recent years to dislodge (once again) the orthodoxies of religious thought. More specifically, theologians have been attempting to undermine the hegemony of systematic theology, to replace it with, or at any rate to subordinate it to, a less dogmatic "intermediary or parabolic theology," justified by the belief that "the theological temper of our time is such that the form which holds the mystery in solution is more needed than the one that confronts it directly" (SP, pp. 2 and 81n).[3] In short, analytical, propositional discourse is at a discount, and biblical parable, far from being, as dictionaries and literary handbooks have it, a simple moral tale, becomes, in Louis Marin's formulation, "a genre . . . whose characteristic is to offer itself immediately to interpretation while making it impossible to confine it to a univocal allegorization."[4]

A distaste for the discursive and paraphrasable is, of course, at the heart of modernism, and there is no question but that in its redefinition of the parabolic tradition intermediary theology owes a considerable debt to modernist literature and criticism. But in its rejection of aesthetic self-sufficiency, in its demand for active engagement on the part of the reader or listener, it clearly exceeds its models and points on the one hand toward a looser, less autonomous conception of form and, on the other, toward a more exigent dynamics of response—that is, in the direction of postmodernism in general and of midfiction in particular. To quote McFague again: "The heart of the new hermeneutic project is . . . not the interpretation *of* the parables, but the interpretation of the listeners *by* the parables" (*SP*, p. 75), a belief that entails, not surprisingly, a stress "on confrontation and decision" (*SP*, p. 73) and an awareness that "the goal of a parable is finally in the realm of willing, not of knowing" (*SP*, p. 80).

Parable, then, in challenging both the passivity of our responses and the completed, perfected, autotelic quality of the work of art, raises fundamental questions about the moral effects and demands of literature upon us. But that problem is one I want to bracket for now, since a more immediate and more strictly aesthetic matter—specifically, how to distinguish parable (and midfiction) from other genres—demands prior consideration. The final point of resemblance between parable and midfiction, I want to suggest, lies in the fact that each is recognizable as such by some technical *écart*, a formal swerve that bends or twists the work away from its own normative procedures. It has, of course, often been argued that literature in general trades in deviance from established patterns (compare, for example, the notion of foregrounding), but parabolic and midfictional works do so to a degree that makes, finally, for a difference in kind. Accomplished in a variety of ways (McFague instances "exaggeration, hyperbole, dislocations" [*SP*, p. 78], and one could add such devices as paradox or radical tonal and narrative shifts), the parabolic swerve, or rather the very possibility of such a maneuver, depends upon the quality of the work's texture, upon a fabric that is neither (as in metafiction) so heteroclite as to blur the presence of the dissonant nor (as in realistic fiction) so uniform as to render the deviant improbable.

On the other hand and in deference to its adaptive capacities, it probably should be said that there exists in all literature the *potential* for parable, as a consequence of which midfiction would appear to be doubly (that is, virtually and actually) parabolic. Yet, while the analogy will continue to prove useful in a general way, one must at last reject the notion of the two as altogether congruous. The rock on which the identification founders is, predictably, religion, since midfiction is essentially secular in spirit;[5] and though McFague, for example, maintains that "parable is the form for a secular people" (*SP*, p. 141), and though she instances *Slaughterhouse-Five* as a parabolic story, still, for all her openness to human complexity and doubt, in the final analysis her eye is on other worlds. It's worth quoting at some length from *Speaking in Parables* to observe the inevitable modulation of her argument as she approaches and then veers away from the consequences of a thoroughgoing skepticism: "When the narrative form lacks integrity, as it seems to for many contemporary novelists, it cannot," she says with conviction, "be insisted upon. It may be that the parable, while itself a story of a certain kind, is a more appropriate genre for our time, for unlike more developed narratives it does not call for the same degree of faith in cosmic or even societal ordering. It is a more skeptical form with regard to such matters, insisting that the gap between the human and the transcendent is closed only through personal risk and decision." So far, so good, provided that one chooses not to dwell on or to make overly explicit the allusion to the transcendent. Nevertheless, the first note has been sounded, and others follow, creating a music that is no less comforting for the distance of its sonorities. The passage continues: "It *only* insists that the secular and the human is the place of God's presence—a presence for the most part hidden under the ordinary events of everyday life. It insists, in other words, on faith, not on an ordered structure built into the nature of things upon which the individual can rely" (SP, p. 141; my italics).

What can one say to this measured and tolerant affirmation other than that *deus absconditus* is *deus* still, and that in his wake follows everything against which postmoderism reacts, notably, depth, distance, essentialism, and the belief that meaning is something not to be forged or generated but, with however much difficulty and uncertainty, to be discovered—and to be discovered, moreover (one is again reminded of modernism) in pursuit of "the desire for fulfillment, for ultimate consummation, of one's entire being" (SP, p. 58)? Postmodernism's aims, at least those of midfiction, are more modest than this, as is its sense of possibility. In place of McFague's "experience of *coming* to belief" (SP, p. 120), midfictionists reveal the consequences of disbelief; instead of "faith in the ultimate reality of order and life,"[6] their stories betray a sense of life's essential disorder; in response to "the basic parabolic impulse, the perception of the extraordinary in the ordinary" (SP, p. 173), they insist that the ordinary, in all its secularity, *is* extraordinary. In brief, what we are dealing with is an attitude I have elsewhere called "suspensiveness,"[7] that is, the recognition of life's randomness and contingency and the acceptance of that awareness as a condition of one's participation in the world. Given this general indecisiveness about the meanings and relations of things and given the nonmodernist willingness to make do without other, compensatory orders (we are, it needs to be stressed, in the presence of something more radical than McFague's "necessarily . . . somewhat hidden and ambiguous" meaning [SP, p. 108]), reflexivism or metafiction becomes an understandable temptation and realism, at its best (witness recent movements like photorealism or an artist like Philip Pearlstein), the fantasticated attempt to recuperate an innocence no longer quite feasible in our self-conscious times.

✳   ✳   ✳

In a humorously plaintive acknowledgment of that impossibility, Max Apple, the first and most realistic-seeming of the writers I want to consider, delivered himself of the following miniature apologia: "This may sound crazier than any of my fiction, but I consider myself a realistic writer. I want to imitate Tolstoy or Chekhov but what happens is just like daily life. A few important characters take over, businessmen, fighters, promoters, aggressive types. When they start making trouble, I'm just a 120 pound weakling with a ball point trying to maintain a little order."[8] The takeover is evident in a story called "Small Island Republics," which, as its opening line ("Inudo was probably the world's tallest Japanese-American"),[9] as well as its title, makes clear, bases itself on the deceptively simple metaphor of size. Obviously physical and territorial in its application, the metaphor functions more importantly as an index to the psychology of its protagonist, supplementing and surrounding Inudo's own sense of contradiction ("He was big, very big, but he felt small and he understood smallness" [pp. 35–36]) with far more subversive paradoxes whose full force emerges only at the story's end. In fact, it is only there, after much talk of helping "small island republics to maintain their identity" (p. 38) and with the hilarious and unexpected revelation (it is the story's *écart*) that Inudo has "saved" Taiwan by leasing it to an American corporation—"Taiwan, a no-man's land, becomes a Disneyland," he announces proudly. "What bananas are to so-called banana republics, electronics is to Disneyland. It was a marriage made in Heaven" (p. 42)—only there and then does the reader grasp completely the complexity of his character. An oversize man dreaming oversize dreams of smallness, his concern with smallness at the mercy of a *folie de grandeur* that means to correct the lapses of history and forge the destiny of the twenty-first century, Inudo is an anticapitalistic capitalist, an anti-Western imperialist, who identifies with history's losers ("Hannibal of Carthage was his hero" [p. 28]) but skillfully masters the modern world's techniques of conglomeration.

But if the complexity of "Small Island Republics" is in part a function of the contradictions embodied in Slim Inudo, it is still more the result of the narrator's ambivalent attitude toward him, which announces itself in the story's first sentences: "Inudo was probably the world's tallest Japanese-American. Six-five-and-a-half barefoot, he also had extra measures of Oriental cunning and agility. He was good at basketball and paper folding. He honored his parents and got all A's at Harvard, where he majored in American history" (p. 27). Blandly reportorial, it seems, the description manipulates its hyperboles and incongruous juxtapositions in such a way as simultaneously to amuse and unsettle, thereby preparing us for the mixture of sympathy and irony that determines Apple's tone throughout. Or to put this another way, the story, as much as Inudo himself, embodies antithetical impulses, namely (and as in the better known "The Oranging of America"), an admiration for enterprise and adventure along with a typically postmodern preference for smallness. Furthermore—and this is the important point—if "Small Island Republics" seems in its final disclosure to pass judgment on Slim, inviting us as readers not only to share its insight into his self-deception but to make that insight the basis of some easy moral lesson, in fact it does something quite different. Recognizing that Taiwan's "merger with a corporate identity" (p. 42) does after all preserve its integrity (in perhaps the only way it can be preserved), we are forced by Apple to agree that if his hero's success is his failure, his failure is also his success.

It follows that "Small Island Republics" accepts the contradictions of which its protagonist is unaware and thus becomes, above all, a study in perspective. The "swerve" of the ending, we come to realize, has been prepared for from the start; and though thematically the story appears to attain a kind of ironic closure as Slim consummates his international deal, formally it opens out into a vision of far more unresolved and reverberating ironies, whose effect is to affirm, or at any rate to accept, the problematic, and whose source is Apple's always genial and quietly spirited voice, establishing the undogmatic tone of the fiction through the subtle variousness of its texture.

Part of this variousness derives from the chorus of other voices (his parents', his girlfriend's, his employer Bo Huang's) that surrounds Inudo and qualifies further our assessment of him and his final coup. For if all of these subsidiary characters agree with Bo Huang that Slim "is a giant, truly a giant, not in body alone" (p. 39), each interprets the perception, ruefully, hopefully, or confusedly, in his or her own way. And each is in turn the object of an irony that undermines that perception, dissolving its kernel of truth in a haze of wishes and desires. "Everywhere," Inudo announces, "the big eat the small. It may be pure physics, the whole universe as hungry as gravity" (p. 38); but it is only fitfully, if at all, that the others glimpse their own status vis-à-vis the world's tallest and hungriest Japanese-American. The story's last words—"A small island republic is just a start. Someday he'll be a senator" (p. 42)—belong to Slim's mother, and they seal our awareness that none of its characters' perspectives is to be received by us as privileged or final. Nor is the aim, as in modernist epistemology, to multiply perspectives until we see beneath the shifting surfaces a stable depth. The intention is rather to call into question the very notion of reconciling depths and the corollary consolations of form that even the most perplexed of modernist fictions provide.

To be sure, Apple as narrator offers us at the last a perspective unclouded by the personal interests of his characters. But that is not to say that he offers us answers.[10] Instead, the openness of the form enacts, as Inudo himself does not, the attitude of suspensiveness I've proposed as one of the characteristics of mid-fiction; and it is left, finally, to the reader to negotiate (or to accept) the story's contradictory impulses. According to Samuel Hynes, the parabolists of the thirties attempted to offer "models of the problem of action" (AG, p. 15). Apple's more hesitant and oblique morality investigates the necessarily ambiguous properties of action and invites us to consider his story not, in the modernist fashion, as "an alternative world" (AG, p. 46) but as a way of inhabiting this one.

The elusive but inescapable presence of the world, or its meaning, is also the subject of Stanley Elkin's *The Making of Ashenden*, which, like "Small Island Republics," but with greater abandon, engages in a send-up of its central character. Surely one of the most outrageous figures in contemporary literature, Brewster Ashenden acts out the fall from innocence that is the novella's most obvious if, finally, only its enabling theme. But the innocence is at the same time (for the two are by no means incompatible) a matter of extravagant pride and self-deception; and no sooner do we hear Ashenden begin to speak than we anticipate not only the inevitability but the precipitousness of his descent. "One of the blessed of the earth," as he describes himself, one among its *only three or four dozen truly civilized men*," he is, by his own estimate, the cynosure of the universe: "I come of good stock—" he says, referring to the source of his ancestors' considerable fortunes, "real estate, mineral water, oxygen, matchbooks: earth, water, air and fire, the old elementals of the material universe, a belly-button economics, a linchpin one."[11]

It is clear already that Ashenden sees himself mythically and his world aesthetically. "A heroic man" (p. 132), he becomes a character in his own elaborate romance. But if, as he puts it, he is "classical, drawn by perfection as to some magnetic, Platonic pole, idealism and beauty's true North" (p. 133), he is still more emphatically a romantic, his potentially glacial assurance neatly compromised by what is, given his age, a somewhat incongruous search for identity. For Ashenden is, and is meant to be, considerably less tragic than comic in his fall; and his need to know, indeed his assertion that he "know[s] *everything*" (p. 149), is in reality hostage to a more urgent need for stability and order, which betrays itself in the hilarious credo that is his final comment on the world's balky diversity: "You can learn almost all there is *to* learn," he tells a friend, "if you leave out the mystery and the ambiguity. If you omit the riddles and finesse the existential" (p. 149).

Whether or not it was so intended, Elkin's novella provides, as will become apparent, a virtual compendium of modernist themes. And when it introduces Jane Löes Lipton, its second major character, it engages what is perhaps the most suggestive of them: the projection of the ego into its double. As the object of Ashenden's quest for perfection and as his mirror, Jane is our major clue to him and to the underside of that vaunted civilization to which both pay tribute. The fact that the two come together for the first time at an estate whose park is an enormous private zoo and whose owner inclines to see his friends in terms of his beasts ("A man concerned with animals must always be conscious of who goes into the cage with whom" [p. 157], he says, worrying about the meeting of his guests) gives us our first hint of what has so far been hidden. The revelation that Jane suffers from *lupus erythematosus*—"the intelligent, wolfish mask across her beautiful face" (p. 162)—is the next. And the last, which proceeds from Jane's refusal of Brewster's proposal (because he has been impure) and which sets him off "to undo defilement and regain innocence, to take an historical corruption and will it annulled, whisking it out of time as if it were a damaged egg going by on a conveyor belt" (p. 164), this final one lets us know for certain that we are in the presence of Romanticism's and modernism's pervasive primitivist dream. For Jane's rejection bespeaks a claim to innocence even greater than her lover's and, since they are doubles, indicates the unwillingness of both to accept the conditions of the fallen world, the imperfections of life in time. Typically, since he is adept at self-justification, Ashenden achieves the impossible (it is the farcical climax of the novella's first part), "the self-loathing that *is* purity" (p. 167) and that, in restoring him to innocence (as he sees it), makes him worthy of Jane: "See, morality's easy, clear, what's the mystery?" (p. 167). But Jane, that flawed emblem of completeness, disappears now, too static to interest us for long, leaving behind unsettling whiffs and intimations of an otherness that will in time overtake and overmaster Ashenden himself. In other words, whereas Jane embodies the state of unreal perfection, Ashenden figures its pursuit: the quest that reveals him, over and again, as a prig of the extraordinary and the victim of his own heroic myth.

Ashenden's swerve, its *écart*, is effected by a switch in point of view, as we move, suddenly and unexpectedly, from first to third person about two-thirds of the way through the work. But though we now see Brewster from the outside, the world remains what it has always been, *his* mirror: "a crèche of the elements" (p. 167), an image of "paradise" (p. 168), a landscape that charms him by its resemblance (here at least he is right) to the works of painters. "I am in art, he thought, and thus in nature too" (p. 172), he adds with a Popean delight in order. The eruption at this point of a ruttish bear into the frame that methodizes nature as Ashenden's myth aestheticizes his life promises a challenge different from any he has heretofore known and, it is to be imagined, one that will lay waste his awesome self-satisfaction. So it does up to a point, urging him into emotions he has not known till now. But habits of mind die hard; and though he is hardly in a position to deny the fact of the bear, the interpretation of the encounter, Elkin indicates, remains very much his: "The confrontation was noble, a challenge (there's going to be a hell of a contest, he thought), a coming to grips of disparate principles. . . . He believed not that the bear was emblematic, or even that he was, but that the two of them there in the clearing . . . somehow made for symbolism, or at least for meaning" (pp. 174–75).

Not surprisingly, since nothing for Ashenden can be simply itself, the presence of the bear repeatedly translates itself (an affectionately parodic allusion to Faulkner here?) into a test: "Oh Jesus, he thought, is this how I'm to be purified? Is *this* the test? Oh, Lord, first I was in art and now I am in allegory" (p. 179). And if in what follows—his unavoidable lovemaking with the bear, the description of which is one of Elkin's most prodigious tours de force—he is at last forced out of his complacence, it is only superficially so. Even while stretching to encompass a new content—"But then I am a beast too, he thought. . . . What this means . . . is that my life has been too crammed with civilization" (p. 179)—his mind retains its fundamental structures of thought and perception. Fatuous to the end, he manages at once to glimpse the truth about himself ("I have the tourist's imagination, the day-tripper's vision") and to transform it into a matter for self-congratulation: "God, how I honor a difference and crave the unusual" (p. 185).

Brewster's post-coital resolution (Jane is now not only out of sight but out of mind) to "book passage to someplace far, someplace wild, further and wilder than he had ever been" (p. 187) testifies both to his inexhaustible capacity for fantasy (still finessing the existential, "fleeing the ordinary" [p. 185], he will, we recognize, always be en route and possibly *en rut*) and to the wonderful plasticity of his innocence. Reconstituted in the aftermath of Jane's rejection ("So innocence is knowledge, not its lack" [p. 167]), it undergoes a more bizarre and paradoxical recovery during his "ecstatic, transcendent" union with the bear (p. 186), for, as he thinks later: "Maybe *I* was the virgin. Maybe *I* was. It was good news" (p. 188). Good news indeed: a gospel of infinite possibility, renewal, and redemption. But Elkin's final comment ("He started back through art to the house" [p. 188]) ensures that we will not miss the irony—not only that Ashenden is off on the track of still wilder myths; or that like Dick Gibson's, in another of Elkin's novels, Ashenden's is an apprenticeship that will never end;[12] and not only that his taste for the extraordinary is undiminished; but that (it is Elkin's most illuminating insight into modernism's thematic ideals and resolutions) the aesthetic and the primitivist are two sides of a single coin: the one, *pace* Forster, Lawrence, Woolf, and Joyce, the echo rather than the antithesis of the other.

At this point, with Ashenden dispatched and unchanged, everything seems to have fallen into place. But has it? Does this reading account for all of the work's complexity and does it account for my use of it as an example of midfiction? In the light of Elkin's other works, even of some elements of *Ashenden*, and especially of remarks made by him in various interviews, some doubts begin to obtrude. "All characters," he says in one of these interviews, "all protagonists, are ultimately sympathetic,"[13] and in another: "Energy is what counts. . . . Whoever has the better rhetoric is the better man. . . . He is as far as I'm concerned the more sympathetic character."[14] Ashenden? Sympathetic? Is that what these comments imply? At stake is Elkin's well-known fascination with obsession, a subject to which he returns repeatedly: "I'm attracted to the extreme. . . . I'm attracted to extremes of personality too. . . . I stand in awe of the *outré*. Those characters who are exaggerated seem, to me at least, more vital than the ordinary character, certainly more energetic. It's this energy which engines my work." And again, speaking once more of his characters: "I don't regard them as losers. The fact that they may be unhappy doesn't mean that they're losers. The fact that they may be outrageous or immoral doesn't mean that they're losers. The fact that they're obsessed, that they have obsessions which would get real people arrested, doesn't mean that they're losers. It means that they are simply demonstrating the kind of extravagance—the kind of *heroic* extravagance, if you will—that makes them, in my view, winners—winners, inasmuch as they impress me."[15]

Brewster Ashenden clearly belongs in the well-stocked gallery of Elkin's obsessive characters. And though he is less intense than, say, Alexander Main in *The Bailbondsman* or *The Franchiser*'s Ben Flesh (largely because the treatment of him is so frequently broad-stroked and farcical), still he does have an incontrovertible vitality, which derives from the fact that Elkin endows him—successfully, if in defiance of even the most minimal verisimilitude—with his own energetic, vivid, and disruptive language. It is that language, indeed, and the texture it sustains that act, even more than in "Small Island Republics," to alert us to the midfictional quality of the work. But to say this is to acknowledge just how problematical the novella is. For if Elkin, like Apple (though for less immediately discernible reasons) reacts ambivalently to his protagonist, and if, as he does, he clearly revels in the bizarre and improbable not only for their ironic potential but for their own sake, how are we to gauge the novella's attitude toward the central question it poses about the ordinary and the extraordinary? The answer is anything but obvious, since *The Making of Ashenden* does not itself tell us unambiguously what—if it were not contravened by Brewster's aesthetic and primitivist impulses—the ordinary might be. Nor, until recently and especially in *The Living End*, does any of Elkin's fiction.[16] His works are—and the image doesn't seem excessive—a battleground in which the lure of the extraordinary, made attractive by an obsessive concern with death, time, and the unknown, is only gradually and never completely countered by a celebration, still wild and fantastic, of what Larry McCaffery refers to as "the beauty and wonder that is normally locked within the vulgar and ordinary."[17]

Perhaps the most one can say is that the good life according to Elkin steers a difficult course between a desired intensification and a possible distortion of the ordinary and that his fiction demonstrates a willingness to risk failure rather than remain passive in the face of life's ineluctable mysteries. But that isn't quite all. The title of this section derives from another of Elkin's novels;[18] and its central metaphor tells us this much at least: that Elkin differs in important ways from McFague, whose language insistently points to a morphological change, a "reform[ing]" or "deformation of ordinary life" (*SP*, pp. 6, 17), that is, to an ultimate, if difficult, transfiguration of the world's body. With his more locative notion of "displacement," Elkin seeks at most—since "there is no conventional wisdom . . . [since] truth comes in fifty-seven day-glo flavors"[19]—a mitigation of inherent contradictions, a way, finally, of coping, which leaves the world in its essence unchanged and us, in part at least, with the job of making sense of it.

So much, then, for parable. And for whatever else midfiction is not. One could, of course, easily enough continue to swell the catalogue of differences, noting, for example, with reference to modernist predilections for symbol and myth and with an eye to New Critical theories of resolution, that the world for midfiction presents itself neither as a veil to be penetrated nor as a disorder to be mastered, and still less as a complexity to be compelled into unity. But my major concern is to distinguish midfiction from other postmodern and contemporary forms; and the best way to do that is probably to propose, even before coming to my final example, a working definition of what the term is meant to imply. To begin with what I've already tried to establish: midfiction describes a narrative form that, whatever its occasional and incidental resemblances to either or both, fundamentally eschews the oppositional extremes of realism and metafiction, offering, indeed creating, its own presuppositions and technical procedures in place of theirs.[20] Further, it seeks to reveal the extraordinariness of the ordinary, frequently and paradoxically by trafficking in limit situations—thereby subjecting to interrogation the very foundations of the writer's (and the reader's) beliefs. Finally, it invites us not *through* but *in* the relationships and actions of its characters—and by way of some strategic *écart* in its fabric—to perceive, obliquely and ironically, the moral perplexities of inhabiting a world that is itself, as "text," ontologically contingent and problematic.

The works I've discussed so far bear out, I believe, the first two segments of my definition, but they illustrate only partially the consequences of the third, especially the fact that inhabiting such a world offers at least the possibilities of generating more positive (if never complete) meanings and values than are allowed for by *Ashenden* or than are directly articulated by "Small Island Republics."[21] In Donald Barthelme's "The Emerald," however, it is precisely the idea of possibility that determines the story's treatment and theme and makes it so eminently midfictional. Having said which, I imagine a murmur of resistance and disbelief. Barthelme a midfictionist? Barthelme, the well-beloved of reflexivist-minded critics, the chief disciple of "the Metafictional Muse" (to borrow the title of Larry McCaffery's intelligent and persuasive book)? No doubt, Barthelme is the most self-conscious, experimental, artful, and playful of the writers I'm dealing with in this chapter; and no doubt, elements of metafictional theory and practice are to be found throughout his work. But with relatively rare exceptions, Barthelme's fiction remains stubbornly referential, acknowledging the pressures of the world it questions and refusing simply to privilege imagination at the expense of Graff's "resisting reality"—any more than it does the reverse.[22]

The best of Barthelme's stories and novels—"City Life," "Engineer-Private Paul Klee," "Rebecca," "The Death of Edward Lear," "The Great Hug," *The Dead Father*, and, not least, "The Emerald"—are in fact (to proceed further into heresy) *moral* studies of how to deal with a world it is impossible either to dismiss or to understand. The attempt in most of these to re-create value and meaning in the felt absence of either accounts for the oddly indeterminate status of these fictions, which are at once among the quirkiest and the most compelling in contemporary literature. Certainly, "The Emerald" gives full play to the odd and fantastic in the premise and development of its plot, which recounts the kidnapping of a precocious, talking, seven-thousand-and-thirty-five-carat emerald, the offspring of Mad Moll (a rather limited and ineffective witch) and the man in the moon, and its subsequent recovery when a reliquary containing "the true Foot of Mary Magdalene"[23] kills Vandermaster, its abductor. And yet, however much the story's incidents lay stress on life's vagaries and absurdities, its techniques—the generally humdrum speech, the predominantly dialogic presentation, the consequent exclusion of comment by the narrator, and a cast of characters who largely assume the authenticity of the situation—all these make for a treatment that is, for the most part, deliberately and scrupulously ordinary. But to put the matter this way may be to suggest, unintentionally, the priority of the ordinary over the marvelous, whereas their relationship, as the evidence of style reveals, is one of mutual qualification. Barthelme's language is always, even when most seemingly matter-of-fact, slightly but persistently stylized, deviant, offbeat. Indeed, in its bland recycling of clichés, in its barely perceptible stiffening of the rhythms and patterns of colloquial prose, in its ubiquitous deployment of linguistic *chevilles* (all as if enclosing the discrete elements of discourse within invisible and ironic quotation marks), and in its not always recognized capacity for modulating on occasion, as in Moll's monologues, into a more ornate and rhetorical register—in all these ways, Barthelme's flexible style, the indelible signature of his midfictional status, serves as the concrete embodiment of a vision that recognizes life's overwhelming dailiness even as it celebrates the human potential for establishing within that dailiness small, unstable, and mysterious enclaves of significance and pleasure.

"The Emerald," to come back to it now, thematizes this double view as fully and suggestively as any of Barthelme's fictions; and in doing so it recapitulates and enlarges on the concerns of "Small Island Republics" and *The Making of*

Ashenden. Thus Moll, with her "memories of God who held me up and sustained me until I fell from His hands" (p. 410), inhabits a fallen world. Her descriptions of it (along with the emerald's)—it is, variously, "this gray world of yours" (p. 398), "the ferocious Out" (p. 399), "the welter" (p. 411), and "the scrabble for existence" (p. 417)—indicate an attitude that is from first to last suspensive, accepting of its drab and fierce confusions. That attitude sets Moll and her child directly at odds with the other characters, for all of whom the emerald is the hypostatized object of a passionate quest for the extraordinary as something perfected, other, and apart: a variably interpretable means of correcting or overcoming life's insufficiencies. So "Lily the media person" (p. 404) and her "editor-king" (p. 407), Mr. Lather (their newspaper, not coincidentally, is called *World*), are after the perfect story, the mob of weirdly-named but otherwise indistinguishable emerald-hunters after still more exotic, if more tangible, gain; but it is only Vandermaster, whose quest is the most outrageous and extreme, that need concern us here. Seeking nothing less than immorality—"In addition to my present life," he tells Moll, "I wish another, future life" (p. 404)—Vandermaster represents desire run wild. But not, perhaps, as wild as all that. The absoluteness of desire may be construed as, among other things, the recurrent dream of art's resolving grace, its power to achieve through form a stability beyond the reach of life's disorders. If this is so, Barthelme's story presents itself, along with Apple's and Elkin's, as a comment on modernism. That is, as "Small Island Republics" contests the idea that man is the measure and *Ashenden* the belief that primitivism offers a genuine alternative to aestheticism, so "The Emerald" gives the lie to the heterocosmic imagination and to the imperialism of art.

Here again, the comment—roughly, the valorization of postmodernism's preference for looser and less determined orders and for smaller, less perfect pleasures—is both structural and thematic; and what the antic choice and arrangement of events intimate, Mad Moll herself expresses. "Diamonds," she says, "are a little ordinary. Decent, yes. Quiet, yes. But *gray.*" And she proceeds then, in paradoxical praise of various gems, all of which are by any usual reckoning more ordinary than the diamond, to assert, precisely, the extraordinariness of the ordinary: "Give me step-cut zircons, square-cut spodumenes, jasper, sardonyx. . . . But best of all, an emerald" (p. 416). The justification of the claim is the substance of Moll's central speech, in which she spells out for Lily's benefit the "meaning" of the emerald and in which, through her, Barthelme adds to his acceptance of the world his assent to its possibilities: "It means, one, that the gods are not yet done with us. . . . The gods are still trafficking with us and making interventions of this kind and that kind. . . . Two, the world may congratulate itself that desire can still be raised in the dulled hearts of the citizens by the rumor of an emerald. . . . Three, I do not know what this Stone portends . . . but you are in any case rescued from the sickliness of same" (pp. 416–17).

The "in any case" neatly qualifies the affirmation, as does the aposiopetic maneuver that leads Moll to suggest abruptly "a small offering in the hat on the hall table" (p. 417). Indeed, the swerve from the vatic to the mundane provides the note of ironic deflation, at any rate of reservation, one expects to find in Barthelme's work. On the other hand, one needn't take literally, as Moll does, the existence of those "tucked-away gods whom nobody speaks to anymore" (p. 401) to recognize on Barthelme's part the wish to restore, along with desire and diversity, some sense of mystery to a radically despiritualized world: the world to which, in other stories, his characters so often react with a kind of wry or aggrieved hopelessness. The phrase that best sums up this intention is perhaps Alejo Carpentier's *"lo real maravilloso"*: "the intrinsic quality of Latin-American experience," as Alastair Reid says, paraphrasing Carpentier and referring specifically to *One Hundred Years of Solitude*, "in which the wondrous and inexplicable are an essential part of ordinary perception."[24] The perception (central to American pop art and French surrealism, as well as to what we have come to call magic realism) is one that Barthelme shares, whether or not it surfaces in all of his fictions. "The Emerald" ends with one of his most felicitous expressions of it. "And what now? said the emerald. What now, beautiful mother?" To which comes the reply: "We resume the scrabble for existence, said Moll. We resume the scrabble for existence, in the sweet of the here and now" (p. 417).

Unlike the paradoxes that translate modernist irresolution into aesthetic stasis, Barthelme's find energy in contradiction and in so doing realize the potential of midfiction. Clarifying Elkin's explorations of the extraordinary, adding to Apple's suspensiveness a hint of possibility (as Apple himself repeatedly does in *The Oranging of America* or in the exuberant "Free Agents"), "The Emerald" invites us into a world where action is neither heroic nor final but in which the scrabble for existence, uncertain at best, offers something more than the self-referentiality entailed by the semiotics of enclosure. Something other, however, than McFague's "parabolic mode—the hidden way of locating the graciousness of the universe within the ordinary and the mundane" (*SP*, p. 95), for midfiction's concern is less with the discovery than with the generation of meaning. Barthelme's Deus Lunus exacts from humans not faith but risk in a difficult balancing act whose existential motto is, in the words of the emerald: "Now is sooner than then" (p. 411). So affirmation, yes, and assent; but local, limited, and temporary. Deus Lunus is a suitable god for a world that remains obstinately stochastic. Commenting on the "rhetorical sacrament" he finds at the end of "The Emerald"—Moll's reiterated reference to "the scrabble for existence"—Elkin writes: "There is a solace in finality and a grace in resignation no matter *what* one is resigned to—death, helplessness, the end of chance, resignation itself. But life's tallest order is to keep the feelings up, to make two dollars' worth of euphoria go the distance. And life can't do that. So fiction does. And there, right there, is the real—I want to say 'only'—morality of fiction."[25]

I'm not sure that Barthelme (or Elkin himself in *The Living End*) would agree that "life can't do that"; but what matters, in any case, is that Moll and her creator direct us not only to the scrabble but to "the sweet of the here and now"—or to both at once. The morality, in short, whether it is art's or life's, bypasses the extremes of experience, deriving its complexity from a vision that immerses itself in less ultimate truths, as Elkin himself acknowledges in a remark immediately subsequent to the passage I've just quoted. Reminiscent of the climactic revelation in *The Dead Father*—"All there is, Julie said. Unfortunately. But this much. This where life lives"[26]—Elkin's final words are no less tempered: "Not much, is it? It's all there is." Midfiction's response, an answer equally to the different faiths of realism and parable and to the invincible doubt of metafiction, can be stated simply: It is enough.

Notes

1. For discussions of metafiction, see Robert Scholes, *Fabulation and Metafiction* (Urbana, Chicago, London: University of Illinois Press, 1979), pp. 105–38; Larry McCaffery, *The Metafictional Muse: The Works of Robert Coover, Donald Barthelme, and William Gass* (Pittsburgh: University of Pittsburgh Press, 1982), chapter one; and Patricia Waugh, *Metafiction: The Theory and Practice of Self-Conscious Fiction* (London and New York: Methuen, 1984), chapter one. Scholes's term "fabulation" is ultimately too general and inclusive for my purposes and, in addition, too aesthetically resolved in its quasi-modernist emphasis on complexity compelled into unity. On the other hand, fabulation comes closer to what I'm after in its emphasis on "a return to story for renewed vigor" (p. 25).

2. Sallie McFague, *Speaking in Parables: A Study in Metaphor and Theology* (Philadelphia: Fortress Press, 1975), p. 44. I am indebted throughout the following discussion to McFague's book, which will be referred to hereafter as *SP*. See also Frederick Buechner, *Telling the Truth: The Gospel as Tragedy, Comedy, and Fairy Tale* (New York: Harper & Row, 1977) and John Dominic Crossan, *Raid on the Articulate: Comic Eschatology in Jesus and Borges* (New York: Harper & Row, 1976).

3. Less radical than some, McFague goes on to say that "neither tradition can do without the other" (p. 81n).

4. Louis Marin, "On the Interpretation of Ordinary Language: A Parable of Pascal," in *Textual Strategies: Perspectives in Post-Structuralist Criticism*, ed., Josué V. Harari (Ithaca, N.Y.: Cornell University Press, 1979), p. 241.

5. Samuel Hynes, untroubled by the religious associations of the word parable, uses it suggestively to apply to works by such writers as Auden, Spender, Greene, Rex Warner, Isherwood, Orwell, and MacNeice. See *The Auden Generation: Literature and Politics in England in the 1930s* (London: The Bodley Head, 1976), pp. 13–15. The book will be referred to hereafter as *AG*.

6. William A. Beardslee, *Literary Criticism of the New Testament* (Philadelphia: Fortress Press, 1970), p. 17. Quoted in *Speaking in Parables*, p. 140.

7. See *Horizons of Assent: Modernism, Postmodernism, and the Ironic Imagination* (1981; pbk. ed. Philadelphia: University of Pennsylvania Press, 1987), pp. 10–11 and part 3, *passim*.

8. The statement appeared in Bantam's 1979–1980 catalogue of "Literature for

Colleges and Universities." Compare Apple's brief essay "On Realism," *The Nation*, 3 February 1979, p. 117, in which the zaniness (his word) of his fiction is ironically traced to the bizarre events of "the whole world singing in tune to reality." For a somewhat different view of Apple's relation to realism, see chapter 7, below.

9. Max Apple, "Small Island Republics," *Free Agents* (New York: Harper & Row, 1984), p. 27. Subsequent references to this story and to the other fictions I discuss will be given parenthetically in the text.

10. See "The American Bakery," in *Free Agents*, where Apple speaks of style as "a truth more profound to me than meaning, which is always elusive and perhaps belongs more to the reader" (p. 90).

11. Stanley Elkin, *The Making of Ashenden*, in *Searches & Seizures* (Boston: David R. Godine, 1973), pp. 129, 150, 130.

12. For a different reading of the ending, see Thomas LeClair, "The Obsessional Fiction of Stanley Elkin," *Contemporary Literature*, 16 (Spring 1975). "The real 'making of Ashenden,'" he writes, "is his freedom" (p. 161). Peter J. Bailey's *Reading Stanley Elkin* (Urbana and Chicago: University of Illinois Press, 1985) provides an admirably comprehensive and persuasive overview of its subject.

13. Thomas LeClair, "Stanley Elkin: the Art of Fiction LXI," *The Paris Review*, 66 (Summer 1976), 78.

14. Jeffrey L. Duncan, "A Conversation with Stanley Elkin and William H. Gass," *The Iowa Review*, 7 (winter 1976), 61.

15. Scott Sanders, "An Interview with Stanley Elkin," *Contemporary Literature*, 16 (Spring 1975), 131–32 and 141–42. The last quotation ends, apparently in acknowledgement of differing interpretations of his characters: "Alas, they put others off." For Elkin's comment on *The Making of Ashenden*, see LeClair's interview, p. 74.

16. See Larry McCaffery's essay on *The Franchiser*, "Stanley Elkin's Recovery of the Ordinary," *Critique: Studies in Modern Fiction*, 21, 2 (1979), 39–51. I have dealt with the subject apropos of *The Living End* in *Horizons of Assent*, pp. 158–61.

17. McCaffery, "Stanley Elkin's Recovery of the Ordinary," p. 40.

18. See *The Dick Gibson Show* (1971; rpt. New York: Warner Books, 1980), p. 274. I should say that there is no clear agreement about the novel or about the scene from which my title comes—or indeed about the phrase itself. In LeClair's *Partisan Review* interview, Elkin says about the book: "The theme of the novel is that the exceptional life—the only great life—is the trite life. It .s something that I believe. . . . To have affairs, to go to Europe, to live the dramatic clichés, all the stuff of which movies are made, would be the great life" (p. 73)—a statement that suggests a more straightforward conception of the ordinary and the extraordinary than the novel seems to me to convey. Asked by LeClair, "Do the characters in your novels, then, have rather conventional notions of what exceptional is?" (pp. 73–74), Elkin's answer is yes. See too LeClair's essay, p. 154; Raymond Olderman, "The Six Crises of Dick Gibson," *The Iowa Review*, 7 (Winter 1976), 130 and 136–37; and McCaffery's "Stanley Elkin's Recovery of the Ordinary," p. 41.

19. Sanders, "An Interview with Stanley Elkin," p. 133.

20. By way of explaining possible resemblances, it has to be said that the practitioners of midfiction are themselves remarkably various and diverse, so much so that the middle grounds they occupy describe a spectrum of considerable range, the far edges of which abut on, although they do not overlap, the territories of reflexive and realistic writing.

21. This is not to deny a more obviously affirmative quality in other of Elkin's and particularly of Apple's work. See *Horizons of Assent*, chapter 5 and also chapter 7, below.

22. For a more detailed discussion of the referential aspects of Barthelme's fiction, see chapter 8, below.

23. Donald Barthelme, "The Emerald," *Sixty Stories* (New York: G. P. Putnam's

Sons, 1981), p. 395. The story originally appeared, with pictures and captions (Barthelme's?) in the November 1979 issue of *Esquire*, pp. 92–105.

24. Alastair Reid, "The Latin-American Lottery," *The New Yorker*, 26 January 1981, p. 109.

25. Stanley Elkin, "Introduction," *The Best American Short Stories 1980*, ed. Stanley Elkin with Shannon Ravenel (Boston: Houghton Mifflin, 1980), p. xviii.

26. Donald Barthelme, *The Dead Father* (New York: Farrar, Straus & Giroux, 1975), p. 175.

two

acts of definition

3

in defense of phenomenology, or who is Thomas Berger?

My subtitle is meant to invoke *Who Is Teddy Villanova?*, the most antic and subversive of Thomas Berger's novels, whose narrator, protagonist, and (more often than not) victim, one Russel Wren, may be thought to figure the traditional reader of well-made novels, that expectant and hopeful devourer of plots, always hungry for answers and resolutions. A strenuous moralist adrift in a self-serving world, burdened besides by an "appetite for the legendary,"[1] Wren brings to bear on the novel's byzantine plot and the stubbornly inexplicable world it articulates the ethical, aesthetic, and linguistic assumptions of an English teacher turned private eye. Trapped by the academic, overblown, but always orderly language his training has imposed on him, Wren is, not surprisingly, a spinner of theories: plausible theories constructed to explain everything, which, in the event, explain nothing—least of all the novel's eponymous villain, whose ubiquitous traces at once announce and obscure his repeatedly suspected presence. And who *is* Teddy Villanova? "The personification of evil" (p. 203), according to one of Wren's many dubious sources of information; but Berger's characters, inhabiting a world of extravagant intrigue, are understandably given to hyperbole. It makes more sense to think of Villanova as the necessary complement to Wren's assumptions, held in the face of all contrary evidence, about life's essential comprehensibility and (on the strength of this parabolic reading of the book) to see imaged in Wren's attempts at detection a quest for that most elusive of contemporary literary figures: the author.

The notion of the integrated, controlling author and, behind it, the concept of the coherent self have, of course, been under seige for close to a century. And yet, looking back from the vantage point of the eighties on the various modernist slogans that exemplify the attack—the intentional fallacy, the loss of the self, the autotelic work of art, and so on—and even allowing for the occasional exception (Nietzsche's "the subject as multiplicity," for example, or Gide's "action gratuite"), one has a sense of no more than minor skirmishes. Banished along with biographical criticism, the historical author resurfaces as the implied author; while the self, increasingly mysterious but far from lost, simply recedes beneath the level of the daily, empirical, recognizable "ego," there to regroup and to recuperate its essential being. Contemporary theory is an altogether different and more radical matter. Or so, at any rate, run its claims. Thus the author is seen to be not only displaced but absent (Jacques Derrida), fictitious (Raymond Federman), dead (Roland Barthes), a textual effect (Jean-Louis Baudry), or finally, according to Michel Foucault, "a certain functional principle by which, in our culture, one limits, excludes, and chooses; in short, by which one impedes the free circulation, the free manipulation, the free composition, decomposition, and recomposition of fiction . . . the ideological figure by which one marks the manner in which we fear the proliferation of meaning."[2]

At best, then, a function, a fiction, an effect: a hole in the fabric of language, to which alone it owes its insubstantial, epiphenomenal being. Moreover, the position is one with which, if I'm reading his deliberately bizarre and fantasticated novel correctly, Berger agrees. Very near the end of the book, having, as he thinks, solved the mystery of Villanova, Wren receives a final phone call from his still evasive, teasing prey—if, in fact, Villanova's is the voice at the other end of the line. Wren's response marks a change in attitude, if not, as one might expect, in his linguistic range: "'It's too late in the game for me to be gulled again,' said I. 'I no longer believe in archcriminals and polymorphous perverts. Quixotism cannot long survive among the Panzas of Manhattan'" (p. 244). Wren's declaration of independence represents both liberation from the need for tidy explanations (as well as from his "appetite for the legendary") and an acceptance of the world's contingency and facticity. Going further still, the novel's Baudelairean epigraph ("We are all celebrating some funeral") suggests that the corpse is the author's and that Berger is at one with poststructuralist critics in celebrating the death of presence, logocentrism, and the autonomous self.

Indeed, it is not only surfictionists and metafictionists who seem determined to dissolve the imperialism and integrity of authorial intention—at least in the reader's mind and, no doubt, occasionally in their own—though their strategies, one can agree, are the more immediately unsettling. What they self-consciously seek to enact, demonstrate, or artfully mirror (in a scriptural behavior that pulverizes plot and character, scrambles traditional narrative elements, and relentlessly plays with coherence by means of disorienting typographical tricks) vehemently and belligerently proclaims the nonreferential or reflexive nature of writing in general. On the other hand, midfiction, Berger's kind of fiction, while it also questions a traditional authorial center and power, preserves in its forms and rhetoric a referential, if not (as I stipulated in an earlier chapter) a representational function. Less spectacular but not for that reason less authentically "experimental," it strenuously interrogates the world without foreclosing all knowledge of it and unsettles rather than topples our certainties and presuppositions by way of parody and other recyclings of fictional, cultural, even metaphysical givens. There is no need, however, to catalogue the techniques of midfiction here. It is enough simply to note that in adopting parody as a dominant mode of registering their encounter with the world,[3] writers like Berger— or Barth, Baumbach, Charyn, and even, at times, Barthelme—risk, perhaps court, the possibility of ventriloquizing themselves out of existence and of producing an *oeuvre* (or, poststructuralist critics would say, a series of *textes*) devoid of any controlling center or developmental force.[4]

Or so it seems. In a recent study of postmodern literature, Charles Caramello argues persuasively that, despite the overwhelming commitment of critics and philosophers to a belief in the dissolution of the integral authorial self (and of the autonomous work), even the most complicitous writers of fiction hesitate finally and fully to endorse these ideas in practice. Postmodern fiction becomes, then, in Caramello's view, altogether more ambivalent, nostalgic, and problematic than theory often imagines it to be.[5] Similarly, toward the end of his remarkably sane and flexible discussion of metafiction, which implies, among other things, the "fictional" status of the author, Larry McCaffery concludes that "experimentalism *per se*—especially experimentalism in the direction of reflexive, nonreferential works—is not nearly as important to writers today as it was a decade ago."[6] But more is at issue than critical tendentiousness or the inevitable taming of the once radical. "The mere fact," Leo Bersani writes, "that every living organism has to accommodate itself to a field of reality in which its needs can never be entirely fulfilled suggests that the self, far from being only an ideological construct, would always have to go through a difficult negotiating process between its own appetitive energies and both a world *and* an internal economy which limit the possibilities of performing our energies and satisfying our appetites."[7] What makes this concession (for that is what it is) so important to the point I'm pursuing is the fact that it is embedded in a subtle and thoroughgoing attack on the stable self, eventuating in a call to resist coherence and to desublimate desire in order to achieve the goal of psychic mobility. In short, A *Future for Astyanax*, even as it asks us to "resist the appeal of that unity of personality assumed by all humanistic psychologies" (p. 310), concedes that "it would . . . be impossible to eliminate all fixed character structures" (p. 314).

The sinuousness of Bersani's argument is, at least in part, the result of adopting a model that, for all its stress on the liberation of desire (or because of it), remains fundamentally psychological; and he goes on to insist that "even the structured self can enter that play of mobile desire" (p. 314). The writers I'm concerned with, midfictionists like Berger, are at one with Bersani in the attempt to demystify the imperial ego: the self as a preexistent "psychic entity"[8] coercing a yielding world into a transparent text. But the "fixed character structures" that are for him the perhaps unfortunate by-product of the struggle between "the bias of centrality" (p. 284) and totally unmediated desire are for them an irrelevance. An irrelevance because what Bersani persists in regarding as an illusion (character as "the *centralizing* of a partial self" [p. 313]) midfictionists conceive of as a creation: consciousness discovering itself in its tentative, ongoing, and experiential relation with the world of which it is part and partner.

But how can one speak of an identifiable self or, conflating the two related concepts once more, of a definable author if, having rejected psychological, essentialist, and linguistic determinisms, one is left with so indeterminate a project as "the perceiving subject undergo[ing] a continued birth"?[9] How, in other words, is one to reconcile the fluidity of the inchoate self with the critical assumption that it is after all possible to respond positively, as Russel Wren finally refuses to do, to Berger's interrogation of the very existence of Teddy Villanova? The answer, as my last quotation suggests, is predicated on a phenomenological approach to current fiction, that is to say, on a belief that the author I've been pursuing is to be found *in* the text and that he exists there not only as "a variable and complex function of discourse,"[10] which in part he no doubt is, but as the initiator of a meaning his acts create.

This is not the place to attempt a full-scale exposition of phenomenology or of phenomenological criticism,[11] but something needs to be said to justify both my subsequent discussion of Berger (as well as other writers to be considered still later on) and the assertion just made that whereas in one sense "the author is never more than the instance writing" (that is, "it is language which speaks, not the author")[12] in another and more important sense the author creates himself in and through language. More accurately, the author creates that phenomenological ego to which we as readers respond and which "*does not exist* anywhere—not in things, which as yet have no meaning, nor in the artist himself, in his unformulated life" (SNS, p. 19). This is at once to acknowledge the determinative powers of *langue* and to insist nevertheless on the engendering force of *parole*: to reserve to ourselves as human beings the capacity to "make sense *out of* our experience from within [the world]"[13] and to claim for ourselves as readers the ability to discover in any writer's works the imprint of an always unique encounter with the unstable boundaries of experience.

What, then, does phenomenology or—to specify the version I intend to adopt in this book—what does Merleau-Ponty's phenomenology have to offer to a theory of authorship? In answering that question I mean to take for granted the well-known beliefs that found and distinguish his thought, namely, "the mutual implication of 'selfhood' and the 'world'";[14] the incarnation of consciousness and, what follows from that, the fact that the body is our fundamental way of seizing the world; and, finally, the intentionality of consciousness. Two consequences of these beliefs need to be stressed, however. First, that human beings are immersed, embedded, in the world, inseparable from it and incapable of attaining some ideal, neutral, detached vantage point from which to take its measure. Second, that because consciousness is situated, it is inevitably partial, limited, and perspectival. The existential cast of Merleau-Ponty's ideas is already apparent, and it is what accounts for his sense that we necessarily entertain an "ambiguous relationship . . . with our bodies and, correlatively, with perceived things" (PP, p. 4). Ambiguous because, as Eugene Kaelin remarks, "the human being is constrained to construct . . . objects from a first, often confused, and always indefinite perception of a situational quality."[15] But ambiguous also because our presence, or self-presence, is less a given than something to be determined, negotiated, and made—all these within the horizon the world offers to us. As Merleau-Ponty says, "the world is not what I think, but what I live through" (PhP, pp. xvi-xvii).

To say all of this is not to imply that we can know the world in itself, things in themselves, in some absolute and transparent way, though it is to admit their solicitation and pressure. Nor is it, as I'll argue more fully in a moment, to attribute to human beings the purity of unmediated vision. But it is to ask how exactly, if our natural, untutored instinct is to project and constitute the world, we can also speak of a mutual or reciprocal relation as the defining quality of our Lebenswelt. Merleau-Ponty's reply amounts to another acknowledgment of ambiguity, as when he argues "both that the world offers itself as prior to perception and that we do not limit ourselves to registering the world but would like to engender it" (PW, p. 124). By way of this generative and experiential paradox, Merleau-Ponty sets his philosophy apart from empiricism and idealism alike and, by implication, from notions of simple mimesis and nonreferentiality as well. In addition, the quotation makes clear why throughout his career his principal concern is with the primacy of perception. Perception is for him no less than our originary way of grasping the (pre-objective) world, of ordering it (to some degree), of making the indeterminate always more, if never fully, determinate, of, most especially, bringing meaning into being. As the transitivity of his vocabulary (seizing, grasping) indicates, perception is an event, an act: "We experience a perception and its horizon 'in action' [pratiquement] rather than by 'posing' them or explicitly 'knowing' them" (PP, p. 12). Indeed, "to be conscious is to constitute" (S, p. 93). But at the same time the act of perception is never more than incomplete, not only because our situation is inherently perspectival but because the world is inexhaustible, because it "envelops and exceeds those perspectives" (S, p. 52). Finally, perception is more than an act; it is a creative act. It "is already *primordial expression*" (S, p. 67).

With this assertion, we come up against one last ambiguity. Just as perception reaches toward expression, expression extends the project of perception. Which is not to say, however, that for all their apparent concentricity, Merleau-Ponty's two models of response are to be construed simply as less and more sophisticated versions of an identical impulse. Instead, we are told that "in one and the same movement knowledge roots itself in perception and distinguishes itself from perception. . . . This mute or operational language of perception begins a process of knowledge which it cannot itself accomplish. However firm my perceptive grasp of the world may be, it is entirely dependent upon a centrifugal movement which throws me toward the world." In short, expression, like other forms of knowledge, "continues without being reducible to perceptual evidence" (PW, pp. 124–25). Still, there exists between these two modes of encounter a relation of homology, if not identity, so that expression too (that is, language and, ultimately, literature or any of the other arts) "*is* the subject's taking up of a position in the world of his meanings" (PhP, p. 193)—meaning being understood here as "only the excess of what we live over what has already been said" (S, p. 83). Which is also to say that, though "never more than approximate" (S, p. 233), expression constitutes man's "existence in act" (S, p. 79).

That last phrase, the notion of a novel, say, providing us with the evidence of its author's existence in act, *as* act, brings us to the central consideration of how, specifically, phenomenology enables us to read. But before broaching that subject, I want to ask once again, and now more directly, what validity phenomenology can claim for itself in the face of poststructuralist and postmodernist objections to its foundational premises. If one accepts the usual description of phenomenology as a philosophy of presence and as a justification of both reference and meaning, is it possible to regard it as other than an exercise in myopic nostalgia and as more than an outworn metaphysics? Different, and different kinds of, answers are required, the most plausible, intelligible, and generally disregarded of which (to take the major poststructuralist attack first) is provided by Christopher Norris' assertion that "deconstruction neither denies nor really affects the common-sense view that language exists to communicate meaning. It *suspends* that view for its own specific purpose of seeing what happens when the writs of convention no longer run."[16] In other words, it is possible to argue that between deconstruction as a dismantling of Western metaphysics and phenomenology as the groundwork of a *practical* criticism there *is* no conflict, insofar as they aim at different levels of awareness or consciousness.

Indeed, Derrida himself appears to endorse the distinction. Maintaining that signs are signs by virtue of the repetitions they enact in their usage, claiming further that there is no expression (or expressing) that can avoid positing and implicating presence—the assumption of presence—Derrida admits that he is not concerned with new or original (nonrepetitive) modes in the *use* of language but goes on to admit their existence nevertheless. "Doubtless," he writes, "this representativeness [discourse representing itself, mirroring its own a prioris and structure] can be modified, complicated, and made to reverberate in original ways, ways that linguists, semioticians, psychologists, theoreticians of literature or art, and even philosophers may want to study."[17] It hardly needs saying that literary critics, whether or not their orientation is phenomenological, are concerned precisely with that originality whose possibility Derrida so offhandedly concedes. They are concerned, that is, with the question of how repetitions of signs can in various ways generate new meanings, new signifieds—and not merely for single but for armies of interacting signs. Critics may, of course, situate themselves outside the perhaps illusory world of the writer, devoting themselves, as deconstructionists do, to the exposure of an operative blindness (rarely, however, the blindness of contemporary, uncanonical writers). Or they may choose to enter that world, viewing it not as it appears to the historical author but as a created nexus of specific, identifiable, and original intentionality. To elect the second of these paths is no doubt to enter what Derrida in "White Mythology" calls the "gap of liars"; but it is also, according to a less skeptical interpretation, to adopt a generous suspension of disbelief in place of an ever vigilant and potentially corrosive cynicism.

To be sure, this community of empathetic readers is no longer, if it ever was, naive. It includes, after all, not only readers of nineteenth-century fiction but those self-conscious, provoked, and battered readers of Cervantes, Scarron, Sterne, and Diderot—not to mention Borges, Cortázar, and the small armies of meta- and surfictionists doing battle once again with realism and its still hardy assumptions. Possibly no reading can proceed, in the face of the slippery, metaphysical foundations and structures of language, without recourse to some *necessary* and occasional foreclosure of doubt. Not even deconstructionists, who seem to reach for a transcendental immunity through the scrupulous wakefulness of their activity, have invented an alternative discourse. Forced to write "sous rature," they write (like Beckett) nonetheless, betrayed, whatever their self-consciousness, into an inevitable retrieval of the same—a sameness or repetition of negativity that matches, even as it deconstructs, the sameness of positivity. In any case, with the settling of the deconstructive dust, critics, who can now spot with a marksman's eye the unintended ironies, contradictions, metaphysical preconceptions, and discontinuities of various strands of rhetoric or tropic discourse, will still be faced with the task of specifying the signifying gesture or, what Derrida allows, the "vouloir-dire" (p. 104) of a text, no matter how ghostly or problematic the "intuition" of its originary "I."

Phenomenology may be, as Derrida suggests, "la voie d'Icare" (p. 117), but it is doubtful that critics, compelled to make use of the metaphoricity of language, can avoid altogether the Fall his metaphor suggests. Language, however, is not the only battleground on which the war against phenomenology is currently being fought. The other potential challenge (more ostensible than real, as we'll see) comes from the direction of postmodernism and has to do with the kind and degree of order that Merleau-Ponty's philosophy seems to imply in its description of how the individual "intends" the world. There is no question but that for him intentionality implies a unifying activity, and he speaks, in a way bound to set the teeth of both poststructuralists and postmodernists on edge, of "the imperious unity, the presence, the insurpassable plenitude which is for us the definition of the real" (SNS, p. 15). He argues, furthermore, that "the perception of forms, understood very broadly as structure, grouping, or configuration should be considered our spontaneous way of seeing" (SNS, p. 49). On the other hand, Merleau-Ponty nowhere suggests either that perception settles the world into a steady and reductive order or that the world *is* order. In fact, his writings insist, again and again, on "the background of non-sense against which every universal undertaking is silhouetted and by which it is threatened with failure" (SNS, p. 4)— a background inexhaustible and (in its totality) unassimilable, an "unfinished task" (PP, p. 6).[18] This tempered estimate of our ability to make sense of things is crucial. Because our experience involves an awareness not only of ambiguity and contingency but of contradiction, irrationality, and indeterminacy (to choose some of the words that thread themselves through his writings); because, moreover, "the perceiving subject undergoes a continued rebirth; [is] at each instant . . . something new" (PP, p. 5), there is "a perpetual uneasiness in the state of being conscious" (SNS, p. 28). Not surprisingly, the writer, who, "as a professional of language . . . is a professional of insecurity" (S, p. 232) partakes of this uneasiness more abundantly still.

What emerges from this highly qualified account of man's capacities is the awareness that, whereas the human task is to constitute the world (or *a* world) and so to expand the potential for meaning, that task, risky at best, is constantly menaced by disorder and failure. Seen in this way, Merleau-Ponty's phenomenology presents itself, for all its talk of unity and a certain lurking transcendental tendency (discernible in its paroxysmic, mysterious abstractions or the occasional Sunday sweetness of its style), not as antithetical to but as in some ways oddly congruous with the emphatically immanent enterprise of postmodernism, and with the aims of midfiction most of all. Rejecting the possibility of totalizing orders, the adequacy of alternative worlds, the distance or detachment privileged by modernist writers together with the (aesthetic) finality, resolution, and closure they aim to achieve, postmodernism adopts, as Merleau-Ponty had, a perspective deliberately located within the world. In one of the most suggestive of his comments on traditional aesthetics, he contrasts "free perception" with "classical perspective," arguing that "what I transfer to paper [when obeying the "laws" of classical perspective] is not this coexistence of perceived things as rivals in my field of vision. I find the means of arbitrating their conflict, which makes depth. . . ." "Once," he goes on, "things disputed for my glance; and, anchored in one of them, I felt in it the solicitation of the others which made them coexist with the first—the demands of a horizon and its claims to exist" (S, pp. 48–49). Readers of meta- or midfiction cannot fail to be struck by the extraordinary familiarity of words like these. Fusing epistemology with acts of inscription, resolutely determined *not* to arbitrate the "conflict" Merleau-Ponty speaks about, but to avow instead a "tolerance for the incomplete" (S, p. 51),[19] they lay the foundation for a more spacious and flexible order than modernism found possible.

To put the matter a bit differently, the antirationalistic, anti-idealistic, and anti-imperialist bias of much contemporary literature discovers its justification nowhere better adumbrated than in Merleau-Ponty's theory, which permits the writer to manifest more accurately in the shape of discourse the dynamics of a perception inseparable from expression: "the experience of a world of teeming, exclusive things which could be taken in only by means of a temporal cycle in which each gain was at the same time a loss" (S, p. 50). Postmodernism may be able to find here a ground for its belief that unity is tentative, provisional, experiential, and therefore always subject to revision and modification; while midfiction, especially, may discover, if not an exact reflection, then a burgeoning (though somewhat suave) anticipation of its own recognition of the irrational and the non-sensical—not to mention its determination both to accept these as conditions of existence and, partially at least, to overcome them. "Partially" because, as I've been insisting, the creation of meaning takes place within and against the background or horizon of the world's never wholly recuperable disorder and because there exists for creators, whose work is by definition projective, no completion, no finality, no end to the acts that define and redefine them.

How, then, or where, are we to locate our elusive author? What coherence can we hope to uncover in, as it seems, so unstable a figure? And, most specifically, what methodological help does phenomenology offer? Toward the end of his exhaustive study of Merleau-Ponty, Kaelin concludes that the phenomenology of perception fails to realize the existentialist criticism it hints at;[20] and in some sense he is right. Nevertheless, it may be that Merleau-Ponty's work remains our best guide to resolving the problem of the authorial self. What we are offered in his various writings are sporadic but suggestive excursions into practice and, more importantly, a way of apprehending the human situation. What we are *not* given is a programmatic approach; and that, I want to suggest (*pace* the impressive counterexample of Roman Ingarden or the model of the "modes" and "contents" of consciousness derived from phenomenological psychology[21]), may be just as well. The case can be made that phenomenology proves more useful in suggesting what criticism ought to look for than in indicating how exactly the search should be carried out; and though so unspecific a set of directions is unlikely to raise up a host of determined epigones, as structuralism so disastrously did, it does at any rate invite the critic to regard the singularity of the artist with a maximum of flexibility and openness.

On the other hand, if phenomenological criticism offers more of an enabling grid than a precise methodology and if, in Spitzerian fashion, it asks us to undertake for every work or body of work we approach a "to-and-fro voyage from certain outward details to the inner center and back again to other series of details,"[22] still it excludes certain approaches and invites certain emphases, the chief of which have to do with questions of what we are looking for and where we ought to be looking for it. As indicated above, the *what* is something other than the empirical author and, indeed, something different from the phenomenological ego considered as a distinct and separable entity. Our quest is rather, as Merleau-Ponty says, for a style, "the system of equivalences that [the artist] makes for himself for the work which manifests the world he sees"; and, better still, for an emblem: "the emblem of a way of inhabiting the world, of handling it, and of interpreting it . . . in short, the emblem of a certain relationship to being" (S, p. 54). The *where* has been defined, variously, as experiential patterns (Magliola), an organizing form (the early Hillis Miller), a spiritual etymon (Spitzer), and most simply, as structures of experience. Or, more accurately, of experiencing, for what these structures testify to—the emblem they offer, which represents all we *can* know of the "author"—is the grasping by a conditional self of a world whose horizon is always shifting and indefinite.

The various definitions I've cited of those elements in a work of art that ought to claim our attention have this in common: they assume the repetitive, if not the self-identical, nature of consciousness. But consciousness repeats itself in a number of ways. Not only different artists but different ages intend their worlds differently and, in attempting to sharpen our focus, we need to take account of the shifting constraints—generic, stylistic, technical—that affect readers and writers alike. Modernist literature, for example, calls preeminently for a study of form. The postmodern writing I'm concerned with demands, on the contrary, that we consider its antiformalism, that we find in its apparent incon-sequences and irrelevances,[23] its rejections of coherence and closure, its hetero-geneity of style or styles, a meaning, a "vouloir-dire," different from what we have known in the past. Furthermore, if our concern remains, in postmodern as in modernist (or any) literature, with structures of recurrence, these must be, paradoxical as it sounds, capacious enough to encompass those disruptive tokens by which so many contemporary writers define themselves: the irresolutions and contradictions of experience, the ragged edges of consciousness's negotiations with a perceived, sensed, imagined, and written *Umwelt*. Finally, in attending to what is obsessive in a single work or an *oeuvre*, we need to seek out what is latent as much as, or more than, what is thematized, to note Merleau-Ponty's fissures and lacunae as well as (they are much the same) Wolfgang Iser's gaps, and, above all perhaps, to make sense of the unassimilated excess that, in a fictional enterprise like Berger's, makes the subtext not only augment but reveal the full dimensions of the text. My allusion, after so many pages, is deliberate. I want to turn (and return) in the next chapter to my point of departure: the problematic identity of the author, whom we may specify in this case, and for the sake of convenience, as Thomas Berger.

Notes

1. Thomas Berger, *Who Is Teddy Villanova?* (New York: Delacorte Press/Seymour Lawrence, 1977), p. 178. Subsequent references to the novel and to most other works quoted will be given, after their first citation, parenthetically in the text. The book will be referred to hereafter as *TV*.

2. Michel Foucault, "What Is an Author," in *Textual Strategies: Perspectives in Post-Structuralist Criticism*, ed. Josué V. Harari (Ithaca, N.Y.: Cornell University Press, 1979), p. 159.

3. And, incidentally, with other authors and genres, since parody is arguably the most overt form of intertextual encounter.

4. On the question of parody, see Margaret A. Rose's exhaustive (and at times exhausting) study *Parody//Meta-Fiction: An Analysis of Parody as a Critical Mirror to the Writing and Reception of Fiction* (London: Croom Helm, 1979) and Charles Moles-worth's lively discussion in *Donald Barthelme's Fiction: The Ironist Saved from Drowning* (Columbia, Mo. and London: University of Missouri Press, 1982), especially chapter 3.

5. See Charles Caramello, *Silverless Mirrors: Book, Self & Postmodern American Fiction* (Tallahassee: Florida State University Press, 1983), chapter one.

6. Larry McCaffery, *The Metafictional Muse: The Works of Robert Coover, Donald Barthelme, and William H. Gass* (Pittsburgh: University of Pittsburgh Press, 1982), p. 261.

7. Leo Bersani, *A Future for Astyanax: Character and Desire in Literature* (Boston and Toronto: Little, Brown, 1976), p. 8.

8. Neal Oxenhandler, "The Horizons of Psychocriticism," *New Literary History*, 14 (Autumn 1982), 92. Oxenhandler uses the phrase in discussing Jean-Louis Baudry.

9. Maurice Merleau-Ponty, *The Primacy of Perception and Other Essays*, ed. James M. Edie (Evanston, Ill.: Northwestern University Press, 1964), p. 6. The

collection will be referred to hereafter as *PP*. References to Merleau-Ponty's other works are as follows (the abbreviations used are indicated): *PhP: Phenomenology of Perception*, trans. Colin Smith (London: Routledge & Kegan Paul, 1962); *PW: The Prose of the World*, ed. Claude Lefort, trans. John O'Neill (London: Heinemann, 1974); *S: Signs*, trans. Richard C. McCleary (Evanston, Ill.: Northwestern University Press, 1964); *SNS: Sense and Non-Sense*, trans. Hubert L. Dreyfus and Patricia Allen Dreyfus (Evanston, Ill.: Northwestern University Press, 1964).

10. Foucault, p. 158.

11. Among the most helpful studies are the following: Eugene F. Kaelin, *An Existentialist Aesthetic: The Theories of Sartre and Merleau-Ponty* (Madison: The University of Wisconsin Press, 1966); Sarah Lawall, *Critics of Consciousness: The Existential Structures of Literature* (Cambridge, Mass.: Harvard University Press, 1968); Robert R. Magliola, *Phenomenology and Literature: An Introduction* (West Lafayette, Ind.: Purdue University Press, 1977); and J. Hillis Miller, "The Geneva School," in *Modern French Criticism: From Proust and Valéry to Structuralism*, ed. John K. Simon (Chicago and London: University of Chicago Press, 1972), pp. 277–310.

12. Roland Barthes, "The Death of the Author," *Image-Music-Text*, ed. Stephen Heath (New York: Hill and Wang, 1977), pp. 145 and 143.

13. Hubert L. Dreyfus and Patricia Allen Dreyfus, "Translators' Introduction," *Sense and Non-Sense*, p. x.

14. Magliola, p. 14.

15. Kaelin, p. 217.

16. Christopher Norris, *Deconstruction: Theory and Practice* (London and New York: Methuen, 1982), p. 128.

17. Jacques Derrida, *La Voix et le phénomène: Introduction au problème du signe dans la phénoménologie de Husserl* (Paris: Presses Universitaires de France, 1967), p. 64. The translation is mine.

18. In the introduction to his edition of *The Essential Writings of Merleau-Ponty* (New York: Harcourt, Brace & World, 1969), Alden Fisher writes: "Reality will yield some necessary structures, but its contingency can never be fully overcome" (p. 11).

19. Merleau-Ponty is speaking of Cézanne and Klee. Compare Donald Barthelme's *The Dead Father* (New York: Farrar, Straus & Giroux, 1975), where his protagonist, Thomas, speaks of being "able to tolerate the anxiety" (p. 93).

20. Kaelin, p. 321.

21. See Magliola, pp. 34–36.

22. Leo Spitzer, *Linguistics and Literary History: Essays in Stylistics* (Princeton: Princeton University Press, 1948), pp. 19–20. On Spitzer's relation to phenomenological criticism, see Magliola, pp. 33–34 and 37. In a review of Magliola's book, "The Lessons of Phenomenology," *Diacritics*, 9 (Summer 1979), 37, W. Wolfgang Holdheim insists still more strongly on that relation.

23. These concepts can only be formulated normatively and in response to a center that may or may not be missing or suggested.

4

the uneasiness of being

"As with all my novels," Berger wrote recently, "the language of this work [*The Feud*] is the theme; but I expect," the statement goes on (half-ironically, half-defiantly), "that as usual the tin-eared will fail to hear the delicate inflections and humorously mistake it for a study in comic anthropology."[1] At the risk of joining the ranks of the tin-eared, I have to say that, whatever else Berger's fiction achieves, it is rarely delicate inflections. Indeed, as an instrument of discrimination and nuance, Berger's style often seems remarkably blunt, even awkward: the manifestation, if style can still be thought to image the man, of a certain uneasiness (more profound than what Merleau-Ponty attributes to all consciousness, or even to all writers) in the face of whatever it is that is being expressed. In other words, although Berger's *intention* in thematizing language may be seen, along with much of contemporary criticism's, as promoting an aesthetics of the reflexive and self-enclosed, his practice, the primary evidence of his *intentionality*, suggests nothing so much as an edgy discomfort with a world too effortlessly dismissed from consideration.

Or is this perhaps to take Berger's mini-credo too soberly and literally? When in his prefatory note to *Killing Time*, he insists that "a work of fiction is a construction of language and otherwise a lie,"[2] one senses a more traditional motive at work: the antimimetic, antiutilitarian bias of most experimental literature of the last hundred years. Like Joseph Detweiler, the antihero of that book, Berger takes a stand against imitation, the re-presentation of a pre-existent reality. But the differences between Berger and his character are as instructive as the similarities. Detweiler, who owns no books, considers reading futile, and has no sense of humor, "never got the joke implicit in imaginative writing" (p. 78); but while he, literalist that he is, deplores art's uselessness (its "joke") and resents its insult to the original it means to copy, Berger, committed to the notion that we cannot know things in themselves, celebrates it—or, more accurately, acknowledges and accepts the fact that art can do no more than supply *a* view of what we choose to call reality.

And yet, to maintain that Berger celebrates (even in this modified sense) art's, and therefore language's, uselessness probably overstates the case. Whereas Berger's attitude can legitimately be compared to others abroad in the twentieth century, its roots are deeper still, as *Sneaky People*, the novel most directly concerned with the problem of language, makes clear. Early in that book, the following exchange takes place between its protagonist and his mother:

"Ralph, do you think that sometimes you are too honest?" . . .
"Maybe," he said soberly. "But the truth is the truth."
"Oh, I don't know," said his mother. "Maybe it's all made up."   (p. 54)

By the close of the novel, Ralph has lost his innocence in more ways than one. In the most important way, in learning to manipulate language to his own ends, he has become one of the sneaky people who populate and control the world. What matters is not simply that the book presents itself as an ironic *Bildungsroman* and, more specifically, as a parable of the Fall—a fall primarily into language—but that it represents a kind of lament. At once cynical, sentimental, and nostalgic, the novel traces but also regrets the end of innocence; and it is more than possible that within its story of deception and frustrated desire *Sneaky People* conceals a primitivist yearning for openness, communication, and transparency. If this is in fact the case, it follows that Berger's principal and enabling conceptual beliefs—that we are, all of us, inevitably subject to a host of linguistic and cultural determinations and that we are consequently the victims rather than the masters of the tools with which we presume to probe reality—these owe as much to structural as to Saussurean linguistics and as much to Romantic as to modernist and postmodernist epistemologies.

I'll return later on to these questions of filiation. First, however, a more important point. Despite poststructuralism's project of dispersing conventional thematic centers (a project Berger appears to share), it is already beginning to be evident that such centers exist in his work, that the novels intend the world in a specific, discernible, and characteristic, if not always unequivocal, way. To say—as Carlo Reinhart, the hero of Berger's tetralogy, does—that "the whole of life, as we know it, is a construct of mind, perhaps of language" (VP, p. 397) is to indicate not the end but the beginning of the problem, which in Berger's case takes the form of a sustained investigation into the responses human beings make to a reality hidden away in and obscured by the impenetrable folds of language. To be sure, Berger's novels are dizzyingly various—one senses that the investigation is no less a self-investigation—and his positioning of himself, in his role of parodist, as the inhabiter of intertextual and cultural semiotic systems insinuates the obliteration of his own identifiable presence. Nevertheless, as one enters, one after another, the discrete realms of Arthurian romance, frontier America, the gumshoe and detective novel, as one traverses dystopias, *Bildungsromane*, *romans fleuves*, and so on, one senses certain emphases, recurrences, *points de repères*: the creation, if not the presumption, of coherence, or at least of a fundamental consistency.

What we are given, though never in quite the same way twice, is a collocation of the elements I've been describing: language, the world, and a collection of characters who admit or, more often, deny the mediative effects of the one (language) on their confrontation with the other (the world). Chief among the deniers—and they include the most vivid of Berger's figures—are the philosophical idealists: "the type of man," as Jack Crabb says of General Custer in *Little Big Man*, "who carries the whole world within his own head and thus when his passion is aroused and floods his mind, reality is utterly drowned" (p. 404). Encompassing a diverse group of egomaniacs, monomaniacs, and solipsists, as well as those given, sometimes as destructively, to abstraction and the ascendancy of the idea, these coercers of reality represent from one end of Berger's career to the other the most intense and single-minded reaction in his fiction to the kind of world he habitually imagines into being. The concretions of the type are manifold, ranging as they do from Reinhart's essentially passive father ("an idealist in the true sense of the word" [*RL*, p. 374]) and aggressive, carping mother to his odious father-in-law and his son ("What he wanted was always right. Why? Because it was what he wanted" [*VP*, p. 242]); and from the much put-upon Russel Wren, constantly confusing literature and life, to Bob Sweet, the cryonics booster of *Vital Parts*, whose aim is to "eliminate the dimension of Time" (p. 124). But if the diversity within the overarching category is impressive, what matters finally is the category itself, the community of obsession, which binds these idealists together. Locked into their certainties, unable to detect the relativity of the cultural givens that (we and Berger know) determine them, they all share the will to impose those certainties on the world. [3]

It would be easy enough to range against Berger's idealists the characters he manifestly admires: the mobile and disengaged like Jack Crabb, who is of two worlds and neither; the Indians in the same book, to the degree that they are able "to open [their] spirit up to the wind" (*LBM*, p. 139); those like Wren at the end of *Teddy Villanova*, who forego their quest for answers and solutions; and, above all, Reinhart, Berger's most enduring (and autobiographical?) protagonist, for whom "soul-searching, weighing of alternatives, and identification of motives were a disordered procedure," partly at least because "receptivity to all points of view was his natural habit" (*VP*, p. 242). Indeed, Reinhart, though generally treated with irony as well as sympathy, comes as close to a hero as one is likely to find in Berger's fiction. The reasons for the choice are obvious. The world according to Berger is one without certainty: as outlandish, unpredictable, and contingent as Earl Keese, overresponding or misresponding to that awareness, takes it to be. It follows that what Berger values is the undogmatic, the open, the imperfect, the power of resiliency and adaptability, and, above all, the capacity—imaged in *Arthur Rex*'s contrast of the vital and flawed Lancelot with the altogether too perfect Galahad—"merely to be human, just to survive" (*ROW*, p. 192).

And yet, for all this conscious and deliberate mapping of alternative ways of engaging reality, the notion of unshaded opposition will not do. Certainly, it fails to account for the tensions that sometimes tilt Berger's sympathies in unexpected directions and still more frequently unsettle the reader's sense of how precisely to react. Thus, Berger's two most idealist characters are, if not his heroes, at least the object of his sustained and intense interest. There is no doubting his affection for King Arthur, but no doubting either the answer to Mordred's question: "Can there not exist monsters of the well-intentioned?" (*AR*, p. 366). As Arthur himself admits, his quest is for "absolute perfection . . . which is impossible of attainment" (p. 97); and like most of Berger's idealists, he seeks, ultimately, "to find an universal principle for all things, which is to say, a fixity, an arresting of time" (p. 315). At once too principled and too abstract, too neglectful of the human and of time as the definition of the human, Arthur aims, by way of his Christian beliefs and chivalric code, to correct nature. Joseph Detweiler, a more contemporary and secular figure (though he is insistently connected with Christmas and an ingenuously eccentric brand of salvation), tries instead to ignore it. His failure to do so makes him not only a more complex character than Arthur but, in his role of guileless murderer, the most perverse, thoroughgoing, and oddly attractive inhabitant of Berger's gallery of unregenerate monomaniacs. "Interested solely in fundamentals" (*KT*, p. 23), Detweiler is after the durable, the eternal, the nonaccidental, the "truth-retaining" (p. 83). Pursuing the goal of what he calls "Realization"—the ability "to translate himself into a new context, using only the mind" (p. 78), to "relive the event itself" (p. 298), in short, to be at one with reality—he understandably resists mediation of any kind: art (he has practiced and abandoned sculpture and taxidermy); his mother's spiritualism; sexuality (he attempts to have his penis amputated); language ("Realization could only be approximated in language, *talked about*, but not *experienced*" [p. 84]); and, in general, all "distortion of wish and will" (p. 298).

Berger's attitude toward the project of Realization is what one would expect; and when, at the end of his trial, Detweiler announces: "Each man kills Time in his own way" (p. 366), it is difficult not to hear instead the voice of his creator commenting on the human tendency to achieve certainty, to snare the absolute, by imposing on the world's multifariousness the shape and set of the individual constraining mind. Berger's feeling for Detweiler himself is another matter, however. One can, of course, easily enough account for his fascination with an artist who sees in art's attempt "to represent life" (p. 133) the commission of a crime. *Killing Time* is, after all, in part a reflexive novel whose parallel but incommensurate discourses (everyone in the novel treats life as art) all and equally fail to explain a "reality" the novelist himself invents: the killing which, in the novel's symbolic detective structure, is also the misdeed of fiction, created in all lucidity and incapable, finally, of solution. But Detweiler is more than a compelling enigma, more than the occasion for a meditation on the pretensions and limitations of art. Thanks to his distractedness, which he both recognizes and deplores; thanks to his zestful enjoyment of the concrete and the phenomenal, of ordinary, sensuous things (he is constantly described in relation to food; he walks through a department store "feeding his senses" [p. 135]), he emerges from the novel as not only fascinating but appealing.

Still, the issue I'm raising has to do neither with the fact of Detweiler's appeal nor with Berger's skill in neutralizing, even reversing, the reader's probable reaction to this demented murderer. The problem is how to explain the appeal of Detweiler to *Berger*. In other words, if, as I've been trying to suggest, Berger's postmodernism locates itself in an unrelenting irony at the expense of those who attempt to control the world's unpredictability, nevertheless the examples of Arthur and Detweiler indicate that he is not necessarily unresponsive to those who seek such control. Something more than a kind of negative capability is at work here. Indeed, something quite different. Enlarging on what I said earlier about his handling of language, I want to propose now, more radically, that Berger's "embodiment," as it emerges in his books, is in general one of uneasiness, discomfort, tension. The novels manifest, along with a determined effort to accept the contingency of reality, a more fundamentally intentional sense of the world as hostile, threatening, disequilibriating, alien, *other*; and, in this perspective, one comes to see why not only Arthur, Detweiler, and Bob Sweet but Reinhart himself "could never accept the passing of time" (*RL*, p. 237)—or, what amounts to the same thing, the indeterminacy of human existence.

Acceptance, then, but denial too. At the center of Berger's fiction there is a paradox that seems initially not only to undermine the goals his enterprise ostensibly claims for itself but even to menace the integrity I've claimed for it. For example, in seeking to deny his authorial identity, Berger, who is unquestionably among the most heteroclite of writers, pushes against the notion of repetition or sameness. But what his work reveals is not merely the impossibility of avoiding repetition but the fear, on the part of Berger's characters—and on his own—of what that avoidance entails: the full embrace of the *différance* so essential to deconstructionist aesthetics. Indeed, one needn't search very far to discover in various of the novels an intransigence in the face of the inexplicable, specifically, a primitivist and even a conservative strain that acts to contravene the suspensiveness Berger seems most often to allege. What I have in mind is something more than the celebration (equivocal in any case) of the Indians in *Little Big Man*, or the regret for a lost innocence that *Sneaky People* implies, or, a more telling example, the recurrence in book after book of Reinhart's army experience, which intimates the ideal of freedom but is in fact an image of control, "a sense of community" (VP, p. 184) rooted in the security of male bonding.

More to the point is the dystopian fantasy, *Regiment of Women*, which, through a kind of Swiftian irony, portrays the oppression of women by imagining the equally plausible, or implausible, oppression of men in the twenty-first century. Asserting, like the other fiction, that everyone is trapped in and by artificially-based, linguistically-generated roles and models, the novel argues more particularly that all sexual interpretations are the mind's impositions on the diversity of experience. So much is clear. Too clear perhaps, for at his least successful, Berger is an elaborator of conceits. The ending, however—an Edenic scene in which the two major characters revert to their "natural" sexual roles—betrays the intended moral. No doubt, the final vision means to suggest a relationship in which no one is master, no one underling. In fact, with civilization increasingly stripped away, biology asserts itself, and nature, assumed to be the biological determinant not only of sexual but of social behavior, emerges as the novel's traditional and inexorable norm, the justification of a division that *Regiment of Women* intends, in theory, to subvert.[4]

The appeal to nature (or Nature)—we will come upon it again—is one of Berger's hedges against a world perceived as totally out of control. Nevertheless, for all his residual conservatism, he generally adopts less peremptory and clearcut solutions to the dilemmas his novels enact. The most complex of his characters, attempting to negotiate the antithesis of the world's mysterious and threatening presence and the mind's coercive power, dramatize instead the risky existential ethic that most fully expresses their author's special perspective on the hazards of modern experience. The basis of the threat and the motive for the idealist reaction are both to be found in that sense of otherness I've alluded to, which, as much implicitly as explicitly, determines the horizon within or against which Berger grasps and constitutes his world. What we are dealing with are those profoundly unassimilable elements of existence that poststructuralism has thrown into relief and that challenge the integrity, even the identity, of the self. As a result, the question Berger's fiction most insistently, if covertly, poses (at the level of character and author alike) is whether it is possible, in the light of this challenge, to recuperate or rather to originate the self, to give it, however tenuously, an operative reality at least.

Variously specified—as time, of course, but also as woman, language, mortality, anarchy, and evil (to offer, for now, an incomplete list), the principle of the Other takes as its first what is perhaps its most traditional form, the problematic figure of the Jew. There is nothing surprising about the choice: *Crazy in Berlin* takes place during the postwar occupation. Nor is there anything unexpected in Berger's attitudes. More realistic (and symbolic) than his later novels, more traditionally humanistic in its orientation, the book offers through the filter of the young Reinhart an unexceptionable moral appraisal of (as it was coming to be known) the absurd: "Did it matter?, oh, hell yes, for all we have in this great ruined Berlin of existence . . . is single, lonely, absurd-and-serious selves; and the only villainy is to let them pass beyond earshot" (p. 282). In aid of these beliefs, Reinhart attempts, at the risk of his own life, to rescue a Jewish friend and, failing that, betrays his friend's betrayer. But to say that Reinhart engages himself in the events around him is not to suggest that the novel's perplexity about the Jews and their "difference" is in any way overcome. It is not. In fact, the Jewish question yields neither to formal nor to logical resolution; and toward the end of the book Reinhart admits to the psychiatrist who is treating his "craziness": "Now the Jews and me. My feelings about them are irrational. Actually the Jews bore me stiff. . . . Maybe, secretly, every gentile wants to kill every Jew, but the Nazis did it in practice and the other Germans, or many of them, didn't care. But you see, *someone must care.*" And when the psychiatrist says in turn, "But you were concerned about the Jews," Reinhart answers: "I am concerned about myself" (pp. 370–71), a statement that gives us, honestly enough, as much finality as the book has to offer. The issue, in brief—and it is what makes *Crazy in Berlin* a paradigmatic work—revolves around Reinhart's ability to accept, on the one hand, the insolubility of the problem and the irrationality of his own feelings, and, on the other, the necessity of proceeding almost despite them: the need to act his values, which is to say, himself, into being.

At the same time, because Berlin represents not only the human condition in all its grotesqueness but also, for Reinhart, a time out of time, away from "the earth-people" (p. 379), that is, ordinary existence, the situation the novel describes is to a degree anomalous. And ambiguous as well. It can be granted that Reinhart commits himself to his beliefs and so ratifies his freedom. But insofar as his sense of freedom derives most fundamentally from the security of his army life and the control it offers, it is legitimate to ask whether external definition doesn't in some sense compromise and exceed self-definition, thereby forestalling a still more radical encounter with an otherness that Berlin's Jews only begin to suggest. Certainly, the problem reappears in Berger's second novel, where, at first, it seems to be more openly and directly confronted. Reinhart, we're told in that book, being "a man, was at any given moment trying to define himself" (*RL*, p. 237). The implied distinction between male and female modes of consciousness—Berger's, I suspect, as well as Reinhart's—has its own fascination, but what needs to be examined first is the notion of definition itself. "True freedom," Reinhart thinks at one point, "is found only by being consistent with oneself" (p. 254), and, even more than in *Crazy in Berlin*, "his quest, of course, remained: freedom" (p. 172). But consistency of this kind is exactly what he is incapable of and what, in large measure, makes him Berger's hero. If definition, at least self-definition (which is what consistency with oneself amounts to here) entails an act performed in terms of something other than the self, then idealism, aggressively reassembling reality according to its own prescriptive needs and desires, describes the ultimate self-definition: a performance *at the expense of* the world. Berger's heroes seek instead (a more precarious enterprise) definition *in terms of* the world, so that otherness is conceived of not only as threat but as a necessary, enabling resistance, the abrasive difference that makes possible the construction, the creation, of a self. In addition, since "to live by the definitions of other people was always to be a swine" (*VP*, p. 199), self-creation is also a way, *the* way, of overcoming otherness. But not in theoretical terms. As in *Crazy in Berlin*, so in *Reinhart in Love*, salvation lies in *acts* of definition: Berger joins Merleau-Ponty in valorizing the dynamics of a concrete and specific encounter with the world.

Such a dynamics in fact energizes Reinhart's climactic speech—"Do, instead of Look. Act, rather than Imagine. Move, in place of Talk" (*RL*, p. 425)—which in its attack on the aestheticizing of life (a form of idealism, of course), its defense of reality against fantasy, triumphantly turns a porn show into a whore house and its heretofore passive audience into a mob of sexual activists, leaving Reinhart himself to announce to the show's owner that "it [the reconstructed "entertainment"] will no longer outrage Nature to anything like the old extent. Just remember, you never have to apologize for normality" (p. 428). We are to understand, needless to say, that Reinhart has accomplished his most elaborate act of self-definition, after which the novel can end because definition, being an ongoing process, is necessarily unfinished: an act in what must be a continuing series of acts. (Again there is nothing that could rightly be called resolution or closure, for in structural terms the climax is, as it were, incidental; the final chapter, following on the one I've been describing, begins: "Reinhart had been sidetracked" [p. 429].)

But this amounts to only half the story. Something more is at stake than a manifesto on behalf of participation, and once again the reference to "nature" provides the clue. Like *Regiment of Women, Reinhart in Love* asserts at the last, and in the teeth of its putative acceptance of freedom and diversity, the appropriateness of man's ascendancy over women. As the "blow against . . . teasing" (p. 429) that Reinhart prides himself on—he is thinking about his disruption of the pornographic spectacle—dissolves into a justification of the normal, there takes place in the novel's deeper moral (or perhaps psychological) economy a righting of things that addresses a felt sense of imbalance. (In the third of the novels devoted to him, we're told that "women had always been Reinhart's nightmare" [*VP*, p. 296].) Whatever Berger's ostensible purpose, then, the scene reverberates in ways that are as dissonant as they are distasteful, and we come to comprehend more fully why, through most of his work, he displays an abiding, if ambivalent, fascination for his idealists, whose inclinations offer a persistent temptation not to come to terms with but to overcome, to shut out, the alien presence of the Other. And what is the cause of this fascination, the ground of this temptation, which subverts the integrity of Reinhart's existential choice, his capacity to define himself *without* obliterating the world? The most fundamental revelation of *Reinhart in Love*, as of *Crazy in Berlin* and most of the other fiction, is of a terror, a fear in the face of the ungovernable, that demonstrably supplies the mainspring of Berger's work, the hidden source of the perplexity that defines, in Merleau-Ponty's phrase, his "intentional arc."[5]

I don't intend, in pursuit of that arc, to track Berger through all of his novels. The patterns I've been describing are recurrent and may be taken for granted— at least until some of the more recent works. But before looking at these, I want to anticipate a possible objection, namely, that the attitudes I'm ascribing to Berger's characters are theirs, not his, and that I have given an account of his ideas instead of his "situation." The question is whether a resemblance does exist, particularly between Reinhart and his creator. Reinhart's four appearances in the series that bears his name run from 1958 to 1981 (his fictional life span is longer still), and, as one would expect, he displays, in the midst of his repeated attempts both to define himself and to avoid the finality of definition (a description of Berger as parodist as well?), a marked if unsteady development. As, I want to argue, does Berger, so that there can be detected not an identity, certainly, but a parallel between the two, manifest most obviously, perhaps, in the gradual tempering of the traditional and unreflective humanism to which both originally subscribe. (By the time of *Vital Parts*, Reinhart is less sure than he once was of the efficacy of his earlier, Orwellian slogan, "common decency.") My concern, however, is with Berger's novelistic strategies, which, as they evolve, mark the gradual transformation of a fairly conventional realist into a postmodernist of considerable originality and, more to the point, into a midfictionist who ploughs up without abandoning fiction's familiar ground. Generally, one notes, beginning with *Killing Time*, a complicating of focus, a multiplying of perspectives, a refusal to espouse unequivocally a single point of view. More specifically, what we find is a skewing of the narrative line, in such a way as deliberately to frustrate and unbalance the reader, and a concomitant blurring of character outline (of those characters, at any rate, who are not villains or grotesques). These technical shifts amount, in turn, to a decreased attention to, even an undercutting of, verisimilitude and depth and an attempt to defraud us of "answers," of stability and closure. In short, from the late sixties onward, we encounter a mode of writing that articulates Berger's emblematic relation to the world: something akin to Reinhart's (and other characters') growing sense of indeterminacy and uncertainty, which is, like Berger's, crossed with an occasional desire to escape completely the burden of contingency.

In sum, the situation is this: Reinhart's increasing receptivity to the uncertain and incomprehensible ("When Reinhart was younger," the narrator of *Vital Parts* comments, suggesting that things have changed, "he had sought control over experience" [p. 175]) finds its counterpart in Berger's structural openness and experimentation. But by the same token, Reinhart's continuing uneasiness ("It is difficult," he admits in the same book, "to deal with freedom" [p. 272]) echoes Berger's own failure to confront the demon of otherness head-on. The first two novels of the eighties, however, suggest at least the possibility of a new and more easeful accommodation with the world, a swerve in, if not a recharting of, the intentionality of character and author alike. In these books, the theme of the world's disorder, along with the problems of freedom and self-definition, becomes—without ceasing to be that—more nearly a celebration of the extraordinary as the ordinary and (ultimately a riskier position) of the ordinary as the extraordinary: a shift in emphasis that has to do, one surmises, with Berger's gradual embrace of suspensiveness—the acceptance of that state "when things did not add up," which for Detweiler, and for Berger throughout most of his career, means "trouble" (*KT*, p. 187).

So it is in *Neighbors*, which adroitly intertwines the plausible and the implausible—or, rather, sets them side by side, thereby keeping the reader as constantly off-base as the incredulous Earl Keese. Predicated on Earl's inability to accept the bizarre as real (and Harry and Ramona, the neighbors of the title, are nothing if not bizarre), the novel gradually transforms absurdist comedy into a parable about the disjunctions of human psychology and, it seems, about the need to make an adjustment to them. To put this another way, what appears at first to be a dramatization of life's palpable irrationality, "a life in which," Earl says, "chance encounters can be brutal" (p. 125), becomes even more, as the novel goes on, a myth of middle age seeking and resisting something on the order of saturnalia. Everything considered, Earl, for all his skeptical resistance, craves the "outlandish"; and Harry and Ramona, outrageous and conscienceless to the end, suggest an objectification of his own repressed desires. When, toward the end of the book, he tells his hardly more predictable wife: "They're free spirits, Harry and Ramona, the world would be a worse place without them" (p. 270), it is clear that he is beginning to be moved by, though he probably still does not recognize, the anarchic, amoral principle his neighbors embody. And when, in answer to Harry's evocative invitation, "All aboard! . . . Connections to all points of view" (p. 273), he decides to leave home, he apparently crosses the boundary intimated by one of his earlier remarks: "It just takes a while to perceive their unique quality, but once you do, *you're not the same*" (p. 271; my italics).

Perhaps. I've used words like "seems" and "appears" a good deal in discussing *Neighbors*, and with reason. If the novel is in fact parabolic, or something like parable,[6] its "moral" is intended less to enlighten than to unsettle us: to make us too confront the randomness and incalculability that exists without and within. Earl's fatal stroke, with which the book ends, may be victory or defeat; it is clearly a summons to recognize the extraordinary as a fact of existence and, like Earl, to come (more or less) to terms with it. As Ramona says, "it could happen to anybody" (p. 275), a remark that, if it fails altogether to clarify, at least generalizes, Earl's confrontation with the Other that is himself.

Reinhart's Women, probably the least hectic of Berger's novels but by no means the least original, is even more suspensive and midfictional: a meditation, one might argue, on the unexpected enchantments of the ordinary. To discuss the book requires, however, an account of one final, fictional incarnation of otherness. At the risk of turning Reinhart too facilely into a mere *porte-parole*, I want to begin with one of his remarks in that book, the latest of the series, taking it as a clue to Berger's own fundamental perspective on the world. "I come from a generation of men who weren't concerned that much with women," Reinhart tells his daughter. "When I was young I was obsessed with whether I was *virile* enough. We young men were all like that: it was our constant preoccupation in the Army, for example. Even our humor dealt with it incessantly: *fruit, fairy, swish, pansy, fag*, the words themselves were enough to provoke a guffaw" (p. 19). The words—I want to say it again—are Reinhart's. What relevance do they have to Berger? A good deal, in fact. The novels are remarkably, extraordinarily, full of references to homosexuality, beginning with *Crazy in Berlin*, in which one of the characters asks: "Why does the girl-man [the coy postwar reference is to a presumed homosexual] stimulate sadism rather than pity?" (p. 69), and continuing on, often with unaccountable excess and gusto and as often as not with a curious air of defensiveness (on the part of the characters, to be sure; one can't quite so easily snare the parodistic, "absent" Berger), through most of the novels. A handful of examples, all from the opening pages of the books quoted, ought to provide some sense of the cumulative and configurative effect of this "experiential pattern":

[1] I should say I am a bachelor of thirty (but heterosexual, as some have said, to the threshold of satyriasis).   (*TV*, p. 2)

[2]   "Don't we know one another?"
      Oh-oh, Reinhart thought instantly . . . *here it comes*, yet found, self-hatefully, that far from assuming a hostile righteousness, he felt weak and guilty.
      The putative fag took two backward steps.   (*VP*, pp. 3–4)

[3] The driver of the second [car] . . . was a fat, morose queer who had no real hopes that Reinhart would accept his offer.   (*RL*, p. 3)

[4] Reinhart was shocked and then touched to see that Dad kiss his PFC on the cheek, and the soldier wearing the Indian Head patch and Purple Heart, no pansy he. (*RL*, p. 6)

[5] Reinhart concentrated on the lighter to avoid the gentleman's lean face, for such elegance conjoined with such geniality, in America, could only mean much inversion.   (*RL*, p. 7)

It would be easy enough to demonstrate that the allusions, here and in other novels, reveal collectively, and despite the humor with which the subject is frequently treated, fear, distaste, scorn, superiority, and even a touch of hysteria. On the other hand, so few citations cannot hope to establish something more important—though I've quoted three times from only slightly more pages of *Reinhart in Love* to suggest the point—namely, the total and unmistakable *gratuitousness* of so many of these remarks. In other words, one senses unavoidably that they are less part of the novels' structures, and still less of their texture, than tell-tale signs of Berger's (not Reinhart's but *Berger's*) ultimate discomfort with a strangeness that unsettles the economy or consistency of the self's negotiations not only with the world but with itself.

Any phenomenological description of Berger's intentionality must come to at least a temporary pause here. What we recognize, finally, is that otherness for him shapes itself not simply as difference (women), disruption (Harry and Ramona), opaqueness (language), or menace (time and mortality)—though it is all of those—but as *deviance*, a veering away from what continues to be taken, at some profound level, as natural: that allegiance to the "normal," which bespeaks, in turn, the depth and extent of Berger's fear. Yet the pause is not, after all, final. Like *Neighbors, Reinhart's Women* works against this fear, bringing it into the open and examining its heretofore unacknowledged causes and effects. Perhaps for this reason, the novel is, as I've noted, far less sensational than most of its predecessors. Full of incidents that are disequilibriating but common, even commonplace, it constitutes the quotidian through a series of small shocks and surprises, which effectively render the domestic absorbing: the ordinary, as never before, *is* extraordinary. Confronted with the discovery that Winona, his daughter and the one member of his otherwise repellant family that he cherishes, is lesbian, Reinhart manages to take the news in stride, if not exactly to embrace it; and the novel derives much of its motive force from the contemplation of what precisely the revelation entails for him. "In emotional moments," the narrator notes, "he took comfort in the crafting of general rules, while knowing, all the while, that only truth is particular" (p. 116). *Reinhart's Women* is a novel of particulars, and its chief truth is Reinhart's love for Winona, which requires of him not only the concession, apropos of homosexuality, that "whatever else it might be, it is a fact" and, even, that "most things of a sexual nature have developed naturally" (p. 42) but also a reassessment of his own self-defining attitudes (the question of his virility, for example), past and present.

As in the other novels, definition means act, and Reinhart's acts are less occasional, more deliberate here than they once were. But also, like the book as a whole, less dramatic. The second half of the plot revolves around Reinhart's newly found passion (discovered since the bleak days of *Vital Parts*) for food and cooking, the one "a great positive, yea-saying force, the ultimate source of vitality" (p. 69), the other "the *only* truly creative art" (p. 78). Cooking, most especially, provides an island of stability and pleasure in an otherwise inexplicable world ("Whatever the state of the world outside, everything made sense when Reinhart was with his pots and pans" [p. 12]) and—a more important point—supplies the novel's major metaphor for the fact of being human. "No other animals did any of these things," Reinhart thinks, specifying, along with flying ("when you weren't born with wings") and reading, "eating cooked food" (p. 21).

Reinhart's reflection leads to another and more central formulation of the problem that preoccupies him here: "If *homo sapiens* in general was a pervert under the aspect of eternity, then why," he asks himself, "jib at a subspecies?" (p. 21). It is worth pursuing the implications of his question, an eccentric variation on Lévi-Strauss's binary opposition of the raw and the cooked, which conjoins his daughter's "specialness" with his own and which, furthermore, founds the novel's central and reversible truth. (According to the fictional logic here, homosexuality becomes not only human but creative, a conclusion surely not consciously intended.) Finally, neither Reinhart's tolerance—his recognition that like tastes in food ("private business if there ever was any" [p. 69]), sexual preferences are incontrovertible—nor the love that promotes that tolerance is the issue. Cooking is: cooking as Reinhart's human definition, his gift "for *making* something" (p. 78), his specific way of creating himself and his life. Given the description of his art as an aberration and of homosexuality as no more deviant than his art, it follows both that to be human is be other *and* that to be other is to be human. Even more than in *Neighbors*, the Other is oneself, the condition or ground of an authentic self-definition that neither abandons itself to nor, in the manner of Detweiler or Custer, seeks to coerce the world's contingency.

To be sure, the world has in some ways never been more puzzling. But though he is as aware as ever of "Fate's inclination towards the arbitrary" (p. 79), Reinhart is emotionally more secure. The acceptance of himself and of homosexuality proves reciprocal and mutually enabling. Not that otherness disappears—Reinhart's creative activity is an answer rather than a denial, a modest response to life's inescapable senselessness—but there is, for now, a mitigation of its threat. Not coincidentally, therefore, Reinhart's new attitude precipitates a different relation with women as well. About a third of the way through the novel he thinks: "He had not had a girl *friend* since [the end of his Army days]. He had never been interested in females whom he had not craved. And when sexual desire came into play, matters of relative power soon took precedence over feelings" (pp. 106–07). By the end of the book he has found just such a friend, who, moreover, emerges in her final scene as another of the novel's symbols of affirmation and life. His decision to pursue his friendship with her despite Winona's likely disapproval confirms what is already implied by his cooking: the need to add to his acceptance of his daughter (and of the irrationality that, in the book's larger design, her homosexuality represents to him) some more active and creative reply. (The order that modernism seeks to impose *on* "futility and anarchy"—to allude to Eliot's famous definition—postmodernism attempts to create, less imperially and absolutely, *within* it.) With wonderfully delicate irony, the novel's last lines register a determination by Reinhart to take Winona as she is *and* to go his own way. "How fatuous," he thinks, "had been the impulse to ask her whether she could permit him to have a girl friend younger than herself. Of course she would have refused! Winona was a notorious prig. Who would want any other kind of daughter?" (p. 295). Reinhart's balance is difficult but sure: he is, as he announces early in the novel, "going back into the world" (p. 60). Or perhaps one ought to speak of *Berger's* suspensiveness and of *his* modificatory, midfictional gestures of assent. Less densely realistic but more convincingly daily than earlier novels, *Reinhart's Women* moves toward an ending that is, thematically as well as technically, open rather than, as in the other Reinhart novels, unresolved. For the first time the world seems, if not determinate, at least largely free of the discomfort that compromises and clouds previous attempts to probe its ambiguities.

Seems again, deliberately, since, all I've said notwithstanding, acceptance is something less than complete. If it weren't, one could hardly argue for the rough continuity of the Reinhart Series (rougher than that of Updike's Rabbit books, for example, but manifesting a community of concerns nevertheless), and one could argue still less for the integrity of Berger's intending, authorial self: the phenomenological ego his novels create in and through their expression. In fact, Reinhart's temperamental conservatism, though subdued, is still very much in evidence, as is Berger's in his conception of his hero. At one point, thinking about Winona and her lover, "Reinhart felt an involuntary wave of revulsion. . . . Nature did assert itself from time to time" (p. 223), and, at another, he says to his son: "That it [homosexuality] would always be a joke with respect to Nature might be considered as certain" (p. 21). There is little enough here to gladden the hearts of the National Gay and Lesbian Task Force, little to suggest that Reinhart's newly won understanding or Berger's less hectic strategies signify a revolution in the way either establishes his "existence in act." The normative references intimate a familiar and continuing, albeit for the moment a less urgent, tension in Berger's fiction; and that, after all, is what one would expect.

If, as I said in the last chapter, consciousness is repetitive but not self-identical, then the "meaning" of any single work designates a variable within a larger situation, which is at once its existential limit and the matrix of its expanding human definition. Like *Neighbors*, and still more than that book, *Reinhart's Women* tests but also confirms that limit. In its willingness to confront otherness directly, the novel thematizes what has up to now operated latently and subversively. In its acceptance of otherness, it makes possible a clearer sense of how the self undertakes its own realization and entertains, in the face of an abiding uncertainty, a more calculated, predetermined response. But in its edgy recourse to the regulative concept of Nature, it corroborates what earlier skirmishes with idealism and primitivism make clear: that the emblem of Berger's "relationship to being" continues to be found in the uneasiness that each of the novels, in one way or the other, betrays. Of all these matters, the most crucial is the one that concerns definition. I've argued that, for Berger, the self authenticates its identity by a process of creation—except when, as in the case of his idealists, an overriding need for control sublates that process. But to conclude that for his heroes, and for Reinhart in particular, there is no stability, no finality, no arresting of time is to offer a commonplace. What makes Berger's fictional enterprise distinctive—and with it the phenomenological ego it embodies and expresses—is its restlessness, its restiveness, its parodistic refusal of generic limits and of narrative or stylistic restraints. All of which may explain why, paradoxically or not so paradoxically, the determining of the self is nevertheless Berger's master theme. For that reason also it would be rash to make too much of the more temperate strategies and accommodations of *Reinhart's Women*. Otherness, even there, remains the horizon of Berger's world; and, in a career that is ongoing, it is safe to predict no more than further, repetitive but singular, acts of definition.[7]

Notes

1. Thomas Berger, "Works in Progress" [the collective title of a series of responses by various writers], *New York Times Book Review*, 6 June 1982, p. 11.

2. Thomas Berger, *Killing Time* (1967; rpt. New York: Delta/Seymour Lawrence, 1981). References to Berger's other novels are as follows (I am listing them in order of composition; the abbreviations used are indicated); *Crazy in Berlin* (1958; rpt. New York: New American Library, 1971); *RL: Reinhart in Love* (1962; rpt. New York: Delta/Seymour Lawrence, 1982); *LBM: Little Big Man* (New York: Fawcett Crest, 1964); *KT: Killing Time*; *VP: Vital Parts* (1970; rpt. New York: Delta/Seymour Lawrence, 1982; *ROW: Regiment of Women* (1973; rpt. New York: Delta/Seymour Lawrence, 1982); *Sneaky People* (1975; rpt. New York: Delta/Seymour Lawrence, 1983); *TV: Who Is Teddy Villanova?* (New York: Delacorte Press/Seymour Lawrence, 1977); *AR: Authur Rex* (1978; rpt. New York: Delta/Seymour Lawrence, 1979); *Neighbors* (1980; rpt. New York: Delta/Seymour Lawrence, 1981); *Reinhart's Women* (New York: Delacorte Press/Seymour Lawrence, 1981).

3. Earl Keese in *Neighbors* is a special and reverse case. Subject to "outlandish illusions" (p. 2), Keese schools himself in skepticism, with the result that when reality does indeed reveal itself to be extraordinary, he is unable to credit his senses. Skepticism becomes monomania, an oblique but equally perverse exertion of the will.

4. In an essay called "Romance Without Women: The Sterile Fiction of the American West," *The Georgia Review*, 33 (Fall 1979), 643–56, Madelon E. Heatherington has a number of perceptive things to say about Berger's attitudes toward women in *Little Big Man*.

5. Maurice Merleau-Ponty, *The Phenomenology of Perception*, trans. Colin Smith (London: Routledge & Kegan Paul, 1962), p. 136.

6. On parable and its relation to midfiction, see chapter 2, above.

7. Published after this chapter was first written, *The Feud* (New York: Delacorte Press/Seymour Lawrence, 1983) and *Nowhere* (New York: Delacorte Press/Seymour Lawrence, 1985) bear out my prediction but also justify my caution. Neither book matches the accomplishments (or confirms the spirit) of the works that appeared at the beginning of the eighties, and it has seemed sensible to relegate a brief discussion of them to a footnote. Like *Neighbors* and *Reinhart's Women*, *The Feud* is tighter and more economical than the earlier fiction, but it is, despite this resemblance, a more conventional and less unsettling work. Violent and melodramatic, the book nevertheless suggests, partly because of its dense and complex plotting, partly because of its distanced and distancing ending, a certain detachment on Berger's part. Like *Sneaky People*, which it resembles in more than its geographical and historical setting (the Midwest in the 1930s), the novel traces the ways in which "the code of normality" (p. 37), the unquestioned cultural conventions (and especially the rampant male pride) of the times, precipitates the feud of the title. Furthermore, in the attitudes of its most vivid character, the short-fused, hostile, aggressive Reverton Kirby, the book broaches again the problem of otherness. But Rev, though he is, "with his extreme way of looking at things" (p. 146) continuously aware of the world's threat, differs from Berger's previous idealists in having nothing positive to oppose to it, no dream of Realization or immortality with which to subdue it to the desires of an imperious imagination. And yet he is, in his monomaniacal paranoia, of their company. What distinguishes him is the fact that his self-defining, uniformly destructive acts regulate the world not by reducing but by exacerbating its menacing terrors. That is, Reverton heightens, dramatizes, and personalizes reality into a state of perpetual war and himself into its militant center, thereby, paradoxically, transforming the actuality of disorder into a myth of disorder ordered and controlled. No less disruptive than Harry and Ramona, Reverton develops their generative anarchy into something more blatantly evil and so becomes, interestingly, not only the opponent of otherness but, for the novel's characters, its unsettling embodiment. The Other, like an unexorcizable spirit, lodges itself, even more than in the two previous books, within. Still, however fascinating this reworking of his basic preoccupation may be, Berger at least partly undermines it by

providing explicit and even extenuating psychological explanations for Rev's behavior, as he does not for Harry's and Ramona's; and it's hard to resist the speculation that in coming more fully to terms with otherness, in bringing it closer to the surface of his work, in, finally, making it, at a remove from himself, the horizon of his *characters'* perceptions, Berger has robbed his obsession of some of its fictional power and resonance.

At least for the time being. *Nowhere*, although for different reasons, *is* unsettling. Adopting Russel Wren as its narrator again (Berger has apparently embarked on a second series of novels, this one to be called *Russel Wren, Private Investigator*), the book reads, unfortunately, like a parody of the already parodic *Who Is Teddy Villanova?*. To put it kindly, the novel is scatter-shot in its satire, which encompasses (among other people and things) authors, scholars, and, always, the graceless, narcissistic self-indulgence of New York and New Yorkers. The major interest of Berger's dystopia (it is revealed finally that Nowhere is everywhere) resides in its confirmation of his somewhat Arnoldian conservatism, his scornful amusement (not for the first time) at the expense of those who "do as they like," which leads, once again, to an obsessive fascination with homosexuality—a fascination that goes so far (alas) as to make a passing joke involving AIDS. Saint Sebastian, the "nowhere" of the title, overflows with men who offer to procure boys for Wren, and while the novel's homophobia generally excludes Russel himself, the gratuitous insistence suggests once more Berger's curious discomfort (and fascination) with the subject. What is perhaps of most interest is the fact that homosexuality continues to be thought of by those who discuss it in the book as "unnatural." "To have a boy," a clerk tells Wren, "is to violate nature, to partake of the forbidden. Now, that's exciting!"; and asked by Russel whether "it's against the law," the same clerk responds: "Of course . . . What country would be so degraded as not to condemn the vile crime of sodomy?" (p. 70). Even the homosexual ruler of Saint Sebastian thinks in these terms: "The pederast has a keen sense of humor—he must have," the prince says, "given the joke he is perpetrating on nature!" (p. 63). To which, later in the book, he adds: "All this is in the royal Sebastiani tradition, like sodomy. . . . I've been deposed now . . . I'm not obliged to be a bugger anymore" (p. 185). Needless to say (I trust), my intention is not to attribute to Berger the sentiments of either the clerk or the prince. It has to be said, however, that although in some ways *Nowhere* may be seen as a book written against ideology, its own covert assumptions continue to affirm the anachronistic correctness of a never clearly defined, though, for Berger, an ambiguously normative, concept of Nature—all the more so, one may conclude, when Saint Sebastian, not entirely unpredictably, proves to have been Wren's dream. The interlude of *Reinhart's Women* notwithstanding, the uneasiness of being has returned with full force.

three

ways and means

5

an intolerable double vision: Thomas Pynchon and the phenomenology of middles

"Middles," one of Barthelme's narrators confesses in an access of metafictional angst, "are nowhere to be found."[1] Pynchon's admittedly more thematic and axiological middles are, by contrast, *everywhere* to be found. Or appear to be. Prompted by his repeated variations on the theme of the mysterious "domain *between* zero and one,"[2] most of Pynchon's critics have understandably directed their energies toward the discovery of whatever values escape the "intolerable double vision" (V., p. 440) that Pynchon shares with at least the more sensitive of his characters. Joseph W. Slade, for example (and typically), proposes that "the foremost [of the guidelines Pynchon offers his readers] is that individuals should not exclude middles, should try instead to occupy the domain of Oedipa Maas and Roger Mexico, the realm between one and zero: between absolute freedom and total control, between the void and the labyrinth, between anonymity and solipsism."[3] In theory, there is nothing to quarrel with in this summary. All of the novels do, in fact, posit an ideal or ideals that finesse their various binary oppositions. How effectively is another matter, however. In other words, what is at issue is not the presence of middles in the three novels, but their status; and that, I want to argue, is effectively notional, epiphenomenal. The postulated middles reveal, upon examination, so many markers of desire and intention, which the novels' intentional structures (a different matter altogether) variously contradict, question, or subvert.

If any of the novels provides an exception to these generalizations it is arguably V., the most schematic and tendentious of Pynchon's books, in which the balancing of opposites—Stencil and Profane, "Right and Left; the hothouse and the street" (p. 440)—is absolute, and in which the absoluteness of the opposition appears to preclude, even as it makes desirable, what Stencil's father thinks of as "the once-respectable Golden Mean" (p. 440). To say this is not to identify Pynchon with the elder Stencil; nor is it necessarily to locate Pynchon's own desire in a sense of things remembered and lost (although an intermittent nostalgia is undoubtedly part of his characteristic apprehension of the world). It is, however, to suggest a fellow-feeling between author and character, which presumably ratifies Pynchon's own attempts to mediate and so to overcome the extremes his book describes.

Or, again, so one would think. One character's (Schoenmaker's) "private thesis that correction—along all dimensions: social, political, emotional—entails retreat to a diametric opposite rather than any reasonable search for a golden mean" (p. 91) offers an alternative way of reading what all of Pynchon's critics have perceived to be the novel's central statement about the nature and possibility of middles: McClintic Sphere's disquisition on flopping ("no love, no hate, no worries, no excitement") and flipping ("That war, the world flipped. [. . .] Every once in a while, though, somebody flips back. Back to where he can love . . ." [p. 273]),[4] which leads, some seventy pages later, to Sphere's formulation of a new and hip gospel of the golden mean:

There came to McClintic something it was time he got around to seeing: that the only way clear of the cool/crazy flipflop was obviously slow, frustrating and hard work. Love with your mouth shut, help without breaking your ass or publicizing it: keep cool, but care. He might have known, if he'd used any common sense. It didn't come as a revelation, only something he'd as soon not've admitted.   (pp. 342–43)

The most obvious question the passage raises is where Pynchon himself stands in V.—with Schoenmaker or with Sphere?[5] The question is anything but simple or, indeed, single. To begin with, flip and flop are, as concepts, less symmetrical and poised than they seem at first to be. Despite the fact that it makes up half of McClintic's motto, coolness is in context essentially a negative, or at least an ethically secondary, notion: a brake or restraint on the explosive, "crazy" possibilities that inhere in the activity of flipping. ("You take a whole bunch of people flip at the same time," Sphere tells Ruby, "and you've got a war. Now war is not loving, is it?" [p. 273].) At the same time, Ruby's comment, "Maybe you have to be crazy to love somebody" (p. 273) makes clear that whatever hope McClintic nourishes locates itself in the vicinity—or in the act—of flipping. All of which is to say that in V., as in his other novels, Pynchon tends to privilege one of his theoretically balanced extremes, making of it the site of possible destruction, yes, but also of potential redemption; and to say too (or therefore) that the idea of the middle in Pynchon's fiction, with all its suggestions of midpoints, halfways, and—a favorite of Pynchon's critics—interfaces, needs to be replaced by the more fluid image of middle grounds: indeterminate ethical or ideational spaces that lie closer to the edges than to the center of his imagined worlds.

One more thing follows from what I've been proposing, namely, that the temptation to embrace the more privileged of the extremes (Profane over Stencil, street over hothouse) threatens always the creation even of those amorphous and ambiguous middle grounds occupied by the likes of McClintic Sphere. To be sure, the risk is one that all midfiction runs, perhaps even courts, since its mode is naturally one of transgression, the exploratory pursuit of limit situations; but in Pynchon's case the risk, as we'll see presently, is especially great, since the forms of perception and conception in his work are—the creation of characters like Sphere notwithstanding—so relentlessly oppositional, so radically intense.

The problem of where (that is, in what fictional space) Pynchon's values are situated matters less, however, in the case of V. than it will when we come to *Gravity's Rainbow* and *The Crying of Lot 49*. For now, the central issue concerns the ways in which readers should or do respond to the values they are offered. And, a more perplexing matter, the ways in which Pynchon himself responds. For reasons that will become apparent in a moment, Tony Tanner, the sanest and shrewdest of Pynchon's critics, comes neatly to hand to play the role of exemplary reader. Commenting on McClintic's "keep cool, but care," he writes: "That last formulation has been criticized as being too easy—slick and glib, like an advertising slogan. But perhaps that is a result of the problem of finding 'right words' in a world in which language seems to be declining like everything else."[6] What Tanner understandably fails to mention is that he is one of those who, in an earlier essay, criticized that "formulation" on exactly these grounds. "The guarded maxim of the black jazz musician," he wrote at that time, ". . . is about as much genuine emotion as the book seems to allow. As such it is unconvincing. . . . You cannot render great emotions in a comic-strip, and 'Keep cool, but care' is just such bubble talk or the sort of slogan-jargon mongered by advertisements."[7] I quote these two comments not to catch in contradiction a critic whom I admire and still less to suggest that critics are debarred from changing their minds, but to propose that Pynchon's own fundamental uncertainty about the validity or feasibility of Sphere's solution itself invites just such disparate readings.

The uncertainty manifests itself in a variety of ways, the most obvious of which have to do with odd echoes of the original cool/crazy opposition and its apparent resolution. What, for example, are we to make of the fact that it is

SHROUD ("synthetic human, radiation output determined" [p. 264]), one of the novel's many representations of the mechanical and inanimate, who tells the departing Benny Profane, "Keep cool. Keep cool but care" (p. 345)? Or of Benny's response: "I'll bet under that cynical butyrate hide is a slob. A sentimentalist"; followed by the afterthought: "There's nothing under here. Who are we kidding?" (p. 346)? And what of the still more curious happenstance that names the two girls Benny and Pig Bodine pick up in Washington Flip and Flop (p. 394)? What, indeed, if not the desire to undermine the wisdom McClintic (and Pynchon?) "as soon not've admitted"—to expose it as empty, sentimental, ludicrous?

Or is the intention—if intention is in fact the matter at issue—rather to test the staying power of that wisdom by exposing it to a defensive, saving ridicule: a maneuver calculated to cut off the enemy, whether external or internal, at the pass? For obvious reasons, a handful of local details will supply no adequate answer to these vexed and vexing questions. What, then, of the novel as a whole? There is no need, I think, to add yet another full-scale interpretation to those that have already been offered of V. Critics are in general agreement that the novel's theme, its obsession, is decadence, the "falling-away from what is human," which one of the characters glosses as follows: "The further we fall the less human we become. Because we are less human, we foist off the humanity we have lost on inanimate objects and abstract theories" (p. 380). More to the point is Robert Sklar's comment that "V. is a complex novel that gets simpler with each rereading."[8] Simpler, it should be said, not because the book yields up all of its secrets to the determined exegete—it does not—but because these secrets (or, better, irresolutions) dwindle before the onslaught of Pynchon's unremitting concern with the devolution of the human.[9]

The disproportion between V.'s impressive scope and the narrowness of its final effect is, then, the central and disabling fact about the novel. For all its richness of detail, its wealth of analysis, its structural complexities and chronological displacements, the book emerges as curiously repetitive and static, not to say ham-fisted in its single-minded application and pursuit of the theory that dictates its every fictional move. Arguably, the problem is, at least in part, the theory itself. Writing about *Gravity's Rainbow* (but the analysis is equally relevant to V.), Scott Sanders objects that "Pynchon has presented a particular social condition . . . as if it were the human condition. . . . He interprets an era of decadence in a particular form of society as proof that we are doomed to fall away from the human, that we are tugged along in a cosmic tide of death."[10] Sanders' reservation seems to me eminently cogent, but my concern for the moment is more particularly with the insistency of what he calls Pynchon's "interpretation": with the clamorous rhythms of theme and variation that shape the novel, whatever its ambiguities and thematic hesitations, into an uncompromising myth of eschatological doom. If it is still permissible to believe that technique *is* vision, and if vision implies not only the object of perception but the nature of perceiving, then V. is finally as much "about" Pynchon's way of apprehending the world as it is "about" decadence, narcissism, fetishism, and the inexorable movement of the human race toward the inanimate. For what the novel's strategies reveal in their habitual structuring of experience is an imagination responsive to, even energized by, the very thing it means to overcome: the irresistible glamor of the extreme.

As already noted, the novel ranges against each other the compulsive patterning of Stencil and the aimless yo-yoing of Benny Profane; and although Benny intermittently suggests greater reserves of feeling and caring, it is clear by the end of the book—with Stencil pursuing "the frayed end of another clue" (p. 425) and Benny running down a suddenly and symbolically darkened street— that there is little enough to choose between them. Which brings us back, inevitably, to McClintic Sphere and to the possible resolution of the stand-off that Benny and Stencil represent. But even to moot that hypothetically desirable alternative is to overlook V. and what she adds to our understanding of the novel's conjuration of the extreme. Obviously, in her willing and willful pursuit of the inanimate, V. figures the fate of twentieth-century woman (and man); and in Pynchon's ambitious pursuit of her through all her many changes there is figured a complexity of reaction which, like Hugh Godolphin's in the face of Vheissu, that "gaudy dream [. . .] of annihilation" (p. 190), amalgamates horror with fascination. Two things follow. First, it is evident that, although Sphere's "keep cool, but care" presents itself as the novel's official answer to the paralyzing binaryism of Stencil and Profane, its validity depends on how effectively it stands up not to them but to V. and the entropic vision she incarnates. In other words, the opposition of McClintic and V. takes precedence over the more obvious contrast of hothouse and street, subsuming it to its own more manifold urgencies. Second, whereas Benny and Stencil provide the book with its parallel and at times interlocking stories, it is V. who defines for us not only the motive force of its plot but its ethos: the recognition and belief that beneath the world's mesmerizing variety of colors and shapes there is—to invoke again the counter-Edenic Vheissu—Nothing.

V., in her own gaudy prosthesis, is perhaps only the approximation of Vheissu, but she is also, especially in her death, its annunciation. What, then, to put the question one last time, are we to do with McClintic Sphere? If for Pynchon the advent of the inanimate is all but inevitable, and if, as I've intimated, his novel betrays, along with its obtrusively intended moral, a subversive fascination with the extremity of the "situation,"[11] then where, in the thematic *or* in the formal structure of the novel, is there room for such counsel of moderation and *bon sens* as Pynchon provides in his supposititious resolution of "the cool/crazy flipflop"? The answer clearly is nowhere, and its implications have great importance for the novel as a whole. "To have humanism," Fausto Maijstral says in his "Confessions," "we must first be convinced of our humanity" (p. 302). Is Pynchon? That, after all, is the central question I've been urging; and if Sphere's tentatively offered advice to Ruby still seems to affirm at least the possibility of a humanistic reading of the novel, it needs finally to be set against the elder Stencil's observation (he is thinking once again of the polarities of street and hothouse) that "in V. were resolved, by some magic, the two extremes" (p. 459).

What we have in this resolution is not only a perversion of "the once-respectable Golden Mean" but a parody of McClintic's "keep cool, but care": the novel's perhaps inadvert admission that V.'s domain encompasses the one and the zero *and* everything between—or, rather, that in the point toward which V.'s lines in every sense converge there is established a single voice that overrides what Bakhtin calls "the realities of heteroglossia," the variety, the tension, the dialogue among different voices that for him constitute the essence of the novel.[12] Critics have, of course, noted the element of deliberate parody in V.,[13] but what I'm attempting to isolate here is something different. Sidney Stencil's view of V. signals a kind of parody that, far from opening out onto new and generative horizons (Bakhtin's "becoming"), forecloses even those possibilities the novel has until now entertained. "She frightened him" (p. 459), Stencil thinks to himself at the end of his summation. And so ought she to frighten the reader, armed with a larger perspective than Stencil's; for what V.—or what this formulation of her power—accomplishes is the effective destruction of any middle ground the novel may have sought to define. McClintic's gospel is born of mediation, the humanistic impulse to replace the peremptoriness of either/or with the more generous accommodations of both/and. V., on the other hand, becomes in the novel's epilogue the dissolving agent of all its hesitancies and discriminations, the parodic negation of whatever counterentropic tendencies it endorses, the mirror of its own deepest doubts and distrusts. She becomes, in short, not only the novel's center but its muse: the visible, if mysterious, sign of Pynchon's penchant for converting a structure of opposites, the book's "intolerable double vision," into the radical evasions and consolations of the extreme. And becomes as well, mutatis mutandis, the presiding spirit of *Gravity's Rainbow,* where the temptations of extremity, at once greater and more indulged, turn the tentative, provisional middle ground of V. into the deceptive shapes and colors of Vheissu.

Imagine Kurtz, not Marlow, as the principal narrator of *Heart of Darkness.* And imagine, further, Kurtz telling his story, or *a* story, from the perspective of the nineteen-sixties and seventies. What values might we expect to inform it? Those of an "extremist," certainly. As the journalist who so describes Kurtz to Marlow says: "He had faith—don't you see?—he had the faith. He could get himself to believe anything—anything."[14] The values too of a man "with moral ideas of some sort" (p. 250), a man with the capacity to utter "burning noble words," to make a "moving appeal to every altruistic sentiment," but also to inscribe the terrifying injunction: "Exterminate all the brutes!" (p. 274). And, finally, those of someone who, having peered into the heart of darkness, found there not only the horror but, in Marlow's phrase, "the fascination of the abomination" (p. 221). Given all this, what kind of novel might we be reading? I exaggerate, somewhat, to make my point, but possibly, not impossibly, the book in our hands could be *Gravity's Rainbow*: postmodernism's most notable discovery and re-creation of the Kurtzian ethos and voice.[15]

Many readers and critics will bridle at this view of the novel. Some will dismiss it because they are chary of *any* view of the novel. Richard Poirier, for example, warns against those who "generally miss the experience in a search for meaning";[16] but it is by no means clear that one can so neatly separate the experience of reading from the need to uncover or disclose meaning (or, indeed, that reading is in any sense an epistemologically neutral activity); and most critics, even those who stress the novel's structural uncertainties and ambiguities, have offered at the last, and understandably so, thematic interpretations as hungry for coherence as any offered by the currently despised New Critics.[17] The problem with such interpretations, however, and especially with those that discover in the novel "a sustained affirmation of possibility,"[18] is not that they are partial (what interpretations are not?) but that they tend to base themselves too exclusively upon the more hopeful and humanistic elements of the novel—on scattered moments of compassion and pity, on fleetingly symbolic revelations of selflessness, on expressed and no doubt desired beliefs that (to quote one often cited statement) "in each of these streets, some vestige of humanity, of Earth, has to remain" (GR, p. 693). That these moments, revelations, and beliefs have an important place in the novel's architecture is no more in doubt than their power to move the reader; and my own aim is only to suggest that the emphasis placed upon them defers, even more than in the case of V., to Pynchon's intentions, evading in the process more fundamental impulses and reactions. The favored metaphor used to describe *Gravity's Rainbow* is theater; the more appropriate one, perhaps, is battleground. And in pursuing it, I am interested less in controverting than in modifying standard readings of the novel, less in arguing for yet one more unequivocal interpretation than in revealing within the novel's fabric the evidence of an altogether different intentionality, which renders the book not merely ambiguous but unresolvably contradictory and further calls into doubt Pynchon's commitment to "the domain *between* zero and one—the middle Pointsman has excluded from his persuasion—the probabilities" (p. 55).

But where exactly is the phenomenological intentionality of the novel to be found? Not in the conscious, deliberate opposition of System and Zone, which pits the deathly and dehumanizing forces of technology, abstraction, analysis, and control against a gallimaufry of uncertain possibilities and likely defeats. Nor in the assertion against both of the middle ground that, we are told, "belongs" to Roger Mexico, lineal descendent of McClintic Sphere. As compared with V.'s hothouse and street, the superficially comparable terms of *Gravity's Rainbow* exist in a state of far more radical imbalance, which, if it does not quite preclude, at any rate makes unlikely the very notion of a middle. All hope centers in the Zone, all evil inheres in the System; and because the evil is absolute and all but triumphant, the reader's interest inevitably follows Pynchon's characters through the amorphous Zone, rooting against the odds for their salvation and redemption.

My point, however, is that the novel's actual terms of salvation are in some ways closer to those connected with the System than to those suggested by the Zone. They depend, that is, not on human-scaled values but on their transcendence. And thus the contrast of death and life, control and drift, is skewed by the more tensively dyadic struggle between those who do and those who cannot follow Kurtz's path into the heart of darkness. Which is not to deny, it needs to be said again, that, when measured against the largely faceless "They"—the wielders of power, the masters of the Rocket-cartel—the Zone's wanderers engage our attention and our sympathy alike. It is, rather, to insist that at a deeper level Pynchon's sympathies are deployed differently: specifically, in accordance with Eliot's dictum that "it is better, in a paradoxical way, to do evil than to do nothing."[19] As this invocation of Eliot (and of Conrad) suggests, what is at issue is an often anguished spiritual tradition that runs from Baudelaire and Dostoevsky to Isherwood and Genet and that valorizes over the *homme* (or *femme*) *moyen sensuel*—the "moderate little men . . . [who go] *so far and no farther*" (p. 598)—those extremists, like the lightning-struck of the novel (p. 664), who transgress both the categories of ordinary life and its boundaries.

In this sense, the roster of moderate little men includes not only functionaries like Franz Pökler but more independent characters like Tchitcherine and Enzian and even members of the Counterforce. Tchitcherine, perhaps, best exemplifies the pattern, aware as he is of "a personal doom he carries with him— always to be *held at the edges of* revelations. It happened first with the Kirghiz Light, and his only illumination then was that fear would always keep him from *going all the way in*" (p. 566; my italics). The phrases I've italicized tell the tale: the failure of nerve; the inability to move beyond the self and, as the Aqyn suggests in his song about the Kirghiz Light, to "be born" again (p. 358); the unwillingness to test the far and, so it is implied, the transformative reaches of experience, where, to quote the Aqyn again, "a man cannot be the same" (p. 358). Furthermore, these phrases, or variations on them, thread themselves together throughout the novel, creating a tough and unyielding fabric of value and belief by which its characters are measured. Tchitcherine, later in the novel, is again classed with those "who are held at the edge": only paranoia, "a secondary illumination—not yet blindingly One, but at least connected" is mooted as "perhaps a route In" for him (p. 703). Katje wonders: "*Shouldn't* I be going all the way in?"; and Weissmann/Blicero comments about her: "But of true submission, of letting go the self and passing into the All, there is nothing" (p. 662). Prentice knows there are "directions he can't move in" (p. 620); Enzian, despite his search for the Center without time, despite his own probable ascent in the 00001 rocket, feels empty, "knowing he's always to be a stranger" (p. 731). Even Pointsman and Mexico, those supposed opposites—Pointsman "who'll never get Into It far enough to start talking about God" and Roger who has "never touched the Other World directly" (pp. 752, 40)—are implicated in the nexus of hesitancies and exclusions.[20]

In short, what unites this otherwise disparate group of characters is a certain "leukemia of soul" (p. 658), the property of those like Katje, the object of this description, who "are meant to survive" (p. 662). But survival, though it is precisely the question that the novel's final page poses as the rocket falls above the theater, does not, at the less immediately apparent level I'm pursuing, constitute one of its values. Indeed, as the following passage suggests, it is the paradoxical emblem of all the moderate little men who remain forever at the edge:

There have happened, though rarely, in geographical space, journeys taken northward on the very blue, fire-blue seas, chilled, crowded by floes, to the final walls of ice. Our judgment lapsed, fatally: we paid more attention to the Pearys and Nansens who returned—and worse, we named what they did "success," though they failed. Because they came back, back to fame, to praise, they failed. We only wept for Sir John Franklin and Salomon Andrée: mourned their cairns and bones, and missed among the poor frozen rubbish the announcements of their victory. By the time we had the technology to make such voyages easy, we had long worded over all ability to know victory or defeat. (p. 589)

"North? What searcher has ever been directed *north?*" (p. 706), the narrator asks a hundred or so pages later, and the answer, one of the answers, supplied is the Kirghiz Light, the site of transformation and of Tchitcherine's failure. All the more significant, then, that the passage just quoted occurs in the midst of an episode that describes Lyle Bland's mysterious voyages outside his body, his discovery (presumably) of "the tremendous and secret Function whose name, like the permuted names of God, cannot be spoken . . . " (p. 590). Bland, in other words, is one of those who does go "all the way in," although why he, hitherto associated with the System, with Them and their control, is chosen seems to defy explanation. Unless, of course, we recall Eliot's paradox of the sinner/saint and so find in the very nature of Bland's earlier actions the then readily explicable grounds of his salvation.

In any case, Bland escapes the book's orderly balancing of System and Zone, elect and preterite, and in the process validates the more covert, more heterodox opposition I have been trying to establish. Along with other, still more unlikely candidates for revelation, he achieves what the obviously well-meaning characters in the novel so conspicuously do not and in the process helps to generate the novel's extremist vision. But before coming to these others, I want to turn first to other aspects of the book, since the immoderateness that radically informs *Gravity's Rainbow* and undermines its official oppositions is, first and foremost, a matter not of characterization, nor yet of the notorious narrative discontinuities that, to the confusion or delight of the ordinary reader, aim at rendering both the complexities and the speed of the contemporary world,[21] but of texture and voice. For here—in the ontological and tonal fractures that appear anomalous even in so heteroclite a novel as this one—the identity of what most truly horrifies Pynchon becomes most apparent.

I want to say again that it is no part of my project to minimize Pynchon's animus against the "They-system" (p. 638) and all it represents, including its infiltration of "each of our brains" under "a cover known as the Ego" (pp. 712–13): the challenge to Western civilization is wide-ranging and, allowing for Scott Sanders' objection, more powerful and effective than *V.'s*. I do mean to insist, however, that the source of the book's irritation and anger is finally less local and specific than even this sweeping indictment would suggest. In fact, what repels Pynchon is life itself, or, more accurately, *human* life and, as the following passage argues, the consciousness that controls it:

The region is lonely and Pan is very close. [. . .] Human consciousness, that poor cripple, that deformed and doomed thing, is about to be born. This is the World just before men. Too violently pitched alive in constant flow ever to be seen by men directly. They are meant only to look at it dead, in still strata, transputrefied to oil or coal. Alive, it was a threat: it was Titans, was an overpeaking of life so clangorous and mad, such a green corona about Earth's body that some spoiler *had* to be brought in before it blew the Creation apart. So we, the crippled keepers, were sent out to multiply, to have dominion. God's spoilers. Us. Counter-revolutionaries. *It is our mission to promote death.* The way we kill, the way we die, being unique among the Creatures. It was something we had to work on, historically and personally. To build from scratch up to its present status as reaction, nearly as strong as life, holding down the green uprising. But only nearly as strong.   (p. 720)

In fairness, it should be said that the passage continues: "Only nearly, because of the defection rate. A few keep going over to the Titans every day, in their striving subcreation (how can flesh tumble and flow so, and never be any less beautiful?), into the rests of the folk-song Death (empty stone rooms), out, and through, and down under the net, down down to the uprising" (p. 720). And it could be, has been, argued that the narrator's reservation ("only nearly") announces "the real 'faith' that Katje, Pirate Prentice, even Enzian [and also Mexico and Slothrop] are looking for."[22]

But how effective can such a faith be in the light of what precedes it? Given the force of the narrator's impeachment, can one read its coda as anything but sentimental and wishful? Indeed, does so global a view (the bow to history and personal responsibility notwithstanding) allow for exceptions? And if it does not, then how exactly are we to explain defections from what is presented not as an aberration but as the very definition of being human? What I'm trying to suggest is that the bitter rhetoric of analysis and the slippery rhetoric of salvation in these paragraphs are at odds; and, as must be clear by now, my own sense is that Pynchon's anger has its way with his hope. But that is not all. However one balances the different elements here—and I admit that disagreements are possible, that the anger may be read as yet another thrust at Them, the promoters of the inhuman and antihuman—still the question remains: What, after all, is the nature of "the real faith" we are offered? What are we to understand by Pan and by the Titans, "the presences we are not supposed to be seeing" (p. 720)? What by "the rests of the folk-song Death"? If it is not always possible to specify exactly what the referents of Pynchon's vitalist, quasi-Laurentian descriptions are, their tendency at least is clear. At stake is something inexplicably mysterious, akin to whatever it is the Aqyn sings about, an ultraprimitivism or mysticism that has as little to do with the modestly and imperfectly human as the death-dealing consciousness to which it is opposed. In either case, and equally, there is implied the destructive will or the imperious need to transcend the middle ground where the most fallible and attractive of Pynchon's characters wander aimlessly or lost.

I don't, however, want to lean too heavily on this passage. Its ambiguities aside, it tells only part of the story, for what defines Pynchon's extremist view of the human is finally less his attitude to consciousness than to its own middle ground: the body that is its necessary relation to the world. How, then, does Pynchon respond to this ultimate pledge of humanity: the fact of incarnation? One hardly needs to document the novel's obsessive concern with bodily functions. The famous (or infamous) scatological humor of *Gravity's Rainbow*, sometimes imaginative and exuberant, at others sophomoric and repellent, demonstrates a dialectic of fascination and repulsion on Pynchon's part that encompasses still larger concerns with decay and death ("Shit is the presence of death" [p. 688]). Also with sex. And, most interestingly, with homosexuality, which will serve as the emblem of Pynchon's dramatic ambivalence toward the body as the vehicle both of mortality and of its transcendence, and, further, as a clue to why there are in his work so few satisfactory relations of any kind.

Pynchon's treatment of homosexuality is fairly constant throughout his fiction. Lacking the sympathy of, say, Barthelme, it yields more than the discomfort one finds in Thomas Berger's novels. Not that his remarks are in general any less gratuitous and negative than Berger's, but on occasion, in the treatment of V. or Blicero, for example, the attitude reveals itself as more complex, more (perhaps?) enthralled. As it does in what may be (tonally as well as substantively) the most startling scene in *Gravity's Rainbow*: the ending of "In the Zone," where the elegiacally homoerotic suddenly displaces, as it is conceivably meant to redeem, Pynchon's more typical and pervasive homophobia. The episode begins with a conversation between Clive Mossmoon (it is in his office that Mexico, urinating everywhere, later undertakes one of the Counterforce's more quixotic gestures) and Sir Marcus Scammony, whose teasing homosexual humor ripples across a discussion of "the Operation"—another variation on the theme of power, inhuman control, the cartel—"where the self is a petty indulgent animal" (p. 616) and where betrayal is as easy as Sir Marcus' jokes. The connection here between homosexuality and the They-system is only one of the many the book makes: a connection forged by way of perverse "masculine technologies" and of its result, the rocket, "an entire system *won*, away from the feminine darkness, held against the entropies of lovable but scatterbrained Mother Nature" (p. 324). Such, Enzian learns when Weissmann brings him to Europe, is "love, among these men, once past the simple feel and orgasming of it" (p. 324).

But that is only the beginning. Pynchon's scapegoating of homosexuality has more profound sources. Slothrop's Boston toilet fantasy is precipitated by, or at any rate related to, a fear of gang rape by a group of blacks: "Shit, now, is the color white folks are afraid of" (p. 688); and shit, as a passage I've already cited indicates, is "the presence of death." Later still, and without reference to blackness now, Gottfried imagines "Blicero's seed, sputtering into the poisoned manure of his bowels . . . it is waste, yes, futility . . . but . . . as man and woman, coupled, are shaken to the teeth at their approaches to the gates of life, hasn't he also felt more [. . .] as he approached the gates of that Other Kingdom" (p. 722). Critics have commented on the way in which Pynchon here "explicitly equates homosexual love with death and heterosexual love with life,"[23] and, though "love" hardly seems the word to describe most of the couplings in Pynchon's fiction, there is no question but that for him "lovers whose genitals *are* consecrated to shit" (p. 722) are emblems of waste and death. But again there is more to all this. Commenting on the sexual conservatism of Pynchon's early novels, Catherine Stimpson acutely notes that "part of his hostility towards homosexuality and such phenomena as sexual cross-dressing derives from the fact that they sever the libido from conception. They are barren in terms of the future of the race."[24] In other words, the heterosexual/homosexual dichotomy is altogether too simple; and if the animus against homosexuality is the greater, is it not because, in precluding conception, it reveals the more starkly the body's other functions and the unacceptable inevitability of its decay?

I seem in these speculations to have lost sight of Mossmoon and Sir Marcus, but it is important to return to them or, rather, to what follows hard upon Pynchon's scathingly homophobic presentation of them. As I've already intimated, the succeeding paragraph, the final one of the section, surprises even in a novel where abrupt tonal shifts are as common as narrative discontinuities:

It wasn't always so. In the trenches of the First World War, English men came to love one another decently, without shame or make-believe, under the easy likelihoods of their sudden deaths, and to find in the faces of other young men evidence of otherworldly visits, some poor hope that may have helped redeem even mud, shit, the decaying pieces of human meat. . . . It was the end of the world, it was total revolution [. . .] and despite it all, despite knowing, some of them, of the betrayal, while Europe died meanly in its own wastes, men loved. But the life-cry of that love has long since hissed away into no more than this idle and bitchy faggotry. In this latest War, death was no enemy, but a collaborator. Homosexuality in high places is just a carnal afterthought now, and the real and only fucking is done on paper. . . .   (p. 616)

How to account for this passage, for its particular contrasts and, given "Pynchon's evident distaste for any form of sentiment,"[25] for its intensity of feeling? In a brief reference to these lines, Paul Fussell comments that "the characteristic 'pastoral' homoerotic tenderness of Great War British male love is specifically contrasted by Pynchon with something superficially resembling it in the Second War and after,"[26] and, following Fussell's lead, Michael Seidel has suggestively taken Pynchon's elegy to represent the novel's sense of the dramatic changes in human history between the two wars.[27] These explanations are entirely plausible; I'm less sure that they are complete, that they respond as fully as they ought to the savagery of the homophobia, the fervor of the homoeroticism, and the mysterious "evidence of otherworldly visits," all of which overlap in these crucial pages.

Surely, what is on display here is both the Kurtzian horror and the no less potent fascination of the abomination, for if homosexuality signifies in *Gravity's Rainbow* the sterile destructiveness of masculine technologies, it represents too, and precisely through its connection with the rocket, a defiance of Nature, entropy, and gravity—a movement beyond those "decaying pieces of human meat" that haunt Pynchon's Swiftianly scatological imagination as the body's form and fate. And so, in the trenches, the men, sogged and mired in the grossly and repellently physical though they are (or because they are), evade their incarnation, it is suggested, by transcending it, thereby realizing once again those sentimental, unitary, and mystical impulses that figure so strongly in the novel. And yet, it would be wrong to create, as Pynchon *apparently* does, too sharp a division between his heroically idealized soldiers and the scornfully caricaturized

Mossmoon and Sir Clive sitting, significantly, "among discarded back copies of *British Plastics*" (p. 615). For the soldiers enact by way of their spiritual loves the same denial of the "lower self" (p. 616) that the Operation more deviously achieves in its own way ("The issues are too momentous for the lower self to interfere" [p. 616]). Obviously, I don't mean to minimize differences; nor do I want to imply that the intended contrasts are without force in the novel. I do want to suggest, however, paradoxical or contrary as the assertion may seem to be, that in some ultimate sense there is little to choose between Pynchon's homoeroticism and his homophobia, that they are in fact mirror images, both of them revealing, as so much else in the novel does, his profound unease with the middle grounds (and the fallible bodies) occupied by the moderate little men he at once cherishes and scorns.

I have come round once more, then, to the underlying extremism of *Gravity's Rainbow*: to those patterns of apprehension and feeling that render so difficult for Pynchon the acceptance of what is most human in human beings and that, at the same time, lend to some of the most discredited of his characters (discredited according to the ostensible norms of the novel) a glamor that eclipses those like Mexico and Enzian whom the novel seemingly intends to endorse. Lyle Bland, roaming free of his body, is in his minor way among these antinormative figures. So too, perhaps, the victimized Gottfried, ready at any rate to "wake, into the breath of what was always real" (p. 754). But it is Weissmann/ Blicero who most fully tests and reveals the nature of Pynchon's sympathies. White man, Western man, self-named for death; by the end of the novel a madman, "his nerves [wired] back into [. . .] the Urstoff of the primitive German" (p. 465), Blicero is connected with decadence, perversity, homosexuality, sadism, decay, and, of course, with the rocket and its technologies—not to say its monstrous, barbaric ascent. And yet, all of this notwithstanding, he is arguably the most vivid character in the book. Why? The old saw, according to which evil always has the best of it in fiction, does not explain his interest. And, still less, the fact that he does more than interest; he attracts. It goes without saying that the reader's attraction to Blicero is contingent upon Pynchon's; and it is surely the case that Pynchon's derives from the awareness that Blicero, more than anyone else in the novel, is an extremist: someone who, like Kurtz, participates in unspeakable—but in *Gravity's Rainbow* all too speakable—rites. Thus Enzian describes him as "changing, toad to prince, prince to fabulous monster. . . ." (p. 660) and adds: "Whatever happened at the end, he has transcended. Even if he's only dead. He's gone beyond *his* pain, *his* sin—driven deep into Their province, into control, synthesis and control" (pp. 660–61). The references to synthesis and control muddy the waters, certainly for us, if not for Enzian, who ends: "I haven't transcended. I've only been elevated. That must be as empty as things get" (p. 661). Or for Thanatz, who thinks that "Blicero, alive or dead, is real" (p. 668).

For the reader, however, Enzian's self-deprecating praise is necessarily more problematic. What kind of transcendence *is* this if Blicero has become like Them! Are we to register irony at Blicero's expense? At Enzian's? Or are we to see, possibly in the absence of the "lower self," a connection between transcendence and the absoluteness of control? In fact, I'm not sure the problem has a solution; and the point may well be that Pynchon's response to Blicero is at least as equivocal as, and considerably less clear-sighted than, Marlow's to Kurtz. Thus, while one might well say of Blicero what Jerome Thale said of Kurtz— that "his triumph is ontological. . . . His tragedy is moral"[28]—it is less certain that Pynchon *intends* so neat a distinction. Blicero's ontological triumph is, after all, not over Conrad's hollow men but over those characters who, for most critics and apparently for Pynchon himself, embody whatever humanistic values the novel conveys. Whether or not he comes finally to see "The horror! The horror!," Blicero hardly conforms to Pynchon's moral contrasts in the way that Kurtz, mediated by Marlow, does to Conrad's. Not, at any rate, to those based on the opposition of System and Zone. My argument all along has been that Blicero, on the contrary, destroys the terms of this opposition and, in addition, that everything in the novel that endorses him and the ethos he represents cuts the (middle) ground from under the feet of all those who seek a human alternative to the usual intolerable choice.

There is no denying that Blicero is given some of the novel's best lines, indeed, that he often speaks Pynchon's essential message—as in the passage on Europe's exportation of "its order of Analysis and Death" and on the "American Death [that] has [now] come to occupy Europe" (p. 722)—and that he gives voice, *is* the voice, of the ultimate desire *Gravity's Rainbow* expresses: "to break out—to leave this cycle of infection and death" (p. 724). That he is also the novel's most potent figure of evil is equally undeniable, but as compared with Pointsman's, Blicero's evil is heroic;[29] and it is the heroism, the heroic extremism, that obviously fascinates Pynchon, that transvalues the abomination of his acts and being into the headier, far from Conradian stuff of salvation. But if Blicero, along with much else in the novel—the Kirghiz Light, the Zero, the North, and those mandalas that over and again bring "opposites together" (pp. 563, 610–11, 620–21)—if he and they figure the possibilities of transcendence; and if, despite the awareness that "this ascent will be betrayed to Gravity," the book nevertheless responds longingly to whatever offers "a promise, a prophecy, of Escape. . . ." (p. 758), then what are we to do with the evidence from which various critics have constructed readings considerably more hopeful than the one offered here?[30]

I have acknowledged already that such evidence does in fact exist. Pökler's gesture of compassion for the woman he finds in the concentration camp; Slothrop's for the young girl found after an air raid; Geli's love for Tchitcherine and Roger's for Jessica (although the first of these is more asserted than dramatized, while the second, as George Levine rightly notes, "has some of the quality of sentimental romance"[31]); all of these, and others, no doubt constitute moments of genuine human feeling: "a few small chances for mercy. . . ." (p. 610). The overall effectiveness of such moments—sporadic, elusive, reluctant as they are, contested as they also are by the context the novel provides for them—is another matter.[32] But not the most important one. *Gravity's Rainbow* also offers, in connection with the blurred categories and "the new Uncertainty" (p. 303) that mark the Zone, a larger hope: the anarchy and anti-paranoia that privilege "the ad hoc adventure" (p. 706) and that manifest themselves both in Slothrop's wanderings and in the Counterforce's pursuit of him. As the Argentine anarchist Squalidozzi says: "In ordinary times [. . .] the center always wins. [. . .] But for a few months [. . .] In the openness of the German Zone, our hope is limitless" (pp. 264–65). None of the ad hoc adventures amount to much, however, and the Counterforce, if it is not subverted by "the Man [who] has a branch office in each of our brains" (p. 712), simply peters out.

Which leaves, to borrow Lance Ozier's phrase, "the debate about What Happens to Slothrop."[33] It isn't my intention to enter this debate, not directly at any rate. Whether one regards Slothrop as someone "unable to love, let alone transcend love and death," someone who "loses his self without having found his Grail,"[34] or, instead, as "a Rilkean Orpheus whose song is 'reine Übersteigung' (pure transcendency)" and whose loss of the self opens him "to the possibility of pure Being"[35] depends probably on prior decisions about how the novel is to be read. Slothrop thinning and scattering, "scattered all over the Zone" (p. 712); Slothrop as "spiritual medium" (p. 622): there is evidence in abundance for both views. I want, therefore, to suggest only this much. If Slothrop "is to be counted, after all, among the Zone's lost" (p. 470), he does no more than Benny Profane to counteract Pynchon's double vision. But if, on the other hand, we choose to focus on the famous passage in which Slothrop becomes "a crossroad" and, "after a heavy rain he doesn't recall [. . .] sees a very thick rainbow here, a stout rainbow cock driven down out of pubic clouds into Earth, green wet valleyed Earth, and his chest fills and he stands crying, not a thing in his head, just feeling natural. . . ." (p. 626); if we concentrate on this and elect, further, to find in the vision Ozier's *reine Übersteigung*, how much closer have we come to a negotiation of the extremes, to a middle ground, indeed to Earth? I am not trying to argue that Blicero's transcendence and Slothrop's are the same, but I do mean to imply that both corroborate the pattern or patterns of binary thinking that dominate the novel. Obviously, Slothrop, even as "tanker and feeb" (p. 738), represents the humanity deliberately denied and excluded by the System. Even at his best, however (that is, as the vehicle of Pynchon's anarchic primitivism), he remains purely and merely oppositional: not the novel's answer to the futile stand-off of System and Zone but its confirmation—just as Blicero's transcendence endorses the more subversive (and unequal) conflict between a lack-luster moderation and the *frisson* of the extreme.

In this sense, if only in this sense, Slothrop and Blicero join together in the novel's moral economy (and behind Pynchon's back, so to speak) to exclude middles or, rather, to demonstrate just how notional they are. In a much commented upon passage, Slothrop, meditating on his ancestor William and his book *On Preterition*, wonders:

Could he have been the fork in the road America never took, the singular point she jumped the wrong way from? [. . .] It seems to Tyrone Slothrop that there might be a route back—maybe the Anarchist he met in Zürich was right, maybe for a little while all the fences are down, one road as good as another, the whole space of the Zone cleared, depolarized, and somewhere inside the waste of it a single set of coordinates from which to proceed, without elect, without preterite, without even nationality to fuck it up. . . .   (p. 556)

"Depolarized" is the central word here, and it hardly needs saying by now that, in ratifying the anarchic openness of the Zone's pole, Tyrone—and, surely, Pynchon as well—perpetuate the very antithetical imagination that is under attack. More interesting is the fact that William's tract itself endorses not the belief that one road is as good as another but the notion that "Everything in the Creation has its equal and opposite counterpart" (p. 555). Tyrone's misreading is perhaps the most suggestive clue we have to the nature of the novel's hope: to a faith that, like Kurtz's, "had kicked the very earth to pieces" (*HD*, p. 293), becoming in the process its own source and justification.

It may be worth stressing one final time that what I'm trying to deny are not whatever articulations of hope critics have found in *Gravity's Rainbow* but their convincingness. Ozier speaks of "a transcendent, atemporal realm of un-circumscribed potential which nevertheless is grounded in the former world and is therefore not pure chaos."[36] My own sense is that what is lacking is precisely such grounding, some anchoring of transcendence in earth, some connection of anarchy and primitivism with the world outside the Zone; and if I fault Pynchon, it is not to impose this or that belief of my own on him but to suggest how thoroughly the novel undermines, through the unreconstructed binaryism of its imagination, the possibilities and probabilities it apparently means to approve. Whatever the consolations critics have managed to extract from the hymn by William Slothrop with which *Gravity's Rainbow* ends, it is hard to deny that the whole last section of the novel amounts to a gloomy prediction of the world going on as always, the powerful still in power, death still triumphant—and inevitably so, given the nature of the book's dynamics. System and Zone are no doubt less equally balanced than *V.*'s hothouse and street, but the obvious tilt toward the Zone in no way undoes the framework of opposition that is Pynchon's prison and mirror—any more than the fact that ASCENT entails DESCENT nullifies the novel's deeper urge toward a transcendence that spells, finally, neither "the idea of transformation" nor "something like mysticism"[37] but, quite simply, a desired escape from a situation that continues to fascinate even as it appalls.

Fascinates *because* it is extreme. The enemy in *Gravity's Rainbow* is not only the They-system; it is, more generally and in a phrase that ends a conversation between Enzian and Katje, "things to hold on to. . . ." (p. 663): the furniture of the ordinary which, for Pointsman, becomes "the elegant rooms of history" that Mexico threatens to wreck with his "symbols of randomness and fright" (p. 56). From the perspective of the narrator, however, these symbols are precisely "the middle Pointsman has excluded from his persuasion." But not only Pointsman. In the final analysis, *Gravity's Rainbow* never quite manages to bring into focus Roger's probabilities, still less the humanistic possibilities to which it seems theoretically committed but which, in its rejection of humanism's complexity of vision, it effectively betrays. For all its manifest difficulties, for all its strategic insistence on discontinuity and the illusoriness of cause and effect, *Gravity's Rainbow* is also a simple novel—simple in its relentlessness, in its impatience with the hesitancies and qualifications that necessarily define the topography of middle grounds. In short, if *Gravity's Rainbow* is Pynchon's updated version of *Heart of Darkness*, there is no room in it for the moderating, deliberative Marlow, Conrad's tertium quid. Kurtz, as I began by saying, remains the plausible analogue; but a still better one, possibly, is the novel's own Byron the Bulb, "condemned to go on forever, knowing the truth and powerless to change anything. [. . .] His anger and frustration will grow without limit, and he will find himself, poor perverse bulb, enjoying it. . . ." (p. 655).

The apocalyptic imagination that dominates *Gravity's Rainbow* and V. is considerably less in evidence in *The Crying of Lot 49*—its concern with entropy and its possible hints of Pentecostal revelation notwithstanding—and the consequences of this difference are of major significance. As are the corollary consequences of adopting, in place of the vastly distant, panoramic perspectives of the first and third novels, one in which "the narrator only knows what Oedipa knows at each step in her quest."[38] Along with V., *Gravity's Rainbow* exhibits what may be best thought of as a baroque sensibility: an approach to the world of experience that heightens and dramatizes but also skeletonizes that world, subordinating it to the abstract polarities that are its coordinates. In saying this, I don't mean to minimize the urgencies involved in so passionately an ideological view, but it is equally impossible to overlook the simplifications such a view entails. By comparison, *Lot 49* is a good deal more nuanced and restrained; and, despite or conceivably because of the fact that it is by far the briefest of Pynchon's novels, it comes a good deal closer to an inside and "ordinary" view of the world and thus to a more human and humanistic, a more tentative and provisional, sense of limitation and possibility alike.

It is for these reasons that I have chosen to deal with *Lot 49* out of its chronological order, and possibly for these reasons that Pynchon seems to have repudiated the book. In his recent introduction to *Slow Learner*, he writes: "As is clear from the up-and-down shape of my learning curve, however, it was too much to expect that I'd keep on for long in this positive or professional direction. That next story I wrote was 'The Crying of Lot 49,' which was marketed as a 'novel,' and in which I seem to have forgotten most of what I thought I'd learned up till then."[39] Most readers will, I suspect, find it difficult to agree with this unexpected and provocative denigration of the novel, but the remarks themselves are clearly revealing. Revealing not as aesthetic judgment but as a clue to what I earlier referred to as the intentionality of Pynchon's work: the perilous attraction of the extraordinary and the extreme that his second novel alone manages to resist. But if *The Crying of Lot 49* differs from the novels that surround it, it does so—as it must, if the notion of intentionality is to have any meaning at all—in ways that stop short of violating the structures which define Pynchon's way of experiencing the world. My point, then, is that the book both is and is not anomalous,[40] that its themes, concerns, even its attitudes resemble those of *V.* and *Gravity's Rainbow* but that, as will become apparent shortly, its view *desde dentro* gives to all of these a notably different slant.

Predictably, then, *Lot 49*, like the other novels, defines itself through an examination of oppositions and of middles. Unlike them, however, *Lot 49* genuinely accepts the indeterminateness of these concepts. Both the specificity of McClintic's motto and the abstract generality of Mexico's probabilities give way to a more dynamic possibility, specifically to Oedipa's ability to imagine or, rather, to *enact* a middle ground. And since what the novel offers is correlative to something potential in Oedipa herself, the middle becomes in a real sense less the object of perception than its form. By the same token, the polarities of *Lot 49*, themselves functions of Oedipa's bewildering and frustrated quest, of the cascading accumulation of uncertainties that almost overwhelm her, are more variously and fluidly conceived. The result is that the modalities of binary thinking which inform all of the novels, but which in *V.* and *Gravity's Rainbow* also delimit the nature of Pynchon's responses, are here transformed into a problematics, an interrogation of precisely those terms by which his fiction constitutes itself.

In saying this, I don't mean to ally *Lot 49* with the ultrareflexive wing of postmodernism. The interrogation I spoke of is equally of self *and* world or, more accurately, it involves a questioning of how the self, through its expressive acts, brings the world into being. Which means, in turn, that the novel parallels the concerns not of metafictionists but of midfictional writers like Barthelme, Apple, and Berger. What underlies this connection, however, and what allows Pynchon to conceive the novel as a problematics is an attitude absent from the other two novels and best summed up in a word I used a moment ago: accept-ance. Acceptance, not in the sense that *Lot 49* endorses, any more than V. or *Gravity's Rainbow*, the inheritance of the past, here identified as "the legacy America" (*49*, p. 137), nor yet in any inclination to acquiesce passively in the wrongs it identifies. At issue is a willingness to accept randomness, contingency, and uncertainty as part of the very nature of things—of what is desired as much as of what is. What follows? The curious and paradoxical fact that Pynchon is, I believe, more authentically, convincingly subversive and also potentially more generative in *Lot 49* than in the apparently more radical experiments that pre-cede and follow it.

Oedipa, however, comes to this kind of acceptance only at the end of her fictional exploration. She begins, and for much of the book continues, as the most modernist of heroines. From the start, as critics have repeatedly noted, Pynchon establishes her alienation from all the conventional supports of Amer-ican civilization. Thus, "Oedipa stood in the living room, stared at by the green-ish dead eye of the TV tube, spoke the name of God, tried to feel as drunk as possible. But this did not work" (p. 1). And, indeed, how could it? Underlying the anomie of her situation is the vaguely existential sense of having fallen from some original wholeness, of "having lost the direct epileptic Word, the cry that might abolish the night" (p. 87). Cut off from this truth (whatever it may be), unable to communicate effectively with those around her, she is forced into indirection and quandary, into what we have come to call the postmodern situ-ation. But initially, at any rate, Oedipa's reaction is as characteristically modern-ist as any one might expect from a character in a story by Virginia Woolf: "*Shall I*," she wonders, "*project a world?*" (p. 59).

The question follows another one prompted by her meditation on Pierce Inverarity's will, her role as executrix, and the revelations she has begun to have about the Tristero, the mysterious organization named in Randolph Driblette's production of *The Courier's Tragedy*. Is it not, she asks herself, "part of her duty [. . .] to bestow life on what had persisted, to try to be what Driblette was, the dark machine in the centre of the planetarium, to bring the estate into pulsing stelliferous Meaning, all in a soaring dome around her?" (p. 58). Clearly, her concern is with order, with order as meaning, and with herself as the source of that order; and since her words directly echo Driblette's ("But the reality is in *this* head. Mine. I'm the projector at the planetarium" [p. 56]), there is no question but that at this point her inclination is, like his, to redeem the world's emptiness by conferring on it a significance emanating entirely from the self.

With this in mind, it is impossible not to notice as well a connection backward to Oedipa's vision of herself as Rapunzel and to the painting by Remedios Varo, "Bordando el Manto Terrestre," whose circular tower provides the necessary gloss on Oedipa's identification. The tower is, of course, another inheritance from modernism: the recurrent image of the self as isolated prisoner; and the painting is precisely a depiction of the idealist tendency I've been describing.

But the attempt to fill the world with the self is seen even by Oedipa as hopeless: "Such a captive maiden, having plenty of time to think, soon realizes that her tower, its height and architecture, are like her ego only incidental" (p. 11). The implications of this awareness are somewhat different from what they seem. Under attack is not, as among poststructuralists, the reality of the self but its imperial pretensions, which soon crumble in the face of "magic, anonymous and malignant, visited on her from outside and for no reason at all" (p. 11). Oedipa's task, in other words, is both to acknowledge how precarious, unstable, and uncertain her ego is and to maintain it. The latter task is the difficult one and requires that she forego her attempts to overmaster the world, attending instead to its not always comforting solicitations. But she, if anyone in the novel, is in a position to do just that. Situated, in terms of the book's characterization, somewhere between her psychiatrist Hilarius and her husband Mucho—the one stubbornly cherishing, the other dissipating or (it comes to very much the same thing) endlessly multiplying the ego—Oedipa figures the latency and potential of being. Which perhaps explains why her alienation is not only more self-conscious but more moving and absorbing than that of any other character in Pynchon's work. If there is a middle ground anywhere in that fiction, it is Oedipa herself.

To reach her goal, however, Oedipa has to face down more than anonymous, malignant forces, has to come to terms with more than the clues to the nature of the Tristero that multiply exponentially around her. The Crying of Lot 49 has been combed over thoroughly and well for all its possible meanings, and there is no need to track Oedipa through every twist and turn of her journey. My concern is with the particular habits of mind that, whether in the tower of Kinneret or in "the infected city" (p. 86) of San Francisco, where her modernist reference points finally and fully disappear, are the most enduring antagonists of the realization she more and more feverishly seeks. Those habits, as I've already intimated, have to do with her entrapment in a series of binaryisms that both reveal and define the conceptual form of her (and Pynchon's) dilemma; and if they are in evidence even in the first chapter, where her thoughts of the tower lead her to set against one another the idealism of Varo's painting and the paranoid force of "magic," they become nothing less than overwhelming in the novel's last ten pages.

By this point, Oedipa's ability to keep the most minimal control of herself and of the menacing, perplexing situation spawned by Inverarity's will and the pursuit of the Tristero has become almost totally dependent upon a mental set whose coordinates invariably take the form of "either" and "or":

Either [she tells herself] you have stumbled indeed, without the aid of LSD or other indole alkaloids, onto a secret richness and concealed density of dream; onto a network by which X number of Americans are truly communicating whilst reserving their lies, recitations of routine, arid betrayals of spiritual poverty, for the official government delivery system; maybe even onto a real alternative to the exitlessness, to the absence of surprise to life, that harrows the head of everybody American you know, and you too, sweetie. Or you are hallucinating it. Or a plot has been mounted against you [. . .] Or you are fantasying some such plot, in which case you are a nut, Oedipa, out of your skull.   (p. 128)

My interest, I've said, is with the *structure* of Oedipa's thought, and in these terms the passage has a good deal to tell us. Reflecting on "the alternatives," she concludes that "she didn't like any of them, but hoped she was mentally ill" (p. 128). And yet the "network" she imagines contains "a secret richness and concealed density of dream"; she can, that is, suppose at least the possibility of "a real alternative" to official America, to the homogeneous and narcissistic culture that surrounds her. Why, then, does she opt for madness?

The answer, I think, lies in the *way* Oedipa sorts out the possibilities. For her, they are "those symmetrical four" (p. 128)—although it might in fact be argued that the four are three: either there is a Tristero, or there is a plot against her, or she is mad (hallucinating/fantasying). In any case, even conceding the accuracy of her arrangement, I'm not sure one can legitimately speak of symmetry. As usual in Pynchon's fiction, one of the extremes is privileged; and the balance, given what we have come to know of Oedipa, surely tips toward the Tristero. Hopeful as well as terrifying, hopeful in a way that her present situation is not, it would seem unquestionably the most attractive to her. Would or *should*. Once more, then, why isn't it? Surely because, however great her disillusion with the America she inhabits and however great her desire for something to replace it, she is stymied by those habitual ways of thinking that make her desire and her disillusion correlative and so vacate the possibilities inherent in the Tristero. "She also wanted to know," we are told earlier in the book, "why the chance of its [the Tristero's] being real should menace her so" (p. 98). The answer by now is clear, if paradoxical: to oppose terms is necessarily to relate them, to situate them within the same ontological context; and seen as one-half of a symmetrical opposition, the Tristero, for all its imagined promise, merely (and intolerably) corroborates the existing order.

I don't, of course, mean to suggest that Oedipa is conscious of these para-doxes, but at some level a resistance to her "captivity" increasingly shapes itself.

Following up "every access route to the Tristero" (p. 127), she struggles against her fears of it but also, willy-nilly, against those elements in herself which, more effectively than any external agents, keep her from acknowledging its reality— and thus the unreality of her own constraining symmetries. What exactly she is able to achieve becomes apparent in the much quoted passage very near the end of the novel, in which Pynchon most directly broaches the problem of middles:

Perhaps she'd be hounded someday as far as joining Tristero itself, if it existed, in its twilight, its aloofness, its waiting. The waiting above all; if not for another set of possibilities to replace those that had conditioned the land to accept any San Narciso among its most tender flesh without a reflex or a cry, then at least, at the very least, waiting for a symmetry of choices to break down, to go skew. She had heard all about excluded middles; they were bad shit, to be avoided; and how had it ever happened here, with the chances once so good for diversity? For it was now like walking among matrices of a great digital computer, the zeroes and ones twinned above, hanging like balanced mobiles right and left, ahead, thick, maybe endless.   (p. 136)

That Oedipa reserves her skepticism about the existence of the Tristero, even as she imagines joining it, is typical. As is the locating *outside herself* the threat she recognizes of binary, either/or choices, characterized here by reference to computers and, more importantly, to the principle of the excluded middle: the logical notion which, in holding that everything is either A or not-A, itself excludes the middle grounds that both Oedipa and her creator in theory pursue. And yet something like a middle ground ("diversity") and a way of achieving it ("waiting") are stipulated. No doubt the idea of diversity is largely unqualified or, as in the passage quoted above (p. 128), qualified by negation and metaphor, but perhaps because it conjures up so directly one of the central tenets of modern humanism, it resonates in a way that the analogous formulations of *V.* and *Gravity's Rainbow* do not.

   I'll return shortly to the related question of waiting, but in the meantime I don't want to simplify what takes place in Oedipa's response to the excluded middle. The specification of what she at once longs for and regrets in no way changes the shape of her thinking, as the conclusion of the meditation reveals:

Ones and zeroes. So did the couples arrange themselves. [. . .] Another mode of meaning behind the obvious, or none. Either Oedipa in the orbiting ecstasy of a true paranoia, or a real Tristero. For there either was some Tristero beyond the appearance of the legacy America, or there was just America and if there was just America then it seemed the only way she could continue, and manage to be at all relevant to it, was as an alien, unfurrowed, assumed full circle into some paranoia.   (pp. 136–37)

Comment on these lines seems supererogatory, as the *eithers* and *ors* cascade down the page. It is enough simply to note that here, on the threshold of the novel's closing scene, Oedipa, *in* confirming her desire by way of the usual oppositions, confirms too the by now familiar habits of mind that render uncertain its actualization.

At this point, as Oedipa regroups and attends the auction in order to find "her target, her enemy, perhaps her proof" (p. 138), it becomes impossible to separate her from Pynchon—or to avoid the question of whether, like her, he remains to some degree trapped and paralyzed by antinomies of zeroes and ones. In fact, the novel refrains from supplying an answer, which explains, no doubt, why it has been the subject of such disparate readings. But no answer *is* an answer: at the least, it is the sign of a willingness on Pynchon's part to see the world very much as Oedipa does, fallibly, partially, and so to problematize—not contravene, but problematize—the dynamics of his own more urgent intentionality. Ironically, however, entrapment, or the acknowledgment of it, becomes a kind of liberation, an opening out, for once, onto the genuine possibilities inherent in the uncertain. To put this in terms of the novel itself, if *Lot 49* has something richer and more generative to offer than the negations of Vheissu or the sterile promise of transcendence, it is not because it proposes more concrete solutions to the problem all three novels engage, but because it is willing to postpone or suspend the need for them.

The emblem of *Lot 49*'s suspensiveness (and of its midfictional quality) is precisely the attitude it shares with Oedipa of *waiting*—an attitude that, as the auction scene defines it, is at once active (or at least potential with activity) and accepting of life's uncertainties. Those critics who take the thrust of the novel to be religious will, of course, find this interpretation unacceptable; and there is no denying the fact that much in *Lot 49* supports their position. All readers will have noted the abundance of religious imagery in the book—miracle, redemption, hierophany, revelation, and so on—and no one can overlook the striking description that ends, or almost ends, it: "Passerine spread his arms in a gesture that seemed to belong to the priesthood of some remote culture; perhaps to a descending angel" (p. 138). At the same time, even if one ignores the fact that lot 49 consists of the Tristero forgeries; that the mysterious bidder may be from the Tristero; and that the name of the "crier," Loren Passerine, perhaps anticipates the idea of the preterite in *Gravity's Rainbow*—all this aside, it is certainly possible, in accordance with Jesús Arrabal's definition of an anarchist miracle ("another world's intrusion into this one" [p. 88]), to give the novel's imagery a nonreligious reading: to find in the metaphor of "another world" an allusion to the "secular Tristero" (p. 124) and to *its* concealed presence and meaning.

To do so, I believe, is to underline and sustain the novel's spirit of inconclusiveness and so to reject the attempt to frame Oedipa's choice, as Edward Mendelson does, "between the *zero* of secular triviality and chaos, and the *one* which is the *ganz andere* of the sacred."[41] Quite simply, *Lot 49* is not about this or that particular choice, however momentous, but about the conditions and possibilities of choice; and our last glimpse of Oedipa, "await[ing] the crying of lot 49" (p. 138)—an image that recalls the earlier "waiting for a symmetry of choices to break down" and the motto W.A.S.T.E. (WE AWAIT SILENT TRIS-TERO'S EMPIRE)—brings us no closer to an understanding of what it is that will or may in time emerge. As compared with the waterspout that kills Sidney Stencil at the end of V. or the rocket that threatens to kill all of us on the last page of *Gravity's Rainbow*, Oedipa's waiting enacts a low-keyed resolution that is no resolution at all. Which is to say that *Lot 49* is both thematically and formally open-ended;[42] and that, like Oedipa herself, we are offered hints and clues or, at most, directions: only the invitation to decode, if we can, "a hiero-glyphic sense of concealed meaning" (p. 13).

The inflammatory conclusion toward which I've been gingerly moving may be put as follows: for all the experimental panache of V. and, especially, of *Gravity's Rainbow, The Crying of Lot 49* is the most insidiously and subtly radical of Pynchon's novels, the one that most authentically discloses to us the universe of postmodern quandary. Indeed, it might even be argued that the earlier and later books are in their strategies and premises neomodernist rather than postmodern works. *Gravity's Rainbow*, for example, although some critics have used its bois-terous iconoclasms as a stick to beat modernism with, exists structurally very much in the modernist mold. Thematically open-ended, its many loose threads deliberately left scattered and uncollected, reveling delightedly in its multipli-cation of ambiguities, equivocations, and irresolutions, the novel is nevertheless formally closed, the hypothetical rocket of its opening balancing and balanced by the hypothetical rocket of the end, while, in between, its heteroclite structure is held in check by the kinds of symbols, rhythms, and allusions that at an earlier time were said to create the "musicalization" of fiction. One might note too the book's heterocosmic imagination and its responsiveness to a primitivism that is so often in modernist literature the obverse of transcendental aspiration. Or, finally, one could suggest that the novel's reflexivity has less to do with "the way in which reality is transformed by and filtered through narrative assumptions and conventions"[43] than, as in many modernist works, with consciousness in a state of crisis, poised between equal and valid polarities, moved by the symmet-rical dead end of that balance to find a way of transcending it.

But there is little to be gained in the multiplication of categories; and it is perhaps enough to say that, on the evidence of *Gravity's Rainbow* and V., Pyn-chon emerges as, at most, a reluctant postmodernist and as a still more reluctant humanist. It is *Lot 49* that stakes out his claim in both areas. A more modest exploration of human possibility, the book is incontrovertibly postmodern, and midfictional besides, a novel of interrogation that, while preserving the referential function of literature, puts into question self, world, and the fictions that express their relations. Like Barthelme's *The Dead Father* and Elkin's *The Bailbondsman*, *Lot 49* offers a comment on and a revision of the typical modernist quest, subverting modernist paradox by turning it against itself. Oedipa, at once heroine and victim, is obviously the instrument of this subversion and, as such, she reflects the novel's deliberate confusions, which are at the same time the basis for whatever hope it conveys—the hope that emerges precisely from the acceptance of its own entrapment in the modes of thought and language it desires in time to overcome.

Earlier on, I identified the middle ground of the book with the idea or ideal of diversity and, earlier still, with Oedipa herself. I would add finally that it announces itself also, and preeminently, in (or as) the form of the novel. Thus, while structure in *Gravity's Rainbow* is oppositional—Pynchon's playful, anarchic, discordant answer to Them—in *Lot 49* it is the mirror of Oedipa's bewilderment, the visible instrument of Pynchon's interrogation of her and of his own perceptual grasp of the world. What the novel achieves as a result of this relentless questioning is not the solution to its many mysteries but an attitude that, in subordinating the attainment of the goal to its pursuit, paradoxically recovers, as process, the diversity for which it can find no absolute correlative. The triumph of *Lot 49*, then, is that the novel itself embodies that attitude and in its structure endorses it. At the last, the middle *is* the waiting; waiting, the middle ground that the other novels parody or deny but that *Lot 49*, if only obliquely and tentatively, enacts into being. For us, as for Oedipa, it is a matter of "nothing specific, only a possibility, nothing she could see" (49, p. 74), but, as the instrument and site of further, if for now unspecified, action, it is more than Pynchon's other acrid and ambitious novels have to offer.

Notes

1. Donald Barthelme, "The Dolt," in *Unspeakable Practices, Unnatural Acts* (1968; rpt. New York: Bantam Books, 1969), p. 65.
2. Thomas Pynchon, *Gravity's Rainbow* (New York: The Viking Press, 1973), p. 55. Subsequent references to the novel will be given in the text, preceded, where necessary, by the abbreviation GR. References to Pynchon's other novels will also be given in the text and are to the following editions: V. (1963; rpt. New York: Bantam Books, 1979); *The Crying of Lot 49*, referred to hereafter as 49 (1966; rpt. New York: Bantam Books, 1972).
3. Joseph Slade, *Thomas Pynchon* (New York: Warner Paperback Library, 1974), p. 246. One of the possible ways of discriminating among Pynchon's critics is to group together those who (like Edward Mendelson in his reading of *Lot 49*) see Pynchon as offering a choice between the one and the zero and those who (like Tony Tanner in his

book on Pynchon) reject the one and the zero in favor of some other possibility. See below for bibliographical information on Mendelson's and Tanner's works.

4. Since Pynchon is almost as fond of ellipses (particularly in *Gravity's Rainbow*) as Virginia Woolf is of semicolons, I have, in order to avoid confusion, enclosed my own ellipses in brackets.

5. Some critics have proposed Paola Maijstral (Ruby) as a center of value in the novel, but her decision to return to her husband is, or at least seems to me to be, too mysterious and unmotivated to sustain the argument.

6. Tony Tanner, *Thomas Pynchon* (London and New York: Methuen, 1982) p. 50.

7. Tony Tanner, *City of Words: American Fiction, 1950–1970* (New York: Harper & Row, 1971), p. 161.

8. Robert Sklar, "An Anarchist Miracle: The Novels of Thomas Pynchon," in *Pynchon: A Collection of Critical Essays*, ed. Edward Mendelson (Englewood Cliffs, N.J.: Prentice-Hall, 1978), p. 90.

9. I have been pursuing one of these irresolutions, and Edward Mendelson, in his "Introduction" to *Pynchon: A Collection of Critical Essays*, puts his finger on another when he observes that "in V., Pynchon finally seems unable to decide . . . whether he is describing an inevitable historical process . . . or whether he is warning of the consequences of actions that we have chosen to make—and we were free to choose otherwise" (p. 7).

10. Scott Sanders, "Pynchon's Paranoid History," in *Mindful Pleasures: Essays on Thomas Pynchon*, ed. George Levine and David Leverenz (Boston: Little, Brown, 1976), p. 158. This is the fourth of Sanders' objections to "Pynchon's world view." All four are worth pondering. See pp. 157–58.

11. The word is Stencil père's, and Pynchon's comment on him at one point is relevant: "The only consolation he drew from the present chaos was that his theory managed to explain it" (p. 174).

12. M. M. Bakhtin, *The Dialogic Imagination: Four Essays*, ed. Michael Holquist, trans. Caryl Emerson and Michael Holquist (Austin: University of Texas Press, 1981), p. 270. See, in general, the essay called "Discourse in the Novel."

13. See, for example, Tanner, *City of Words*, pp. 171–72.

14. Joseph Conrad, *Heart of Darkness*, in *Three Great Tales* (New York: Random House-Modern Library, n.d.), p. 301. Subsequent references will be given in the text, preceded, where necessary, by the abbreviation *HD*.

15. Pynchon's association with Conrad and with *Heart of Darkness* can be traced back to the short story "Mortality and Mercy in Vienna," *Epoch*, 9 (Spring 1959), 195–213. On the story, see Slade's discussion in his book, pp. 20–25 and Tanner's in *Thomas Pynchon*, pp. 26–29. While the comparison I have been drawing is mine, not Pynchon's, Conrad's presence is apparent in both *V.* and *Gravity's Rainbow*.

16. Richard Poirier, "Rocket Power," in *Pynchon: A Collection of Critical Essays*, p. 177.

17. David Leverenz's fascinating meditation on *Gravity's Rainbow* and on his responses to it provides a notable exception to these generalizations. See his essay, "On Trying to Read *Gravity's Rainbow*," in *Mindful Pleasures*, pp. 229–49.

18. Lance W. Ozier, "The Calculus of Transformation: More Mathematical Imagery in *Gravity's Rainbow*," *Twentieth Century Literature*, 21 (May 1975), p. 207. I cite Ozier precisely because his interpretation of the novel is so persuasive and so intelligently argued.

19. T. S. Eliot, "Baudelaire," in *Selected Prose*, ed. John Hayward (London: Penguin Books, 1953), p. 194.

20. See Slade, p. 213, for a different interpretation of what it means to be on the edge of things.

21. See Poirier, p. 168.

22. Leverenz, p. 240. Leverenz attributes the vision that this passage represents to Geli Tripping, but though she is certainly its starting point, it belongs, I think, to the narrator.

23. Lawrence Wolfley, "Repression's Rainbow: The Presence of Norman O. Brown in Pynchon's Big Novel," in *Critical Essays on Thomas Pynchon*, ed. Richard Pearce (Boston: G. K. Hall, 1981), p. 122, n. 14. David Cowart in *Thomas Pynchon: The Art of Allusion* (Carbondale and Edwardsville: Southern Illinois University Press, 1982) presents a more nuanced reading of the passage: "Gottfried approaches the gates of death . . . But nothing in Pynchon is that straightforward, least of all mortality itself . . . [and] the imagined possibilities of an otherworldly kingdom—whether Forster's or Eliot's—are very much part of his program" (p. 117).

24. Catherine Stimpson, "Pre-Apocalyptic Atavism: Thomas Pynchon's Early Fiction," in *Mindful Pleasures*, p. 32.

25. Thomas H. Schaub, *Pynchon: The Voice of Ambiguity* (Urbana: University of Illinois Press, 1981), p. 133.

26. Paul Fussell, *The Great War and Modern Memory* (New York and London: Oxford University Press, 1975), p. 277.

27. See Michael Seidel, "The Satiric Plots of *Gravity's Rainbow*," in *Pynchon: A Collection of Critical Essays*, pp. 204–10.

28. Jerome Thale, "Marlow's Quest," in *Joseph Conrad's Heart of Darkness: Backgrounds and Criticism*, ed. Leonard Dean (Englewood Cliffs, N.J.: Prentice-Hall, 1960), p. 164.

29. For Neil Schmitz, in "Describing the Demon: The Appeal of Thomas Pynchon," *Partisan Review*, 42, 1 (1975), Pointsman and Blicero represent "the Bourgeois and the Heroic" (p. 124). Schmitz's argument goes in different directions from mine, but this contrast bears on the point I've been making.

30. David Cowart, for example, argues that Pynchon's "world picture begins to appear more complex and more optimistic than the bleak vision formerly imputed to him. . . . Pynchon may in fact take a relatively sanguine view of things" (p. 4). See too the essay called "The New Jeremiad: *Gravity's Rainbow*" by Marcus Smith and Khachig Tololyan in *Critical Essays on Thomas Pynchon*, pp. 169–86.

31. George Levine, "V-2," in *Pynchon: A Collection of Critical Essays*, p. 186.

32. Compare Sanders: "There are in *Gravity's Rainbow*, as in the two previous novels, a few interludes of tenderness and compassion between human beings; but these are so fragile and evanescent that they only accentuate by contrast the general drift toward brutality" (p. 149).

33. Ozier, p. 195.

34. Slade, p. 201.

35. Ozier, p. 198.

36. Ozier, p. 203.

37. Ozier, p. 203 and Cowart, pp. 114–15.

38. Richard Pearce, "Where're They At, Where're They Going? Thomas Pynchon and the American Novel in Motion," in *Critical Essays on Thomas Pynchon*, p. 220. Pearce speaks, in the same sentence, of "the stable omniscient perspective" of V. Pearce's chapter also appears in his stimulating book, *The Novel in Motion: An Approach to Modern Fiction* (Columbus: Ohio University Press, 1983). On "the Orphic voice" of *Gravity's Rainbow*, see Schaub, pp. 123–24: "this voice is omnipresent but not omniscient; it is a fragmented voice that is everywhere at once . . . ."

39. Thomas Pynchon, *Slow Learner: Early Stories* (Boston: Little, Brown, 1984), p. 22.

40. In a complex argument, James Nohrnberg describes the novel as "intertesta-

mental." See Nohrnberg's essay "Pynchon's Paraclete," in *Pynchon: A Collection of Critical Essays*, pp. 159–60. In a footnote to Nohrnberg's discussion, Edward Mendelson adds his own, rather fantastic reason for finding *Lot 49* "apocryphal," which has to do with "Pynchon's otherwise incomprehensible refusal to incorporate characters from *Lot 49* into *Gravity's Rainbow*. . . . Since it is clearly Pynchon's practice to make connections between his books, the absence of Dr. Hilarius from *Gravity's Rainbow* amounts to its author's rejection of *Lot 49*, the book that introduced Hilarius, from his own canon" (p. 160).

41. Edward Mendelson, "The Sacred, the Profane, and *The Crying of Lot 49*," in *Pynchon: A Collection of Critical Essays*, pp. 130–31.

42. In "Pynchon's Endings," *Novel*, 18 (Winter 1985), Richard Pearce maintains that "the conclusion of *The Crying of Lot 49* does not answer the novel's main question either seriously or parodically, but it does provide a formal climax" (p. 147). I am, as my summary remarks indicate, less certain about this. Pearce's subtle discussion of all the novels' endings is well worth consulting.

43. I am quoting part of Larry McCaffery's definition of metafiction. See *The Metafictional Muse: The Works of Robert Coover, Donald Barthelme, and William H. Gass* (Pittsburgh: University of Pittsburgh Press, 1982), p. 5. For a persuasive contrast of Pynchon with metafictional writers, see Schaub, pp. 149–52. See too, for a situating of Pynchon among his contemporaries, chapter 1 of Peter L. Cooper's *Signs and Symptoms: Thomas Pynchon and the Contemporary World* (Berkeley: University of California Press, 1983), pp. 1–44.

6

shooting for smallness: realism and midfiction

> At what point do you become yourself? Never, wholly, you are always partly him.
>
> Donald Barthelme, The Dead Father

As Barthelme wryly demonstrated in the mid-seventies, it requires a good deal of effort to bury even a dead father. Worse, according to his novel's intercalated "Manual for Sons," sons are bound, after a fashion, to replicate the attitudes and actions of their fathers. "Your true task, as a son," the section on (and against) patricide counsels, "is to reproduce every one of the enormities touched upon in this manual, but in attenuated form. You must become your father, but a paler, weaker version of him. . . . Your contribution will not be a small one, but 'small' is one of the concepts that you should shoot for."[1] The Manual's cautionary prescriptions notwithstanding, patricide is very much in the air these days, and its intended victim, as the Dead Father may further help to suggest, is the presumably discredited but stubbornly persisting humanist heritage, whose refusal quietly to give up the ghost has driven a generation of structuralists, *nouveaux romanciers*, and poststructuralists, as well as a good number of post-modernists, to frenzy and despair.[2] Still, if, like Barthelme's Thomas, critics are everywhere "abroad in the city with murderinging in mind" (*TDF*, p. 46), the resemblance among them stops there. The arguments alleged against the common enemy differ, sometimes radically, as do the motives that impel them; and there is hardly more agreement about what humanism is (or was) than about what ought to displace or supersede it. After all, the burial of the dead with which Barthelme's novel ends does nothing either to settle the status of the Dead Father ("You'll bury me alive?" "You're not alive, Thomas said, remember?" [p. 175]) or, more urgently, to clarify the ambiguous responses of his heirs: "Intolerable, Thomas said. Grand. I wonder how he does it" (p. 176).

Thomas' remark acknowledges, grudgingly, the vitality of the "dead." But his reluctant admiration does nothing to stop the interment. Critics, always more peremptory, have long since taken their seats at the wake. Predictably, the most elegant, aesthetic, and theoretical attacks on all that humanism may be thought to embody or imply originated, or at any rate effloresced, in the theories of Parisian structuralism and poststructuralism. (Poets like Charles Olson and novelists such as Alain Robbe-Grillet had, of course, anticipated in their opposition to formalism or metaphor much of what was to follow.) Dissolving man into language and reference into a hall of mirrors or a semiotic echo chamber, these philosophies of absence and deferral undercut the traditional humanist credo: the notion, in Pierre Francastel's words, of "l'image d'une Nature'distincte de l'homme, mais à la mesure de l'homme et de ses réactions."[3] So Roland Barthes, in the name of free play, plurality, and *jouissance*, celebrates the text "read without the father's signature . . . without its father's guarantee"; and he goes on to say of the author that "his signature is no longer privileged and paternal, the locus of genuine truth, but rather, ludic. He becomes a 'paper author.'"[4] So much, then, for the substance and substantiality of the father/author/self. The metaphor of the organism gives way, as we move from work to text, to "that of the *network*" (p. 78), and the concept of the individual, so central to all definitions of humanism is, more than dead, dispersed: nothing more than an old wives' tale perpetuated by human beings unwilling to face the truth of their condition.

Barthelme's critique is less monolithic, if no less ironic, and so too are the objections of most American (and, indeed, French) critics—except for those who have swallowed whole the aesthetics of the Text. Most, of course, have not, whatever their debts to the panjandrums of current theory. The fact is that the majority of critics tend still to espouse more flexible and eclectic methodologies and to retain at the heart of their various enterprises a moral imperative, an ethical center (though that word, above all, is suspect today) that humanizes even the most avowedly antihumanist of perspectives. So Charles Altieri, for example, despite his talk of personality "as a centrality but not a centre"[5]—a description that recalls poststructuralist disquisitions on the fictionality of the self—offers nevertheless as a feature of postmodern poetry "a kind of anarchic individualism" (p. 613) and in place of the Barthesian notion of endlessly deferring codes points to a "contemporary distrust of mediation" (p. 630). Similarly, in his attack on the humanist implications of the Harvard core curriculum, William V. Spanos demands a concern with "ambiguous immediate experience" and attention to "human dwelling on this earth, in *this* time, in *this* place": to "man 'grounded' in his occasion."[6]

Nevertheless, for all such contrasts, there is a fundamental resemblance among these writers, which locates itself finally in what they define, with remarkable unanimity, as the stubbornly complacent impediment to a realization of the qualities they variously argue for: immanence (Altieri); temporality and dissent (Spanos); play (Barthes); and, most familiarly, *différance* (Derrida). The obstacle itself is, naturally, Barthes's and Barthelme's father, emblem of a humanism whose aim, as Robbe-Grillet contended over twenty years ago, "is precisely to recover *everything*, including whatever attempts to trace its limits, even to impugn it as a whole."[7] Spanos' indictment, modeled on Heidegger and Foucault, is the angriest and most comprehensive, a counterargument to "the recuperation of a lost and absolute origin and thus, ultimately, of a disciplinary panoptic model of the college or university [but not only of those] in which the center or core (a rational, sane, healthy, 'standard') corrects or 're-forms' the eccentric, the err-atic, the ex-orbitant, the ab-normal, or de-generate (fallen) impulse to de-viate: to stray from the right (normative) way" (p. 11). In short, what each of these writers and critics deplores is a recuperative maneuver that, on behalf of order and stability, privileges the spatial, the formal, the resolved, and that, by way of achieving those ends, seeks to contain and, most of all, to *control*.

If humanism today in fact conforms to this definition, if it is as uniform and coercive as its detractors insist, then perhaps it should, as the Dead Father ultimately does, accept the fate so many have wished upon it. But isn't it possible both to acknowledge the dangers of excessive control and yet to insist that humanism encompasses more than the strategies of power, the perpetuation of privilege, and a self-serving nostalgia for lost origins and orders? And isn't there, more to the point, something paradoxical about an enterprise that seeks (more in some cases than in others) to subvert humanism with the help of what appear to be its own traditional values? To be sure, the term humanism designates a variety of beliefs, and it would require considerable agility to supply an all-purpose description that managed not to stumble over the pressures of changing times and circumstances. Nevertheless, from the Renaissance onward, one can at least identify certain tendencies and attitudes that—and this is my point—are more congruous with than antithetical to the kinds of arguments presented by Spanos and Altieri at least. I'm referring, for example, to humanism's confirmation of the restless and inquiring mind (both the mind's openness to experience and the tentativeness of its approach); to humanism's valuing of the individual and his or her capacity for taking pleasure in the world; and, most of all, to its insistence on tolerance, that "very dull virtue," as E. M. Forster once described it,[8] which entails, among other things, a pushing against limits, a respect for differences ("Tout ce qui est ne peut être ni contre nature ni hors de nature," Diderot said[9]), and a consequent enlarging of our notions of normality and deviance.

All of which is not to offer a refutation of Spanos or of Altieri and the postmodern poets he discusses, still less to equate humanist difference with Derridean *différance*. No doubt certain aspects of humanism have calcified and turned imperial; no doubt modernism sought, in the Eliotic formula, to subdue anarchy to the symbolist imagination, tidying up a world threatening incoherence; and no doubt we have come to understand the fatuity of imagining that we can distance and detach ourselves from a world in which we are not masters but participants. But my remarks *are* intended to call for a discrimination of different kinds of humanism: to set in opposition to the dogmatic desire for control a more modest need to experience, entertain, and enjoy our *Lebenswelt* in all its diversity and concreteness. (And, it should be added, to allow others to do the same!) Some commentators have in fact proposed a distinction (more sinuous than Olson's, closer perhaps to Robert Duncan's) between what Roger Shinn refers to as open and closed humanism. Following Shinn, John Macquarrie notes: "Open humanism refers simply to the pursuit of human values in the world . . . The second type of humanism [which is the subject of Spanos' and Altieri's essays] carries a further implication, namely, that man is the sole creator of meaning and value in the world."[10] Merleau-Ponty's attempt to distinguish a specifically modern humanism is more interesting still and deserves to be quoted at length:

> If there is a humanism today, it rids itself of the illusion Valéry designated so well in speaking of "that little man within man whom we always presuppose." . . . There is no longer anything decorous or decorative about today's humanism. It no longer loves man in opposition to his body, mind in opposition to its language, values in opposition to facts. It no longer speaks of man and mind except in a sober way, with modesty: mind and man never *are*; they show through in the movement by which the body becomes gesture, language an *oeuvre*, and coexistence truth.
>
> Between this humanism and classical doctrines there is almost an homonymous relationship. In one way or another the latter affirmed a man of divine right (for the humanism of necessary progress is a secularized theology). When the great rationalist philosophies joined battle with revealed religion, what they put in competition with divine creation was some metaphysical mechanism which evaded the idea of a fortuitous world just as much as it had. Today a humanism does not oppose religion with an explanation of the world. It begins by becoming aware of contingency. It is the continued confirmation of an astonishing junction between fact and meaning, between my body and my self, my self and others, my thought and my speech, violence and truth. It is the methodical refusal of explanations, because they destroy the mixture we are made of and make us incomprehensible to ourselves.[11]

Like Shinn's open humanism, Merleau-Ponty's vision of the fortuitous and contingent, of those astonishing junctions and mysterious mixtures that rationalism maps into unbridgeable oppositions, situates human beings in a world to which their acts bring value and meaning but not the finality of predetermined "explanations," that is, of either static definition or definitive truth.

Predicated on the activity of becoming, Merleau-Ponty's credo substitutes for the recuperative tactics anathematized by antihumanists projective strategies that ground a revitalized, more flexible humanism, thereby helping to explain, whether as model or by way of contrast, the perspectives of the writers I mean to deal with here and hereafter. My concern, I should say, is not finally with the confident humanism that Spanos attacks, which probably finds its purest literary counterpart today in popular fiction, nor yet (in this chapter) with the equally confident antihumanism espoused by poststructuralists and translated most obviously into the works of meta- and, especially, surfictionists. I want instead to focus on what takes place between these extremes, on yet another middle ground where humanism offers to artists not simply provocation (or reassurance) but the uneasy challenge of a problematics, as it does in different ways to midfictionists and to contemporary realists. To put the matter briefly and provisionally, both realism (as currently practiced) and midfiction speak to Barthelme's notion of "turn[ing] down" (*TDF*, p. 145) the still operative power of Fatherhood. Both, that is, present the humanist ethos "in attenuated form," as they aim for, or at least realize, the goal of smallness (the example of Pynchon— except, significantly, for *Lot 49*—notwithstanding). But whereas realism illustrates, somewhat meagerly, the arts of coping and survival, midfiction responds, with a greater sense of risk, by acts of redefinition and creation, by an imaginative reinterpretation of the place human beings hold, or may hold, in the world. Unreflective at the deepest level, realism takes for granted what midfiction deliberately and continuously interrogates: the question of self and world. Which is why, as I'll eventually argue, realism supports the idea of humanism's obsolescence, whereas midfiction promises a revitalization, if not of the entire tradition, then of whatever in it deserves to outlast the particular embodiments by which we currently and inevitably judge its worth. But that is to get ahead of myself. The last word, properly, belongs to Barthelme: "Patricide is a bad idea . . . because it proves, beyond a doubt, that the father's every fluted accusation against you was correct" (*TDF*, p. 145).

✻   ✻   ✻

> "When your sins are washed away, you are born all over again. It'll come to you, Maureen. And you too, Lola. I'm confident it will."
> "I sort of have my own religion," Maureen said.
> "Sleep," Lola said.
>
> Mary Robison, Oh!

> She said: "D'you know what I think? I think people do what they have to do, and then the time comes when they can't any more, and they crack up. And that's that."
>
> Jean Rhys, After Leaving Mr. Mackenzie

Whether, as J. P. Stern maintains, realism names "a perennial mode of representing the world and coming to terms with it"[12] is still an open question. To those who would restrict the term to the nineteenth century have recently been added others, like Barthes, who effectively dismiss it altogether as a kind of secondary, self-deluding form of mimesis. Furthermore, even if one were to accept Stern's position, it would be hard to overlook the fact that realism remains among the most vexed and nebulous of critical designations or to ignore the disconcerting evidence of how extraordinarily few novelists from Cervantes to Virginia Woolf have not at one time or another, by one critic or another, been pressed into service to stabilize or distend its protean, vertiginous potential for meaning. It makes more sense, perhaps, to substitute for the notion of "a perennial mode" the metaphor of an arc, and to trace its curve as it takes rise in the eighteenth century, reaches its high point in the nineteenth, and descends in our own century with sporadic, though on the whole diminished, promises of recovery. In other words, realism may be best thought of as coterminous with what we sometimes spaciously call the modern or post-Cartesian age and may be imagined as sharing its presumed, if still not fully determined, fate.

To restrict and historicize Stern's definition is not, however, to eliminate the need for specifying those elements that identify a work of art as realistic. On the contrary, the need grows as we confront a movement that appears to exhibit, with however many swerves and discontinuities, with whatever lurches and jolts among its various phases, an integrity responsive not to the abstraction of human nature but to a particular segment of human history in all its concreteness. Obviously, it's easier to talk about integrity than to demonstrate it, but two recent studies, each of which examines the phenomenon of realism at its nineteenth-century summit, isolate features that may help to explain its most recent and apparently very different incarnation as well. Both Leo Bersani in A *Future for Astyanax* and George Levine in *The Realistic Imagination* agree that realistic fiction of the nineteenth century enacts a struggle between opposing forces: the anarchic or monstrous on the one hand, the orderly or shaping on the other. To be sure, the stress falls differently in the two books—Bersani's intention, as one might expect, is to expose the radical suppression of desire; Levine emphasizes the self-consciousness and doubt of the Victorians[13]—but the tension they point to is the same. In Levine's words, realism at once manifests an "ambivalence about established authority" and "embodies in its very texture the controlling force of the established order of society and history" (p. 24). Of course, the same might be said of much nonrealistic literature, and additional discriminations are evidently in order. Why and in what way exactly does realism embody the idea or ideal of control "in its very texture"? And what explains, to quote Bersani now, the realist's "*a priori* choice . . . in favor of a particular kind of world which . . . he severely judges but also (perhaps unintentionally) supports"?[14] As I suggested in my first chapter, Stern seems to me to supply the most plausible answer to these questions, and it is worth referring to his argument again. Partly because realism "is philosophically incurious and epistemologically naive" (OR, p. 54), its adherents, he insists, "merely take reality for granted" (OR, p. 145). Which is to say that realists leave in place the *fundamental* assumptions of the world they set out to describe and often violently to attack, *not* because their conscious aim is compromise or accommodation and not because their objective is, like the modernists', at all costs to contain disorder, but because at the deepest level and despite all seemingly contrary evidence, they participate in and share the preconceptions of their age.

Critics, needless to say—and not only those who reject out of hand the idea that we can in any sense "know" reality—have maintained that taking it for granted is precisely what we *can't* do in today's atmosphere of radical skepticism.[15] And yet to concede that this position is one with which most artists and critics of the twentieth century have agreed, even to agree with it oneself, is not to deny the existence of a whole range of constraints—cultural, linguistic, and so on—that in fact determine and shape the lives of most human beings. On the other hand, the nature of those constraints changes with time, and it is certainly the case that both for those who acquiesce in its givens and for those who contest them (a group that includes meta- and midfictionists alike), the age presents itself not only as less stable but as less expansive than that in which realism once flourished. Consequently, if I conjoin contemporary realism and postmodernism, it is simply to suggest, along with Barthelme, what is in some respects the diminished scale of both enterprises.[16] But the resemblance ends there. Postmodernism, after all, and not realism, envisions new possibilities of action and definition within a world whose randomness and contingency they equally acknowledge. And it is postmodernism that, in seeking to reverse or undermine the modernist heritage, reinterprets the essentials of the humanist venture too.

But of this, more later. My immediate concern is with the more sinuous and ambiguous relation of humanism to a strictly contemporary realism. On the face of it, the suggestion of a connection between writers like Joan Didion, Ann Beattie, or Raymond Carver, with their endlessly repeated evocations of drab, bleak, and disappointing lives, and the confident, coercive humanism Spanos, Altieri, and Bersani deplore[17] is as unlikely as it is bizarre. And yet, if humanism, at any rate "closed" humanism, signifies a regulating, a controlling, of the world in man's image and according to his measure, and if that is the world realists, however grudgingly, take for granted, the nature of the link begins to emerge. But obliquely. Assuming that things are as they must be, affirming and reaffirming (no doubt despite themselves) the reality of "the age," these most recent realists reveal through their characters and in their own voices not the direct image but the reverse side of humanist control: the experience, terrifying and reductive, of *being* controlled. Thus, as the last stronghold of an unexamined humanism, contemporary realism, for all its aggrieved talk of negation, randomness, and inconsequence, betrays as its most basic, operative, and yet unacknowledged assumption about the nature of things a conviction not of the world's meaninglessness but of its *limits*.

The sense of life as fixed, predictable, and, in a curious way, reliable, if only, paradoxically, in its unreliability, can be illustrated by a story that appears in Raymond Carver's most recent collection, *Cathedral*. "Chef's House" focuses on the reconciliation of a married couple, he a reformed alcoholic, and on their few months of happiness in a house loaned to Wes by a friend. With remarkable economy the story implies the unsatisfactory shape of their past life and with still more remarkable restraint intimates the collapse that will inevitably follow in the wake of the owner's decision to reclaim the house. It is as simple as that, simpler perhaps, since the suggestions of "collapse" are too dramatic for what happens. In fact, the story leaves the details of marital breakup and of Wes's return to drinking for the reader to fill in, ending instead on a note of weary and drained submission to the unavoidable. "I went in to start supper," the wife and narrator says. "We still had some fish in the icebox. There wasn't much else. We'll clean it up tonight, I thought, and that will be the end of it."[18] The resignation of these statements, as laconic and disconnectedly paratactic as what precedes them, conveys the fatuousness of having believed, however briefly, that things might have been different, even better. Fate, "Chef's House" proposes, looks malignly on those who infer from random moments of pleasure or from occasional good fortune the likelihood of what seems to them a reasonable or satisfying life. But there is more to it than that. Earlier in the story the narrator asks her husband to join her in contemplating a different scenario for their lives: "I said, Suppose, just suppose, nothing had ever happened. Suppose this was for the first time. Just suppose. It doesn't hurt to suppose. Say none of the other had ever happened. You know what I mean? Then what? I said." To which Wes replies with obvious frustration and self-pity but not, one suspects, without Carver's essential approbation: "Then I suppose we'd have to be somebody else if that was the case. Somebody we're not. I don't have that kind of supposing left in me. We were born who we are. Don't you see what I'm saying?" (pp. 31–32). She does, and we do. There is no breaking out of the situation in which the couple find themselves locked because they, Wes in particular, cannot imagine or experience their lives and the world as being different from what they are. And if they could, if they were able, as the narrator and other of Carver's characters sometimes are, to "suppose," they would still lack the resources to translate their exiguous hopes into realities. All that can be relied on is the leaden, enthralling certainty that everything wearies, stales, and disappoints.

Consequently, Jerry Bumpus, reviewing *What We Talk About When We Talk About Love*, seems to me to misinterpret the spirit of Carver's work when he praises "its evocation of the indomitability of the human spirit" and its "seemingly stoic tone."[19] Finally, neither phrase applies to what the fiction most deeply intimates and reveals. Instead, the descriptive adjective that best suits the responses of Carver's characters and the strategies that interpret them is *catatonic*, although I should say that I'm using the word with something less than clinical precision to express, approximately and metaphorically, a certain range of disabling but not, or not always, totally crippling behavior. Wes and his wife typify those of Carver's protagonists who, in the face of frustration and misery, the eroding of pleasure and the all too evident spectacle of the waste of their lives, demonstrate a terrible blankness that suspends the activities of the self and, except in fantasy or violence, betrays its effective lack of control: its inability to do other than mirror what his characters experience as the insensateness of the world. As for Carver, his narrative voice is invariably marked by coolness and distance, lack of comment, a scrupulous, more than Joycean, meanness of style, and a levelness of tone that add up, one senses, to a defense against desire and despair alike. At once profoundly knowing and "dumb," offering "the barest information, nothing that was not necessary,"[20] he charts the limits of possibility, circumscribing a territory in which the only available reactions (his or his characters') are tense acquiescence or fury. I'll come back shortly to the second half of Carver's dyadic formula: "hopelessness and outrage."[21] For the moment, it is necessary to note only that his particular rendering of the contemporary scene, at the same time strained and restrained, presents a limit-case of sorts. A minimalist of realism, he finds nothing in the world to sustain or delight, nothing that makes possible an alteration, much less a transgression, of things as they are.

If Carver's is an especially gloomy view, deliberately uncompromising in its narrow focus, it is not unique in its essential attitudes. Among those who may be thought of as catatonic realists, the role of prophet belongs, surely, to Joan Didion, whose *Play It as It Lays* renders almost perfectly—more completely perhaps than it intends—the major features of their shared vision: the beliefs that any change is likely to be for the worse, that there is nothing whatever to be done about this state of affairs, and that, as Didion's protagonist announces at the beginning of her story, "to look for 'reasons' is beside the point."[22] Others,

Maria Wyeth says, "will misread the facts, invent connections, will extrapolate reasons where none exist" (p. 4). She will not, Maria insists, but if she avoids for the most part the temptation to make sense of her messy life, it is no less true that throughout the book she continues to envy anyone who, like the character she has played in one of her husband's movies, "seemed to have a definite knack for controlling her own destiny" (p. 20). In other words, Maria's acceptance of inconsequence is less complete than she likes to think; and it is tempting to draw a parallel between her and Didion, in whose plots—so much more conventionally dramatic, even melodramatic, than Carver's or Beattie's—the shadow of "intelligibility" (to use her own word) persists despite her conviction, constantly repeated in *The White Album*, that narrative formulas have lost their relevance. In any case, Maria's rejection of logic and connection constitutes only part of what Didion means us to identify as defining her protagonist's specific way of encountering the world. The other part emerges through the contrast of Maria with her friend and potential double, BZ, who, sharing with her the novel's central ethical and metaphysical certitude that nothing matters, kills himself as she, unresisting, holds his hand. Maria opts instead to *"stay in the action"* (p. 210), though why she does so is no clearer and somewhat less convincing than are the reasons Beckett's characters choose to go on. *"I know what 'nothing' means, and keep on playing,"* she says as we last see her, and, responding to BZ's imagined question, *"Why,"* she answers, characteristically, *"Why not"* (p. 214).

One can hardly imagine a more passive or cynical reply, a more total submission to whatever life proposes. And yet there is no mistaking Maria's pride in not taking BZ's path and no misunderstanding Didion's approval. If not at first, then gradually, we come to recognize that Didion means us to regard Maria not only as victim (of men, of her particular society, and of the universe) but as heroine; to see in her mere persistence a small but not insignificant act of existential courage. So far, so good. But Didion asks more of us, asks us to believe that Maria's capacity for survival grounds, or at least makes possible, further acts of creation and self-creation. Not that there is anything inherently improbable about this entailment. Midfiction, as I've often noted, is distinguished precisely by its determination to create meaning in despite of what it takes to be reality's essential meaninglessness. But *Play It as It Lays*, with its nostalgia for a lost coherence and its failure ever to contest the limits of the given, persuades us neither of its acceptance of the world's fundamental disorder nor of its assent to those possibilities of human action that nevertheless inhere in such a world. In other words, Maria's nihilism—her imagination of what, somewhat glamorously (that is, with none of the hard-earned meanings of various nineteenth- and twentieth-century explorations of nothingness, *le néant*, and the void), she calls "the hard white empty core of the world" (p. 162)—is as facile as her resolves are unconvincing. Both come together near the end of the book:

*I used to ask questions, and I got the answer: nothing. The answer is "nothing." Now that
I have the answer, my plans for the future are these: (1) get Kate* [her brain-damaged
daughter], (2) *live with Kate alone, (3) do some canning. Damson plums, apricot preserves. Sweet India relish and pickled peaches. Apple chutney. Summer squash succo-
tash.*   (p. 210)

Despite its midfictional bow to the ordinary, the passage lacks both specificity
and solidity. Unsupported in the book as a whole by an enabling context of value
or belief—other than the injunction to play it as it lays—the plums and preserves conspicuously lack any resonance or evocative force. As, for that matter,
does Kate. Indeed, Kate provides the most telling clue to the confusion at the
heart of the book. Presented, along with Maria's aborted child, as the sole object
of her mother's affection, she is meant, apparently, to ratify Maria's capacity for
feeling; but since she is herself a blur, it is difficult to take seriously the obsessive
concern directed at her. In addition, her role as fellow victim (like her mother,
Kate has been institutionalized) only dematerializes still further her fictional
substantiality by turning her into a symbolic mirror, the reflex of Maria's im-
placable, uninflected self-absorption. Whether Didion intends us to make this
judgment is another matter. In fact, the novel's voice, uniformly manifest in its
lackluster style and tone, is indistinguishable from Maria's—a coincidence that
suggests Didion's inability to distance herself from or, possibly, fully to engage
herself with the throttled space her heroine occupies, and so to temper her engagement, such as it is, with a much needed irony. In the final analysis, the
story of Maria reduplicates itself in its telling, making clear not only her own
but the novel's imperfect acceptance of the senselessness to which it nevertheless
(or consequently) resigns itself.

I want to make clear the distinction my argument rests on. To accept the
world (which for postmodernists and catatonic realists alike defines itself in its
randomness and contingency) is at once to abandon the anthropocentric model
and yet, in repeatedly testing the limits of possibility, to carve out a space for acts
of human encounter and definition. On the other hand, to acquiesce in its
apparent disorder is to conflate the personal and the metaphysical and, in making the intractability of the universe the measure of possibility at all levels of
existence, to assume the pointlessness of any action whatever. The second, of
course, is the way of Maria and of Didion, and of the other writers I'm considering along with her, but Didion's case is especially revealing. "Order and control are terribly important to me," she has been quoted as saying,[23] and one
suspects that this hankering after the regulative and determinate explains, by
their absence, the narrow and bitter resignation of her novel, as well as the
uncertainty of its focus. Writing of Didion's work (among others'), Vivian Gornick argues suggestively that "these novels have abdicated thinking. They do not
wish to think. . . . The old fear of sex is now openly, less euphemistically, fear

of the genuinely knowing self. . . . The trouble is this preoccupation with self does not go deep enough, the act of introspection is shallow rather than pro-found."[24] The remark seems to me exactly on target. Ultimately, the way these writers intend their world amounts to a failure of imagination and nerve, which leads in turn to a continuous, nagging resentment and frustration on the part of the characters in whom they embody their own discontent.

Interestingly enough, Gornick's comment is echoed by a character in Mary Robison's self-consciously eccentric and comic novel *Oh!*: "'It isn't the chaos,' [Virginia] said. 'It's the hopelessness. . . . Not one of you can save himself or stop himself from harming the others because you just don't *think*. You have lost the habit of thinking.'"[25] She is right. Right especially if thinking is equated with kinetic, enlarging acts of consciousness. The Clevelands are, one and all, feckless, immature, self-indulgent. But does Robison agree? The dust jacket's description of the novel warns us, none too subtly, that "only those too dense to detect the underlying utility of the Cleveland brand of horse-play would mistake this extraordinary family for another American disaster zone"; and Robison so effectively undercuts the priggish Virginia as to make us question her judgment and ours. Nevertheless, and at the risk of admitting to denseness, it has to be said that the Clevelands, unwilling, incapable, or insufficiently imaginative to do anything with their lives, are ultimately unimportant and anything but ex-traordinary. More buoyant than Didion, Robison apparently shares her disabling inability to understand fully the sources of her characters' limitations, which, as I've been arguing, derive from a willingness to equate cosmic carelessness with human inactivity and to excuse the second by easy references to the first. As Katha Pollitt astutely says in a review of *Oh!*, "one could argue that the vision these writers [Robison, Beattie, Carver] share, of a pared-down, emotionally drained, random world, reflects less the failures of contemporary America than some obscurer failure to connect on the part of the writers themselves."[26]

With Beattie, however, particularly in her most accomplished collection of stories, *The Burning House*, one senses a clarity and steadiness at any rate, if not an enlarging, of the typical catatonic perspective. Wiser and more knowledge-able than most of her characters, Beattie nonetheless perceives life essentially as they do, with a disillusioned and cheerless glance that plays relentlessly over life's dailiness and finds it without exception pinched, meager, and limited. We have come to the zero degree of contemporary realism, where the relative activ-ity of playing it as it lays gives way to the still more defeated gesture—inscribed in the title of Beattie's second novel—of falling in (but not into) place. Not that her men and women are any less miserable, angry, or resentful than Didion's, but they and her narrators are, by and large, too mannerly to raise their voices, too dispirited to imagine alternatives to what they are already doing. "What will happen can't be stopped," ends "Learning to Fall," the first story in the volume, adding by way of coda: "Aim for grace."[27] For Beattie, grace is a matter of style, the achievement of a sophisticated delicacy, understatement, and restraint that are her hallmarks as a writer. For her characters, grace translates into a style of life: the capacity, at best, to hang on, to take things in stride, to make, as the story's model heroine does, the best of one's lot and ask nothing more.

Not that everyone in *The Burning House* manages to achieve even this much grace. The placement of "Learning to Fall" in the collection serves to expose, but not finally to judge (failure, after all, is more plausible than success in Beattie's joyless, claustrophobic world), the unhappiness and disappointment of those who continue to struggle against or at least to resent the fates dealt to them in these stories. The airlessness of Beattie's writing derives in part from the fact that her characters are unable to take comfort even in the consolations of memory and desire. Or nearly so. More attenuated than in *The Waste Land*, thoughts of a different and better past or future only confirm in their unrealizability the sense of entrapment in the present. So at the end of "Afloat," the narrator drifts "between [her husband and her step-daughter] knowing exactly how each one feels . . . knowing that desire that can be more overwhelming than love—the desire, for one brief minute, simply to get off the earth" (p. 197). And at the close of "Winter: 1978,"[28] one of the characters, typically transposing the limits of individual consciousness into other, in this case historical or cosmic, inevitabilities, relates a parable of decline from a more impressive time:

Benton told [his son] this fact of evolution: that one day dinosaurs shook off their scales and sucked in their breath until they became much smaller. This caused the dinosaurs' brains to pop through their skulls. The brains were called antlers, and the dinosaurs deer. That was why deer had such sad eyes, Benton told Jason—because they were once something else.   (p. 121)

The emblematic significance of the deer requires no elaborate gloss, but the tone of the narrative deserves some notice. Self-consciously wistful, the more so for its wryly amusing inventiveness and charm, the tale oozes self-pity in its account of inexplicable metamorphosis and irreversible loss, while in its assumption of narrowed horizons and diminished expectations, it justifies the freight of weary, submissive hopelessness that threatens almost to sink *The Burning House* under its weight.

If these remarks display a marked lack of sympathy, it is because, as James Wolcott rightly notes, "Beattie's characters aren't beaten down by life; they're defeated by their own defeatedness."[29] And if, for all the book's manifest subtlety and stylistic felicities, one is tempted at times to dismiss it as minor work, "it isn't," to quote Wolcott again, "that Beattie's vision of contemporary life is false, just that it's so drab and limited, so willfully puny." Benton's story becomes, then, more than a comment on "Winter: 1978"; it reflects, inadvertently, on the whole of Beattie's enterprise, and not only on hers. Life has indeed become for the realists I've been discussing "much smaller." But smallness is a notion that adjusts itself to the requirements of differing, sometimes incompatible contexts, and I don't mean to confound Beattie's use of the word with Barthelme's. The summons to smallness in "A Manual for Sons" is by way of being a deliberate and purposeful act of retrenchment: at once an attempt to overturn the heroics, certainties, and all-encompassing orders of the past (that is, of the Dead Father) and the determination to generate, tentatively and open-endedly, energies, meanings, and values in the midst and on the very surface of the fortuitous and problematic. Beattie's acquiescence, on the other hand, constitutes a more fundamental, though not necessarily conscious, acknowledgment of limits (the self-imposed limits of consciousness itself), and if her characters, like Didion's, choose to "stay in the action," it is only because they resist the threat of total inanition, the fear that, as someone says to his lover in "Running Dreams": "[If you] let me go . . . I'm going to be as unmovable as that balloon in the tree" (p. 212).

Still, if most of the characters attempt to preserve a balance this side of literal catatonia, their hopes and even their demands are minimal. "Girl Talk," the story that best sums up the mood of *The Burning House*, makes the point. Visiting the family of her supposed husband, the narrator describes, with apparent dispassion and detachment, the relatively unexceptional but unmistakably repellent relations gathered for a weekend birthday celebration. Only at the end, as she suspects she is going into labor, do we understand fully both the feelings that subtend her narration and the assumptions that keep them at so low a boil. "There is every possibility," she says, "that my baby will be loved and cared for and will grow up to be like any of these people. . . . I am really at some out-of-the-way beach house, with a man I am not married to and people I do not love, in labor. . . . I smile, the first to hold out my glass. Pain is relative" (p. 38). No doubt. But there is something about the final remark that grates. Too easy in its transparent defensiveness, too lazy in its conviction of life's inexorable sameness, it is finally as complacent, as self-congratulatory in its presumption of virtue in mere endurance, as it is reductive. Nevertheless, there is no suggestion that we are to do other than applaud this instance of psychic immobility. "What do you do with a shard of sorrow?" (p. 220), one last story closes; and the answer, more persuasive than in *Play It as It Lays* because it roots itself more firmly in the quotidian, is again nothing.

One has to admire Beattie's consistency and control, her faithfulness to the boundaries of her elected world. But one has also to wonder at how much, even by the standards of contemporary realism, is excluded. Minimalist though he is, Carver encompasses a wider range of responses, and I want to return to him now to explore the ways in which his fiction challenges (or seems to challenge), even as it confirms, the insights and reach of his fellow catatonic realists. The closest Carver comes to a credo is in the anomalously reflexive story, "Put Yourself in My Shoes," which rejects the three anecdotes it encloses—anecdotes that, as told to its artist-protagonist, attribute to narrative a concern with the exceptional, the dramatic, and the consequent—in favor of the banal account of ordinary life that it itself describes and is. But what makes the tale so revealing is not its conventional realist aesthetic but the unpleasantness and cruelty of its hero, whose confidence of superiority to his wretched hosts at least hints at Carver's own treatment of his characters. Of course, cruelty in Carver's work has its shades and degrees, and the salient fact about it is that it intensifies in direct proportion to the extent of the hopes his pathetic men and women cling to in assessing themselves and their lives. The irony directed, for example, at the miserable but relatively unexpectant protagonist of "The Student's Wife," who can do nothing but pray wretchedly for change, or even at the slightly more self-deluding narrator of "Fat," whose momentary expectation that her "life is going to change. I feel it" (WYP, p. 6), deceives neither us nor, ultimately, herself is as nothing compared with that aimed at the initially so much more confident and ingenuous main character of "Will You Please Be Quiet, Please?." Centering on Ralph's discovery that his wife has been unfaithful, the story traces, with an astringent and remarkable lack of sympathy, his romantic, dramatic, but (to the reader) altogether understandable reactions to what he has learned, and presents him to us in the process as a naive and self-pitying fool, whose presumption that things might or should have been different constitutes in itself sufficient cause for Carver's mockery and scorn. Clearly, Carver is more comfortable with those of little hope, and his sympathy, such as it is, goes to those who don't choose, as Wes's wife does, to "suppose." The need and desire for happiness are seen, in fact, as not only impossible of realization but as unreasonable and fatuous. And when, in "Neighbors," for example, there is a random moment of fulfillment, the glimmer of something better, it is not, as in Barthelme, a small pleasure, an achievement of will or perception in the face of indifference and senselessness, but a tease, the predictable prelude to inevitable letdown.

Indeed, pleasure, whether longed for, or (rarely) achieved, seems to be for Carver not only a delusion but an affront; and it is hard to resist the suspicion that his grudge against those who wish or expect life to be perfect stems from a desire on his part for just such perfection. If I'm right about Carver's subterranean longings, it's easier to make sense of the cruelty in his fiction, which on this reading can be accounted for by his underlying resemblance to the very characters he shows least sympathy. And easier to understand too why, in the light of his frustrated idealism, hopelessness finds its inevitable complement in outrage—in the excitement and violence that are the other face of catatonia. This kind of anger and resentment is pandemic in *What We Talk About*, which, like the earlier volume I've been discussing, but more grimly and acridly, focuses on failed relationships and wasted lives. To be sure, much of the violence is aimless or minor: one husband carries on low-scale guerilla warfare against his estranged or ex-wife, destroying her Christmas pies, cutting the cord of her telephone ("A Serious Talk"); another, deserted by his family, throws rocks from his roof ("Viewfinder"); a third stabs a needle into his embroidery, displacing his bitterness at his wife's illness and his spoiled evening ("After the Denim"). Nevertheless, the outrage is more general than in *Will You Please Be Quiet, Please?* ; and in some of the stories the ante has been raised considerably. In one, a character kills his wife with a hammer and drowns himself ("The Third Thing That Killed My Father Off"); in a second, an idle flirtation born out of boredom and discontent, ends in brutal murder ("Tell the Women We're Going"). There is no need to multiply examples. The effects of frustration permeate the volume, testifying to a desire for completeness and permanence that is almost painful in its intensity. But since the desire goes unacknowledged, if not by all the characters, then by Carver himself, its genuinely tragic potential dwindles into an irritated resentment that directs itself less against life than against those who, paradoxically mirroring their creator's profoundest wish, would have it otherwise.

With Carver, then, we come to contemporary realism's most skillful but also most self-contradictory rendering of what it feels like to be controlled. But controlled by what? It is too simple to invoke the ineluctabilities of age and illness and death, though these certainly help to darken the background of his work. Even more than in Beattie's and Didion's fiction, the emphasis falls on the world of human relations—on needs that can't be regulated, on wants that can't be fulfilled. As in the title story of *What We Talk About*, even the actuality of love is shadowed by the fear of its probable transience. And yet the sketchy anecdote in the same story of an elderly couple whose love has evidently survived whatever drives the younger men and women of the other stories apart suggests that there is something especially bitter and unstable about life in the present (at *this* time, in *this* society), that, as for Beattie, life has become, with what results are apparent, "much smaller." It is unclear, however, which of these "truths"— the conviction of living at the fag end of a more spacious age or the belief that merely to be human results in disappointment—is meant to prevail. What *is* clear is that as the first justifies hopelessness, the second excuses the intuition of fatedness that Carver shares with Didion, Beattie, and Robison. In fact, all four represent a particular cultural moment, the moment of humanism's contestation. Or at any rate part of it. Unable, as I've been arguing, either to accept the reality they perceive or to envision alternatives to it, they substantiate in their fictions the idea of humanism as a closed system, to which they and their characters pay the ironic tribute of protesting not its governing principles but their effects. Which is to say, in sum, that catatonic realism concedes without finally recognizing the boundaries that constrain its responses; that its values are in the last analysis implicitly normative and closural; that it jumbles together the metaphysical, the social, and the individual in a confusion of what does and does not yield to human perception and effort; and that, as Carver's stories demonstrate, its outrage proves no more liberating than its resignation. No character in the works I've looked at can say with the justified conviction of Barthelme's Thomas: "I don't suggest I understand [the larger picture even] now. I do understand the frame. The limits" (*TDF*, p. 32). It is midfiction that, comprehending (and accepting) its inability to master or construe the larger picture, manages *for that very reason* to create for itself the possibilities of purposeful, if modest, action.

☆ ☆ ☆

I am cheered by the wine of possibility.

Donald Barthelme, Great Days

I've been calling upon Barthelme throughout this chapter to intimate a less reductive assessment of contemporary life than that suggested by Carver and the other catatonic realists; and if in turning now directly to his work I choose one relatively brief story to set against the massed weight of their fiction, I'm only confirming a judgment, as much about value as about differences, already implicit in earlier remarks. The question, of course, is what underlies and justifies the judgment. According to Terrence Doody, the idea of realism "does not posit any single organizing idea of its own except that of the world's intelligibility to man's cognate intelligence."[30] My point all along has been that for realists of the kind I've been describing, the world, however contrary to human desire, is—or at some uncontested level is assumed to be—intelligible: the already given is not only the boundary but the determinant (the sole determinant) of being and doing.

But it is precisely this notion that Barthelme disputes. "I believe," he said in a recent interview and with predictable self-mockery, "that my every sentence trembles with morality in that each attempts to engage the problematic rather than to present a proposition to which all reasonable men must agree."[31] Abstractly considered, the antithesis neatly sketches the realist position and the very different way in which Barthelme grasps the world. But the tone of the credo prepares us for still something more. After Carver's stories especially, with their lives of gloomy, numbing routine or of occasional, transitory, and deceptive pleasures, Barthelme's enchant with their buoyancy. But how, given their sense of life's sadness and drabness, its uncertainties, disappointments, and incompleteness, do they manage this? The answer seems to be that in bringing the realists' covert assumptions of limits into the open and in challenging the fictional strategies that articulate those limits, Barthelme releases or makes available an energy and inventiveness which, more than anything else perhaps, set postmodernism (that is, in different ways both meta- and midfiction) apart from realism's inverted, submissive model of control. Without foregoing altogether traditional paradigms of character, narrative, and referentiality (as metafiction at least claims to do[32]), Barthelme puts all of them—and reality itself—into question by means of his manifold rejections of depth and his persistent interrogations of the possibility of fixed, stable "meanings." Or, as he has himself said: "Our Song of Songs is the Uncertainty Principle" (AF, p. 200). And yet, for all its avowal of instability and incoherence, Barthelme's midfictional enterprise suffers from none of modernism's (or realism's) anguish over the unconformability of the universe to human needs and longings. In short, what modernism contends with, the disorder it seeks, if only aesthetically, to shape and overcome, and what contemporary realism (a less confident humanism) acquiesces in, Barthelme, like postmodernism in general, accepts: life's quandaries are no more to be resolved than to be taken for granted.

Acceptance is a threadbare sort of word, however, and if it describes accurately Barthelme's willingness to live with perplexity, it doesn't do full justice to the unexpected lesson of his fiction, which is that the uncertain may actually breed affirmations of a kind available neither to totalizing modernists nor to those realists who, like Beattie, aim for a minimal grace. The paradox of Barthelme's densely human but still relentlessly mysterious novels and stories is that in coming to terms with randomness and even absurdity, their characters (some of them, at any rate) discover in themselves the capacity to make a world that remains stubbornly stochastic yield up, even if fleetingly, visions of moderate, local content. Acceptance, in short, leads to, or at least makes possible, a mode of assent that, playfully but dynamically, works to create meaning within (but not to the exclusion of) life's insistent and confusing dailiness.[33] As it does in the story called "Overnight to Many Distant Cities," an altogether genial instance of supervenient grace in the midst of disjunct reality. No single work, of course, can be made to stand for the whole of Barthelme's literary production, and I don't mean to give that kind of weight even to what seems to me (along with "Basil from Her Garden") the most successful work he has published since the appearance of Sixty Stories.

In fact, while "Overnight" confirms as much as most of Barthelme's fictions his typically ironic and disruptive view of the reality we both create and are created by and, in addition, reveals the suspensive attitude that describes his acceptance of it, the story is in other ways less characteristic—or, rather, comes closer in spirit to his more recent books. Not that all critics find a pattern of development in his career. Charles Molesworth, for example, maintains that "the question of growth becomes cloudy in his case" (DBF, p. 80), and Larry McCaffery finds "relatively unimportant [the] way his work has evolved" (TMM,

p. 100). For myself, I would propose that, without abandoning altogether its arguably metafictional properties, Barthelme's fiction has become over the years—though not consistently or steadily—more affirmative, more moral in the largest and broadest sense. If this is true, then a story like "Overnight to Many Distant Cities" represents a movement, however tentative, toward an exploration of the opportunities for assent and, equally, of midfiction's potential: an exploration that modifies, but doesn't cancel, the skepticism of Barthelme's fundamental vision.

"I think," Barthelme has said, "the paraphrasable content in art is rather slight. . . . The *way* things are done is crucial" (*AF*, p. 199); and it is certainly the case that, like most midfiction (indeed more than most), "Overnight" resists paraphrase. Perhaps all that one can usefully say about it by way of description is that its apparently casual assortment of anecdotes, which take the form (possibly) of a series of unrelated journal entries punctuated from time to time by what seem to be irrelevant reports on the weather (once even on the stock market), expresses the narrator's sense of life's inconsequence, haphazardness, and generally amiable absurdity. As for the anecdotes themselves, what they convey is at once the kaleidoscopic variousness and the stubborn ordinariness of existence, as well as its serendipitous pleasures and inevitable disappointments (in matters of love especially). If there results at last from these bits and pieces, from the fracturing of the narrative, the heterogeneity of the texture, and the staccato, disjunctive rhythms of the prose, a unity of effect, its source, as Barthelme suggests, is to be found in the manner of the telling, in the cool and equivocal voice that offers the reader not the finality of order—certainly not the negatively reductive order of the catatonic realists—but the consistency of a perspective: the testimony of Barthelme's ironically and kinetically intentional relation to the world. Furthermore, though it is so patently serial and nonprogressive, an album of unassorted photographs or a collection of random *faits divers* (to choose other and equally appropriate metaphors for its form), the story nevertheless contrives to close in a way that tempers, though it doesn't efface, the prevailing mood of unrelatedness:

> Lunching with the Holy Ghost I praised the world, and the Holy Ghost was pleased. "We have that little problem in Barcelona," He said, "the lights go out in the middle of dinner." "I've noticed," I said. "We're working on it," He said, "what a wonderful city, one of our best." "A great town," I agreed. In an ecstasy of admiration for what is we ate our simple soup.
> Tomorrow, fair and warmer, warmer and fair, most fair. . . .[34]

Taken by itself, the passage may legitimately be read as threatening sentimentality. But in the patchwork context of other memories and cities, even the final ecstatic, cadenced sentences constitute not a vision of all-embracing unity but a deliberately limited gesture of assent. In addition, the narrator's "admiration for what is" necessarily encompasses "that little problem," an instance, perhaps, of what Barthelme calls "offsetting material, things that tell the reader that although X is happening, X is to be regarded in the light of Y" (AF, p. 194). Y in this case specifies the fickle lights of Barcelona and, more broadly, the authorial tactic they imply: the destabilizing irony that allows Barthelme to qualify in the very act of praising and to praise what he fully recognizes to be a world "stippled with uncertainty."[35]

As for the Holy Ghost, Himself the instrument of a flawed creation, His presence intimates the midfictional morality of Barthelme's story. No more to be taken literally than the "tucked-away Gods" of "The Emerald,"[36] He embodies the problematic as well as a way of responding to it. Like Barthelme's narrator in the rest of the story, but more explicitly, the Holy Ghost accepts the world in all its imperfection; and His apparently contradictory promise to overcome that imperfection, far from negating the provisional character of assent, only underscores it. Hypothetical, uncertain, and, as the verb form indicates, progressive ("We're working on it"), the proposed change demystifies the ideal of completion and control and turns it into acts of process: into ongoing, creative affirmations of what is—and what may be too. Singularly unattached to perfection, the Holy Ghost, recalling the artist-hero of "Engineer-Private Paul Klee" or Mad Moll in "The Emerald," takes impermanence to be the condition of life (as Carver & Co. do also) but in addition testifies, with complete awareness, to the extraordinariness of the ordinary, to the world as, potentially at least, "most fair." Which is to say, finally, that in adding to his acceptance (and so to his skeptical vision of the quotidian) the risky but luminous possibility of assent, Barthelme engages not only the problematic but the supposititious in a way that Carver and his characters, seeing their ultimately immutable and claustrophobic world from within, neither do nor can. For all the modesty of its aims, it is midfiction that opens reality most persuasively to new and generative significations and, in the process, redefines humanism as the limited and flexible answer human beings are capable of when confronted with their own and the world's contingency.

✻ ✻ ✻

> *Truth, being alive, was not halfway between anything. It was only to be found by continuous excursions into either realm, and though proportion is the final secret, to espouse it at the outset is to insure sterility.*
>
> E. M. Forster, Howards End

To say that midfiction validates the possibilities of an open, projective humanism is not to suggest a programmatic bond among its practitioners. My attempt has been, rather, to indicate some common ground, some assumptions that reveal a shared awareness of the difficulties implicit in an enterprise that seeks neither to control nor to be controlled and that, furthermore, bases itself, in Merleau-Ponty's words, on "the methodical refusal of explanations." I've suggested already that in eschewing both the confidence of an older humanism and the acquiescence of the catatonic realists, midfiction puts itself deliberately and continuously at risk. But at this point further discriminations are necessary. Although midfiction refuses the constricting vision of contemporary realism, it rejects as well the belligerent, theoretically antihumanist stance of postmodernism's more doctrinaire experimentalists, those metafictionists (and, more particularly, surfictionists) who conceive the world, aesthetically and reactively, not only as mediated by language but as existing, thanks to the reflexive and constitutive powers of the imagination, wholly within the word. Midfiction, to be sure, doesn't hope or pretend to master the world, but it does admit its solicitation, so that, in admitting too the need of consciousness partly and cooperatively to shape experience, it holds itself accountable to the existence of a vital and independent, if never totally knowable, reality.

In other words, here as elsewhere, midfiction rejects the extremes of current literary theory and practice. Yet even that formulation is too simple. The paradoxical nature of midfiction inheres in the fact that it simultaneously transgresses and reasserts its commitment to the ordinary, that it tests limits and crosses boundaries not to outrun or deny them but the better to discover in what the extraordinariness of the ordinary consists. To put the matter formulaically, the limits that oppress Carver, Beattie, and Didion—and that metafictionists, in their celebration of the untrammeled imagination, deny—provide midfictionists with an opportunity for establishing a probative and existential definition of human endeavor. Thus, even if midfiction finally endorses smallness, or, at any rate (to define its aims less narrowly), refuses to impose a logic of certainties on the problematic world that anchors and invigorates it, it doesn't hesitate to reach its goal by forays into the inexplicably mysterious and strange.

Barthelme's restless and playful experimentation—a dismantling of traditional narrative conventions and the assurances they give us about the stability of reality—is one sign of this tendency, but it is only one. And not necessarily the most radical. Other writers, even while ultimately confirming their midfictional allegiance, have gone still further in entertaining challenges to its validity and sufficiency. The fact is that postmodernism's determination to break the stranglehold of catatonic resignation (and of less extreme realist positions too) renders plausible, if by no means inevitable, the craving to escape altogether the concreteness and specificity of human possibility: to reject or overreach any limits whatever. A persuasive examination of the temptations and dangers involved in just such an unconditioned pursuit of the extraordinary and transhuman can be found in Ted Mooney's ambitious first novel, *Easy Travel to Other Planets*, where the yearning desire of one of Barthelme's characters "*to go somewhere*

where everything is different"[37] becomes the occasion for an exploration of a far more dramatic range of extremes. Barthelme mocks the urgency of his speaker: "The old babe," his narrator comments, "demands nothing less than total otherness." When someone in *Easy Travel* echoes almost the same words—"All I want is to go someplace where everything is different"[38]—our response is more complex and, at least initially, more sympathetic. Sympathetic because the context Mooney establishes for his characters more than justifies the longing. Living some time in the near future, in a too thoroughly humanized world (the very Barthelmean disease of the age is "information sickness"), and at the edge of apocalypse (a global war impends over uranium deposits in Antarctica), the novel's men and women understandably seek, in a variety of conscious and subconscious ways, to evade their situations: to reestablish, by fleeing the world's control, their own. Mooney's point, however—or so I take it to be—is that in their effort not simply to interrogate limits and boundaries but to pass well beyond the threshold of the human, they do not so much reenact as parody the intentions of midfiction, turning its tentative and self-aware explorations into a self-indulgent form of psychic travel.

The emblems that translate the characters' frayed and aggravated responses to their thickly overloaded surroundings suggest, variously, compulsive movement and speed (flying, skydiving, stock car racing), violence (the war, an aborted strangling, a gun that passes ominously from hand to hand in the course of the book), death (one character is dying, another steps from a taxi into a stream of cars and is killed), and liminal experiences of different kinds and intensities (sleepwalking, sex, dreams: the novel is filled with dreams). There is, in short, a sense throughout of everything exploding centrifugally toward or beyond the verge of what can any longer be calculated or controlled. All of this, however, is by way of orchestrating the novel's central narrative theme, which announces itself early on in the sexual coupling of its protagonist, Melissa, with a dolphin named Peter, a relationship that, as it evolves, subsumes *Easy Travel's* other elements to a master emblem of irrevocable violation and transgression: the imposition of "the dry [that is, human] world . . . [where] everything divided up into . . . *things*: separate, disconnected" (p. 223) onto the alien fluidity of the dolphin's. But if Melissa's seduction of or by Peter (it isn't clear which describes what happens) provides a limit case, her "accelerating life" (p. 38) reflects accurately enough the general obsession with death and the future in the book— "a future [that] seemed to demand a less monolithic vision" (p. 35) but that is so unspecific as to represent no more than the state of "want[ing] to want" (p. 155) or, alternatively, a fear "of everything that stopped" (p. 245).

There is no need to pursue here all of the relations the novel intertwines. Enough to say that the tact and subtlety with which Mooney depicts even the most bizarre of them bespeaks in another way the sympathy I alluded to above.

More than that, Mooney's deformation of his narrative line—particularly the periodic shift into captioned, present-tense sections that generally interrupt its progress by countermovements in space or time or by the engagement of other levels or kinds of consciousness—this characteristic deformation in some sense mirrors strategically the transgressions of his characters. And yet it is also the case that just as Mooney's midfictional swerve is less dramatic and unsettling than the techniques of the surfictionists above all, so his feeling for his characters stops considerably short of endorsing their maimed and bungled lives. What Melissa's mother imagines the elderly Freud thinking—"that life on the frontiers of human consciousness is not all it's cracked up to be" (p. 171)—may be taken as a more accurate summation of the book's position. I'm suggesting, then, that in the final analysis *Easy Travel* enacts a cautionary tale or rather that, despite (possibly because of) the ventriloquial skill with which it renders the nonhuman from its own perspective (Peter's and, in one fantasticated sequence, the moon's), the novel constitutes an ironic meditation on what Melissa's colleague calls "the exquisite pangs of one state of being glimpsing another" (p. 132)—a pang that apparently doesn't extend to the butterfish being slammed against a tank for Peter's dinner in the immediately sequent paragraph.

Again, Melissa offers the reader the clearest evidence of what Mooney is after. Characterized (by the narrator? by herself?) as "the scientific method continued by other means" (p. 253), she betrays her detachment—which is perhaps better described as her fevered curiosity—without fully confessing its loss, and the loss of something more. Thus Jeffrey says to her: "Can't you see . . . you're becoming more and more inhuman? . . . You're *not* a human being anymore" (pp. 117–18). And later he notes, this time commenting on her: "She knows how to want a thing. It's just that she hardly ever settles for anything so mundane as the possible" (p. 134). Whether or not Melissa comes to recognize these things about herself hardly matters. She has gone too far, as have most of the novel's characters, and the climax of the book occurs with her deliberate shooting of the dolphin. The irony is patent: unable to deal with the transgression she has provoked in crossing the threshold of the human, she ends by reasserting control in the cruellest, most human way. Or, to put the matter a bit differently, the nonhuman falls victim to the mutually implying extremes of the inhuman and the too meddlesomely human, which, as everything in *Easy Travel* demonstrates, lead inevitably to destruction and self-destruction. (The closest intrahuman counterpart and complement to Melissa's act occurs when her friend Nikki, who has in the past encouraged her lover to "games of physical violence and threat" [p. 214], flees what she mistakenly thinks is his intention to kill her—with the gun that Melissa uses to rid herself of Peter—and destroys herself.)

The novel's final image, the substance of a section titled "WHERE WE LIVED AND WHAT WE LIVED FOR," involves Melissa's memory, which follows (incongruously it appears) shortly after the shooting, of her mother driving *"at a speed that seems, then and at all other moments, incredible"* (p. 274). But the incongruity is only superficial. In fact, the image generalizes the meaning latent in Melissa's killing of Peter by stressing its root cause: the facile disregard of boundaries, the easy travel, that leads her and the others to abrogate their human definition. Whether the answer lies in redefinition along specifically human lines or, rather—since that does seem to be implied—*how* the task is to be undertaken, is not completely clear. There are allusions throughout the novel to "a new emotion, one that no one had ever felt before" (p. 182), which perhaps "actually began years ago with the whole ESP thing" (p. 104) and which seems related to the fact that "everything in America was getting lighter, stronger, and more transparent" (p. 182). Certainly, the prescience of various of the characters and the increasing ability of Jeffrey and Melissa to read each other's mind bear out the likelihood of some sort of breakthrough in the area of *human* communication. (Significantly, Jeffrey decides not to mention their power when they last see one another.) In any case, we are given, perhaps appropriately, no more than hints and suggestions. The way of midfiction is, after all, one of tentative exploration; and if Barthelme offers on occasion affirmations of "what is"—small enclaves of pleasure and possibility—they are set forth with an awareness of just how provisional and modest the offering is. What matters is the grounding of these affirmations in the specifically human concreteness of experience. And so with Mooney. Despite some occasional and homeopathic highflying in *Easy Travel* (that is, the way in which, entering Peter's mind, he makes his own imaginative leaps to "other planets"), the novel, like midfiction in general, is of this world worldly. Which is, I'm aware, what has traditionally been said of realism. But realism, in its latest manifestation at least, has lost its confidence and exuberance; and as for the world, there is no need to stress the fact that it, or our perception of it, has become less solid and reassuring, and manifestly less compliant to human desire.

A casual piece of description in *Easy Travel*—"In the sky, bird events took place" (p. 26)—intimates the necessary boundaries of human comprehension; but it is also true that the novel as a whole only reconfirms the need for men and women to come to terms with what willy-nilly surrounds them. To call upon Barthelme's Thomas one last time, midfiction recognizes the existence of limits but manages nevertheless to keep its options open. In other words, the acceptance of realms and, more, of a disorder beyond human control yields to, or is at least mitigated by, a belief in the capacity of human beings not only to host but to create values, anthropic but not anthropocentric values, in the world. In this way, midfiction enacts, by questioning its own and the culture's preconceptions, the feasibility of the kind of humanism I've been defending throughout this chapter. Intent on exorcizing the ghost of its too imperial past and on overcoming the bleak submissiveness of realism's response, contemporary humanism claims, in answer to its critics, not that man is the measure of the world's meaning but that he is its agent or partner in the task of bringing meaning into being. But to say, in an age only slightly less apocalyptic than the one depicted by Mooney, that this new humanism, and the midfiction that articulates its assumptions, together generally court an ideal of smallness is not to deny the vitality and resiliency of their undertaking. However unspectacular and seemingly antiheroic the aims and anticipations of both (as compared, say, with those of groups as various as the modernists or the Black Mountain poets), they are as far from Beattie's rueful vision of dinosaurs become deer as from the equally extreme nay-saying of so much current theory. Between them, Barthelme's "Overnight" and Mooney's *Easy Travel*—the one through ironic affirmation, the other through ironic contestation—describe the range within which humanism and midfiction deploy their speculative energies and express their commitment at one and the same time to the facticity of the ordinary and, within limits, to its plasticity. As one of Barthelme's characters says, and I take the statement and what it implies to be symptomatic of midfiction as a whole: "Mine is the art of the possible, plus two,"[39] the last words acting to stretch but also, presumably, to qualify the extent of possibility. One could do worse.

Notes

1. Donald Barthelme, *The Dead Father* (New York: Farrar, Straus, & Giroux, 1975), p. 145. Subsequent references to the novel and to all other works quoted will be given, after their first citation, parenthetically in the text. Where necessary, the book will be referred to as *TDF*. Barthelme's parable both confirms and rings changes on the by-now familiar theories of such critics as Walter Jackson Bate and Harold Bloom.

2. Elsewhere I've invoked Barthelme's remarkably overdetermined symbol in connection with modernism. See *Horizons of Assent: Modernism, Postmodernism, and the Ironic Imagination* (1981; pbk. ed. Philadelphia: University of Pennsylvania Press, 1987), pp. 19 and 45–47.

3. Pierre Francastel, *Peinture et société* (Paris: Gallimard, 1965), p. 212.

4. Roland Barthes, "From Work to Text," in *Textual Strategies: Perspectives in Post-Structuralist Criticism*, ed. Josué V. Harari (Ithaca, N.Y.: Cornell University Press, 1979), p. 78. The next quotation comes from Barthes's essay as well.

5. Charles Altieri, "From Symbolist Thought to Immanence: The Ground of Postmodern American Poetics," *boundary 2*, 1 (Spring 1973), 627.

6. William V. Spanos, "The End of Education: 'The Harvard Core Curriculum Report' and the Pedagogy of Reformation," *boundary 2*, 10 (Winter 1982), 14, 26, 27.

7. Alain Robbe-Grillet, "Nature, Humanism, Tragedy," *For a New Novel: Essays on Fiction*, trans. Richard Howard (New York: Grove Press, 1965), p. 51.

8. E. M. Forster, "Tolerance," *Two Cheers for Democracy* (New York: Harcourt, Brace & Co., 1951), p. 45.

9. Denis Diderot, *Le Rêve de d'Alembert*, in *Oeuvres philosophiques*, ed. Paul Vernière (Paris: Garnier, 1956), p. 380.

10. My quotation is from John Macquarrie's *Existentialism* (Baltimore: Penguin Books, 1973), p. 14. Roger L. Shinn's book, which is his starting point, is *Man: The New Humanism* (Philadelphia: Westminster, 1968).

11. Maurice Merleau-Ponty, "Man and Adversity," *Signs*, trans. Richard C. McCleary (Evanston, Ill.: Northwestern University Press, 1964), pp. 240–41.

12. J. P. Stern, *On Realism* (London and Boston: Routledge & Kegan Paul, 1973), p. 32. The book will be referred to hereafter as *OR*.

13. For Levine's discrimination of his position from Bersani's, see *The Realistic Imagination: English Fiction from Frankenstein to Lady Chatterley* (Chicago and London: University of Chicago Press, 1981), p. 331, n. 25.

14. Leo Bersani, *A Future for Astyanax: Character and Desire in Literature* (Boston and Toronto: Little, Brown, 1976), p. 67.

15. See Damian Grant, *Realism* (London: Methuen, 1970), p. 4 and Bernard Bergonzi's comment in "Realism, Reality, and the Novel: A Symposium on the Novel," ed. Park Honan, *Novel*, 2 (Spring 1969), 200. Stern argues that "there is no such thing [as an age without common norms of meaning]: 'an age' *is* a system of agreed meanings in time" (*OR*, p. 158).

16. I had better state at once that in speaking of realistic literature I'm referring to a generation of writers younger than Bellow or Updike. *Rabbit is Rich*, to choose a notable example of a more confident realism, reveals itself in a variety of ways—in its structural and thematic paradoxes; in its valuing of intensity, intricacy, unity, complexity, and scope; in its flirtation with extremity and transcendence; and, most of all, in its great formal resolution—as closer in spirit to the modernist than to the postmodernist age, even while it remains true to its own realist assumptions. In other words, modernism for Updike functions as a series of lessons and paradigms to be pondered with the self-conscious knowledge that coming after inevitably entails, and my point is simply that *Rabbit is Rich* serves as a commentary on (rather than as an addition to) the modernist canon. The ending of the book helps to make the point. In modernism, formal closure overrides, arrests, thematic openendedness. Knowing how unstable closure is but still attracted by its resolving force, Updike offers us an ending that is, so to speak, a kind of existential grace, a surplus that does not radically change our sense of what we have read but that changes it nevertheless.

17. Unlike Levine, Bersani sees no diminishing of "control" as we move into the twentieth century, and he locates the continuing source of its power in the unifying assumptions of "all humanistic psychologies" (p. 310).

18. Raymond Carver, "Chef's House," *Cathedral: Stories* (New York: Alfred A. Knopf, 1983), p. 33.

19. Jerry Bumpus, "Gut Shot," *American Book Review*, 4 (January-February 1982), 8. A better case for Bumpus' description, as some of my students have insisted, can perhaps be made on the basis of a few stories in *Cathedral*, notably, "A Small, Good Thing" (a rewriting of "The Bath" from *What We Talk About When We Talk About Love*), "Fever," and the title story. On the whole, however, the spirit of this latest volume and of stories that have appeared since its publication seems to me very much that of the earlier books.

20. Raymond Carver, *What We Talk About When We Talk About Love* (New York: Alfred A. Knopf, 1981), p. 48.

21. Raymond Carver, *Will You Please Be Quiet, Please?* (1976; rpt. New York: McGraw-Hill Book Co., 1978), p. 183. The book will be referred to hereafter as *WYP*.

22. Joan Didion, *Play It as It Lays* (New York: Farrar, Straus & Giroux, 1970), p. 3.

23. Michiko Kakutani, "Joan Didion: Staking Out California," *New York Times Magazine*, 10 June 1979, p. 50.

24. Vivian Gornick, "Let Me Hear a Woman's Voice," *The Village Voice*, 18–24 February 1981, p. 39.

25. Mary Robison, *Oh!* (New York: Alfred A. Knopf, 1981), p. 179.

26. Katha Pollitt, "Family and Friends," *New York Times Book Review*, 23 August 1981, p. 14.

27. Ann Beattie, *The Burning House* (New York: Random House, 1982), p. 15.

28. My attention to endings is not accidental. Beattie remains, like Carver especially, structurally conservative. Her stories generally build to, or expire in, melancholy epiphanies.

29. James Wolcott, "Ann Beattie's Heartbreak of Psoriasis," *The Village Voice*, 20 April 1982, p. 59. The next quotation appears on the same page.

30. Terrence Doody, "*Don Quixote*, *Ulysses*, and the Idea of Realism," *Novel*, 12 (Spring 1979), 202.

31. J. D. O'Hara, "Donald Barthelme: The Art of Fiction LXVI," *The Paris Review*, 80 (Summer 1981), 199. The interview will be referred to hereafter as AF.

32. Asked whether he doesn't "write more about the mind than about the external world," Barthelme responded: "In a commonsense way, you write about the impingement of one upon the other—my subjectivity bumping into other subjectivities, or into the Prime Rate" (AF, pp. 200–01). The statement, it seems to me, effectively separates Barthelme (and midfiction) from metafiction's habit of privileging imagination at the expense of the world. For a fuller discussion of this subject, see below, chapter eight. In earlier chapters, I have referred to two books on Barthelme worth consulting: Larry McCaffery's *The Metafictional Muse: The Works of Robert Coover, Donald Barthelme, and William H. Gass* (Pittsburgh: University of Pittsburgh Press, 1982) and Charles Molesworth's *Donald Barthelme's Fiction: The Ironist Saved from Drowning* (Columbia and London: University of Missouri Press, 1982). The books will be referred to hereafter as TMM and DBF.

33. On the subjects of acceptance and assent, see *Horizons of Assent*, chapter five.

34. Donald Barthelme, "Overnight to Many Distant Cities," *Overnight to Many Distant Cities* (New York: G. P. Putnam's Sons, 1983), p. 174.

35. Donald Barthelme, "The Photographs," *Guilty Pleasures* (New York: Farrar, Straus & Giroux, 1974), p. 159.

36. Donald Barthelme, "The Emerald," *Sixty Stories* (New York: G. P. Putnam's Sons, 1981), p. 401.

37. Donald Barthelme, "Florence Green is 81," *Come Back, Dr. Caligari* (Boston and Toronto: Little, Brown, 1964), p. 15. The next quotation appears on the same page.

38. Ted Mooney, *Easy Travel to Other Planets* (1981; rpt. New York: Ballantine Books, 1983), p. 187.

39. Donald Barthelme, "The Abduction from the Seraglio," *Sixty Stories*, p. 370.

7

dayanu: Max Apple and the ethics of sufficiency

The conventional tags that generally fill out the titles of short-story collections—"five stories," "eight stories," sometimes the spare and humble "stories," and, most often, as in the case of *The Oranging of America*, the serviceable, formulaic "and other stories"—all leave open the question of what, if any, unifying principle binds together a volume's title story and its remaining, otherwise unspecified contents. Picking up books with names like *Dubliners*, *Winesburg, Ohio*, *Tropismes*, *City Life*, or *Fizzles*, on the other hand, the reader is led to expect a more absolute and demonstrable coherence, as one is when approaching Max Apple's second and larger collection, *Free Agents*, which falls at least nominally into this category. But only nominally. In this case the title signifies not the essential focus of the book's various pieces but their status, which effectively thwarts or denies the very possibility of focus.

The stories, Apple has said, were themselves to stand and function as free agents, and the book's organization, an apparently haphazard juxtaposition of jostling moods and modes, was meant to defeat the temptation (urgent enough, given the obviously personal genesis of so much that is included in it) to read it biographically.[1] In other words, the heterogeneity of *Free Agents* is intended to sublate traditional notions of aesthetic and psychological order, and the intention is in fact amply rewarded. In its continual disruption of the reader's expectations, in its confounding of all efforts to establish thematic patterns or to identify strategies of progression and development, *Free Agents* deliberately attempts to emulate and even to augment the equivocal effect Apple has heretofore sought only in individual works. "It's that ability to understand that there's more than one way of seeing the same thing that I've always been interested in," he said in a recent interview, speaking of "Understanding Alvarado" and *Zip*. "That's the texture I'm after: given all the same events, there are always many possible interpretations. I don't want to create those single, simple interpretations in my works because you can't do that with the world. . . . I want to be clear and then, through reverberations, pass along that fertile unclarity which is in my mind in a straightforward narrative."[2]

The phrase "fertile unclarity" neatly expresses the reader's experience both as he encounters the twenty seemingly straightforward narratives and essays of *Free Agents* and as he tries to distill from the random, at times abrasively disjunctive, couplings of the book's sequence some controlling perception or centralizing response. But the apparent absence of either is exactly the point. If, at first glance, Apple's remarks suggest modernism's epistemological probes into the multiplicity and variability of consciousness and if, furthermore, they evoke New Criticism's hunger for ambiguity, paradox, and qualification, the resemblances are superficial and misleading. There is in *Free Agents* no comparable effort to impose on complexity a final *formal* unity, an aesthetic coherence that, in transcending the fractures of experience, resolves them—or at any rate means to. Apple's tactics manifest, instead, a very postmodern acceptance and, more, a welcoming of diversity, contradiction, tension, friction, and conflict—a confirmation of these things, moreover, for their own sake and not for the "achieved harmony" (to borrow Cleanth Brooks's phrase)[3] they can in theory be made to subserve.

To discriminate between modernist complexity and postmodernist contradiction is not, however, simply to contrast ideas and ideals of form. Nor is it to restrict oneself solely to the aesthetics of the text. Commenting on the work of Georges Poulet and Jean-Pierre Richard, Leo Bersani writes: "Nothing could be more alien to this 'artistic' criticism than a fragmentary or a collective art—or, at the extreme, an art without authorship." And again: "The critic perhaps can't help but seek out—or invent—a 'self' whose unifying design he finds."[4] In short, text and author, for phenomenologists at least, proceed hand in hand; but as structuralist and poststructuralist critics have reminded us, the reality of the author has become questionable at best.[5] Must we, then, if we are to respond to postmodernism's more open and flexible sense of order, consign the writer to the graveyard of superseded concepts? Yes: criticism, regrouping in the wake of some hundred years of psychological exploration and revision, has called into question first the validity of the writer's intentions and, more recently, his existence as anyone other than "the scriptor [who] no longer bears within him passions, humours, feelings, impressions, but rather this immense dictionary from which he draws a writing that can know no halt."[6] Criticism has, in other words, willy-nilly made us skeptical of what it means to speak of an "authorial voice." But also no: to acknowledge the complication of that voice and the dispersal of its singular authority does not, need not, require the additional belief that the writer is simply sucked into the vortex of language, losing him- or herself irretrievably in metafiction's airless, reflexive funhouse.

How, then, is one to negotiate the extremes of the old-fashioned integrated and the newly fashionable absent self? In fact, the problem for the contemporary critic who, conceding the primacy of language (*langue*), believes nevertheless that what matters is the irreducible witness of individual expression (*parole*)— the problem, that is, for all *practical* critics—is to discover a way of admitting the variousness, the deliberate "incoherence," that postmodern writers frequently claim for their novels and stories, and that Apple claims for *Free Agents*, without denying the distinctive configuration that necessarily embraces (embraces, not resolves) the discrete parts of any author's work. Rationally contradictory but experientially interwoven, these parts demand the notion of a more elastic, pro-cessive unity than the one modernism typically provided. And it is possible to supply one; for what is at issue, what we regularly and rightly identify in our reading, is no more, but also no less, than the individual, exemplary life inevi-tably defining itself in acts of creation and self-creation.

The attempt to identify and defend a noncoercive order that will do justice to even the most antiformalist work of art entails the further recognition that in our poststructuralist age the dynamics of a writer's development are as much in question as the integrity of his works. Can one, when examining the careers of writers like Barthelme, Berger, or Pynchon, call upon the familiar adjectives of an earlier, organic criticism and speak of growth, evolution, maturation? And can one, given the parodistic gestures with which these writers defy identification and classification, resort to psychologies based upon a faith in the stable self? The answer to the second question can be found in Merleau-Ponty's assertion: "Although it is certain that a man's life does not *explain* his work, it is equally certain that the two are connected . . . that *this work to be done called for this life*."[7] The unity of the career, in other words, is existential rather than genetic; and what we are to look for is not the essential self lurking behind the work but the phenomenological consciousness embedded in it: the inscription and man-ifestation of a continuity apparent only after the fact.

As will become clear shortly, the distinction between development and con-tinuity applies to the career of Max Apple; and perhaps because he has published considerably less than the other writers I've considered, the difference is both exemplary and dramatic. A more unified book than *Free Agents*, a postmodern work that nonetheless remains amenable to New Critical analysis, *The Oranging of America* coheres by virtue of tone, attitude, theme, and, above all, because of a demonstrably recurrent narrative pattern, the nature of which can be suggested by looking at the endings of several of its stories:

[1] Mildred said, "Howard, you can do anything," and closing the doors of the U-Haul, she joined the host of the highways, a man with two portable freezers, ready now for the challenge of Disney World.   ("The Oranging of America," p. 19)[8]

[2] "That's capitalism," I said. "Mary," I called to the back room. She arose from her computer, stepped over a small hill of puts and calls. I held my arm out from my body at the elbow. She fit like destiny and moved in.   ("Selling Out," p. 27)

[3] Kathleen hesitated, then she slipped off her short black apron, put down her green order pad, and in a long and fluent stride, side by side with Ferguson, headed south. ("Vegetable Love," p. 46)

[4] His words and his music are like Christmas morning. I go forth, a seer.   ("Inside Norman Mailer," p. 60)

[5] I buckle up, Ellie moves close. Careful on the curves, amid kisses and hopes I give her the gas.   ("Gas Stations," p. 103)

[6] "If I get the Dome, do anything you want with it," I said. "Just save me room for the world's largest liquor store." In the midst of the bubbles, I joined her. We sparkled like champagne.   ("My Real Estate," p. 120)

Rhythmically and syntactically similar, sometimes insistently so, the quotations resemble one another in more immediately apparent, if not necessarily more important, ways. Specifically, one notices the recurrence of certain attitudes and values: the confidence and prowess of the (invariably male) narrators or protagonists; the compliance and gratitude of the often vaguely sketched women; and, most obviously, the exuberance, the affirmative, up-beat quality of these final lines, which, however vague or unspecified the future they posit—or because that future is so vaguely and unspecifically rendered—endow the characters (and us) with an overwhelming sense of possibility.

Naturally, the endings by themselves reveal less about the incidents and conflicts that lead up to them than about their outcome, but "The Oranging of America"'s, at least, implies the typical dynamics of the stories in the collection. Briefly, the pattern involves an encounter with obstacles of various kinds; the recognition and overcoming of them by the stories' heroes; and a consequent reward, which, the suggestion runs, is as inevitable as it is appropriate. Needless to say, this description encompasses a good deal of narrative literature, but when one adds that much of what transpires here is fabulous, fantastic, and (in its disregard for causal entailments, as for precise, detailed psychological motivation) unverisimilar, it becomes clear that both structurally and thematically *The Oranging of America* resembles nothing so much as a collection of fairy tales.

To be sure, these are highly sophisticated, self-conscious, ironic, and eccentric fairy tales, which situate themselves not in never-never land but in the concrete, if highly selective, particularity of an America whose defining landmarks include the stock market and the Astrodome, Disney World and Howard Johnson motels, and Oasis, "the world's largest [gas station], eighty-three pumps, forty-one urinals, advertised on road signs as far east as Iowa" ("Gas Stations," p. 97). In fact, the best of Apple's early stories are about two Americas, which once and once only in the volume coexist without antagonism or strain. Thus in the title story, innocence and enterprise, benevolence and expansionism combine in the ambiguous name of Howard Johnson's "civilizing instinct" (p. 8), an impulse so seamless in its reconciliation of contraries that we are led to interrogate not the myth of Howard Johnson but our own response to it.[9] In other stories, however, the integrity of Howard Johnson dissolves into opposition, and Apple's pioneers and explorers, his hopeful Adams and hapless Quixotes find themselves the object of skepticism, misunderstanding, or scorn on the part of those who, like the Big Boss of "Gas Stations," have outlived their illusions, or who, like the Colonel of "My Real Estate," have lived nicely without them.

The complexity of Apple's vision lies, however, not in the oppositional interplay of these figures but in its recognition that they are in the final analysis related—that the moguls and captains of industry who represent individualism in its latest and least attractive phase derive inexorably from the small-scale dreamers whose vivid sense of adventure and enterprise makes them Apple's heroes. As in a Blakean cycle, innocence begets experience; and when in the untypical but perhaps inevitable "Noon," the narrator, himself a product of the television age, kills Larry Love, the game-show host who represents to him "one of the seven deadly sins, the electric version of Horatio Alger" (p. 124), it becomes clear that for Apple fairy tales contain within themselves the potential for nightmare.

I want neither to over- nor to underplay the significance of "Noon." It's true that in various ways—in the sourness of its mood, the extremity of its action, and the coarse, angry, cynical tone of its narrator—the story is the collection's anomaly. And yet it is no less certain that, in revealing the dark underside of *The Oranging of America*, the story exposes much that Apple's geniality leaves otherwise unstressed: not only the implicit connection between his heroes and their antagonists (or, more accurately, between what each group represents in its working out of the American dream) but the fact that the book's chief adversary is neither technology nor capitalism but death. Crosshatching with its shadowy intensity the luminousness of story after story, the persistence of death (it is a force to be reckoned with in seven of the tales) provides *The Oranging of America* with a complexity that Apple simultaneously acknowledges and contains.

The sense of containment derives from the pattern I've been describing, the sense of complexity from the limitations Apple imposes on that pattern. Distancing death's reality and specificity, domesticating its urgency, the fairy-tale quality of *The Oranging of America* creates a space in which the characters are allowed to postpone the inevitability of the fate that haunts them and their creator. But only to postpone it; these are fairy tales, not exercises in wish fulfillment, and the transcendent hints of "happily ever after" are, deliberately, never quite realized. In the same way, the openendedness of the stories signifies less an irresolution or uncertainty about the future, as in so many modernist novels, than a brief, if undefined, suspension of time's intractability. As one of Apple's beleaguered idealists says (he is speaking of the Israelites' sojourn in the wilderness): "For forty years they lived on this [manna] and then, only then, were they ready to pick up the business of destiny. This was a time out in history, just like during a football game. This is built into the organism" ("The Yogurt of Vasirin Kefirovsky," p. 73). In other words, Apple's characters—Millie, trailed by her portable cryonic freezer; Kefirovsky, obsessed with the life-prolonging properties of yogurt; and especially the narrator of "Selling Out," who, motivated by his father's death and his own " 'stroke potential' . . . decide[s] to strike" (p. 24) by conducting a manic raid on the stock market—all of them are fully as aware as their ironically sympathetic author of what awaits them.

My point is that, like fairy tales themselves, the analogy I've been pursuing has its limits, even as it, and they, have their uses. The resolution of tensions that the stories *seem* to provide is in fact a psychological "time out" in the history of the characters: an opportunity to learn ways of accepting and coping with the physical reality, the transiency, of their existence. In asserting this, it may seem that I am overmoralizing, not to say solemnizing, Apple's delicate and buoyant studies of the contemporary American psyche; and it is true enough that, tonally, most of the stories appear to levitate into the realm of the unconditional and the unconditioned. But this is, surely, to read superficially, at any rate partially. And such readings do scant justice to a writer who has described his work as "steeped in irony" [10] and who has insisted on "the comic spirit" as "a corrective to the way things are in the world" (*IMA*, p. 27).

The notion of correctability needs to be glossed, however. In the interview from which I've just quoted Apple goes on to connect comedy with play ("Comedy is not a vision carved in stone, so there's room for play" [*IMA*, p. 27]); and it is probably more accurate to regard his moral position as a function of his sinuous, mobile irony than to reduce that irony to the instrument of an explicitly normative enterprise. Apple, in short, is only incidentally a satirist,[11] and his wry observations of American vernacular culture tend naturally to prefer the interrogative to the declarative mood. The fact, for example, that Apple so regularly disclaims awareness of his own creative processes[12] suggests the tentative and exploratory nature of his imagination: the attempt not to master or control but to open himself to the world of goods and services and of competing ideals that his stories illuminate. On the other hand, to the degree that these attitudes describe a specific way of confronting the world, they do after all constitute, however undogmatically, an ethic. Continuously alert to the presence of death—recommending oatmeal instead of eggs to the thirty-year-old narrator of "Gas Stations," Ellie warns him: "A man your age can't be too careful" (p. 99)—Apple's characters provide him with the opportunity to take stock of their responses and, in a manner of speaking, to invent his own. Invent rather than rehearse or proclaim, since, as I've been arguing, Apple's awareness of death's inexorability, its absoluteness, is matched by a temperamental resistance to the competing absolutes that various of his protagonists—beginning with Howard Johnson and his lifelong battle against "that something alien [that] might be there to resist [his] civilizing instinct" (p. 8) and ending with "Noon"'s homeopathic murderer—oppose to it. Consequently, Apple's is a necessary middle ground: an unstable arena where, between the illusory hope of perfection and the undeniable certainty of death, his heroes enact the morality of suspensiveness, the effort to achieve in the face of their mortality (indeed because of it), and with complete awareness of the uncertainties that their acceptance entails, the fullest possible realization of the self *in* the world.

The belief that such a realization is feasible, that life's metaphysical limits not only define but, for those willing to admit them, create its existential possibilities and the further belief that within those limits the possibilities are all but boundless explain, finally, the strong forward thrust of the endings I've quoted and give to *The Oranging of America* as a whole its special élan. This is to generalize, of course, perhaps excessively; and in noting common characteristics, I don't want to imply that the stories are merely copies of one another, or of some quintessential ur-story that resides in a platonic Apple-heaven. While some only apparently reverse the usual outcome (in "Inside Norman Mailer," the narrator's epic confrontation with his literary antagonist leaves him "a prone loser" [p. 60], but in losing he in fact gains something more significant[13]), others are more ambiguous, and in them the assigning of sympathies becomes a more difficult matter. Not, however, because, as in the triumphant title story, the central character rises above our classificatory impulses (Howard Johnson is at once the innocence of American enterprise and its inevitable corruption) but because Achilles Alvarado ("Understanding Alvarado"), Jack Spenser ("My Real Estate") and Sonny Williams ("Patty-Cake, Patty-Cake . . . a Memoir") call into question through their victimization, complicitousness, or complacence the volume's general emphasis on the generative effects of action.

Nevertheless, none of these exceptions, neither the equivocalness of "My Real Estate" nor the bleakness of "Noon," does more than stretch and *test* the unity of *The Oranging of America*; and it might even be argued that in submitting the volume to the pressures of deviance, in challenging its coherence and cohesion, Apple only strengthens and enlarges its focus, as, on a smaller scale, he does in the case of what is arguably its most representative story. Less magical perhaps than the mini-epic of Howard Johnson, "Vegetable Love" is more central, a compendium of the book's moods and themes and their most persuasively irresolute resolution: an emblem of the zest with which Apple, at this early stage of his career, confidently sets against the abstract (but also real) terror of death the superabundant (if still partly theoretical) redemptiveness of life. "Vegetable Love" opens with an incident that is at once funny, painful, and prophetic: the meeting in a supermarket aisle of Annette Grim and Ferguson, the story's hero, who "turned to capture, full force, [her] loaded wire cart upon his groin" (p. 31). Needless to say, Ferguson's experience is tangible, physical, and concrete. Annette, it gradually emerges, is none of these. There is no need to pursue here in detail the ups and downs of their relationship. Enough to note that Annette, an ardent vegetarian, increasingly wins Ferguson over to her meatless ways and then, abruptly, leaves him when, in celebration of his graduation from law school, he joins his classmates at a local steakhouse. Or almost enough. For vegetarianism is, in fact, a secondary issue in the story, a *fausse piste*: "This he did not deserve for one steak," Ferguson thinks after a month without Annette. "She knew it, he knew it. It was something else" (p. 39).

And indeed it is. Even at their first encounter, there is about Annette something theoretical, detached, disengaged, abstract. The comfort she offers the agonized Ferguson, though apparently direct enough ("she put her long fingers under his zipper"), is nevertheless offered "as nonchalantly as if she were helping a blind man across the street" (p. 31). And what is hinted at here finds full expression in Annette's theory of spots, and particularly of *her* spot. "The center of my consciousness," as she calls it, it is "a sort of Cartesian pineal gland" (p. 33). For her—and, even after she has left him, for Ferguson—it is the invisible but irrefutable pledge of her identity, the assurance of the integrity, stability, and authority of her being, as well as the justification of her rejection of his marriage proposal and of her subsequent desertion of him. Puzzled, Ferguson pursues Annette from Houston to Dallas, searching as intently for his own spot as for her; and when, for reasons that he can't himself explain, he registers at a Holiday Inn under the name of Glass, it becomes apparent to the reader at least that what he is after is a transparency of sorts, a window onto some controlling principle, some central core, that, bedazzled by Annette, he has come to feel must exist within him.

Apple's comment on this perfervid exercise in essentialist exploration comes in a simile that makes clear its delusive, if compelling, impossibility: "There sat Ferguson . . . seeking his center like a dog after its own tail" (p. 43). And if it takes Ferguson longer to recognize that Annette exists not only beyond his grasp but beyond his desire, he too comes eventually to share the reader's awareness that her brief for health and purity has little enough to do with life, and that her order and stability, her perfectionism, are only other names for the death with which she is in fact obsessed. In short, what we have been witnessing is the contention between two different value-systems, the one based on a belief in depths, essences, and centers; the other commited to surfaces, existence, and acts. And in the final section of the story, Ferguson comes first to recognize and then to accept the unpredictability, the randomness, the contingency of the world he perforce inhabits:

> For the first time Ferguson wondered about the spots of the great. . . . If important people had spots and listened to them, things would not go wrong in the world, Ferguson reasoned. Yet starting from himself and stretching right to the farthest astronaut hitting a golf ball on the moon, there was a line of chaos as direct as the plumb line that went through Ferguson. Who had absolutes? Even the Pope changed his mind. Only his Annette heard the hum of the rhythm of her body, while a tone-deaf world scrambled around her.
> "I have tried," Ferguson said aloud in the shadow of the grassy knoll where thousands had watched the motorcade speed up and curve toward Parkland Hospital. (p. 45)

The "I have tried" sounds a note not of resignation but of defiance: a dismissal of his spot (at least as he has been led to conceive it: "You were my spot and your spot didn't know it" [p. 46], he addresses the absent Annette); a rejection of the paralyzing self-consciousness she has imposed on him; and a repudiation of all claims to absolutes and certainties. But this is very likely to phrase things too negatively. As indicated, Ferguson's meditation bespeaks acceptance too—of himself first (of his fallibility and therefore of his humanity), and then of what surrounds him. His final run through Dallas marks both the "loose and lucid" moment of his definitive liberation from Annette and his embrace of a more varied, diverse, uncontrolled and uncontrollable world than he has known, including, as "deeply he inhaled the city, its desert air and [even] its poisonous oxides" (p. 46).

Ferguson's attainment of suspensiveness is not, however, all there is to "Vegetable Love"; and as the seemingly incidental allusions to the Kennedy assassination begin to ramify, the reader becomes aware that Ferguson's situation (and, by extension, the book's) is historically specific. The clash throughout the volume of two Americas, the old and the new (the old for Apple, whatever its roots in the myth of the American Adam, being understood as the period between the Second World War and Viet Nam), here finds its emblem: the watershed on one side of which stand Apple's youthful optimists, on the other, their descendants or later selves, the Big Bosses, the Colonels, and the Larry Loves. In a sense, then, Ferguson establishes his hope on private and public disillusion alike, and the complexity of his thoughts in these last pages brings together, though without resolving, the tensions of *The Oranging of America* as a whole. And yet, the final lines of the story, quoted earlier, work to thin out this complexity. Parabolically, the gesture of departure could not be more consistent, as Ferguson heads south with Kathleen, the student and waitress, "herself not completely vegetarian" (p. 44), who, having helped him to look for Annette, now joins him. What we have in the replacement of one woman by the other is, so to speak, an exchange of the self-centered and metaphysical for the relational and existential. But the point is precisely that the ending is and remains parabolic, unanchored, unspecific, a generic swerve away from the historical to the mythic. Not, it should be said, that this transformative strategy affects the story's aesthetic success. Indeed, it serves to establish its midfictional quality and status. Still, to stress the point, something disquieting does emerge at the last. Although "Vegetable Love" involves an access of understanding and self-awareness and although Ferguson is ready to accept the limitations of an imperfect and opaque world, the final paragraph tells another story. As in so many of the other tales, it transports us into a different, ethically less examined mode, whose euphoria half denies the hard lessons Ferguson has learned and the suspensiveness he has attained. Blake may give his angel the last words in the "Proverbs of Hell" when he allows him to answer sardonically: "Too Much"; but in *The Oranging of America* Apple is of the devil's party. In a spirit of excess and energy, "Vegetable Love" proclaims for the collection in general the illimitable possibilities of "Enough!"

Something very different takes place in *Free Agents*, where the concept of sufficiency—the stipulation of what attitudes and acts are adequate to the task of neutralizing or overcoming the impediments and antagonistic pressures of Apple's imagined world—undergoes a radical change. Or sometimes does. I began this chapter by stressing the deliberate structural and thematic "incoherence" of *Free Agents*; and if one allows the accuracy of that description, it follows inevitably (or so common sense suggests) that useful generalizations about the book are next to impossible. One might, of course, in the teeth of Apple's deliberate frustration of such impulses, attempt to reorder the sequence of the stories, imposing on them not the congruence of *The Oranging of America* (a task beyond any organizational skills, however compulsive or draconian) but the no less comforting illusion of logical, progressive development. A hypothetical tinkerer would no doubt place at the volume's center those apparently autobiographical pieces that take as their point of departure the death of the narrator's wife or, rather, in stories like "Eskimo Love" and "Bridging," its aftereffects: death actual now, irrevocable, no longer a menace on life's horizon but its intrusive and umbrageous partner. He or she would, further, surround them on one side with those tales that seem to extend the mood and concerns of the earlier volume and, on the other, with those that, following the loss, abandon fairy tales altogether, substituting for them the darker intensities of realism.

There is a certain plausibility to this scheme, although its large meshes allow various of the book's contents to escape the net it casts. Some of the stories do, after all, as their endings indicate, echo the spirit and design of *The Oranging of America*:

> She doused me in Gatorade. "At any pace," she said, "there is infirmity and disease. Carbo-loading will never be enough."
> We bronzed our shoes and toasted one another in Body Punch.
> "When our electrolytes balance," she said, "we'll live happily ever after."
> We showered and went into training.   ("Carbo-Loading," p. 83)[14]

> Full of myself, on tiptoes I bounce on the grass, ready for everything. ("Free Agents," p. 114)

With its metaphor of running, its boundless sense of futurity and possibility, and its adoption of a quasi-parabolic mode, "Carbo-Loading" once again, in ways familiar to readers of the first collection, makes the ordinary extraordinary and makes plausible through its comic play the transcendence of limits that are admitted only to be denied.

As for "Free Agents," that most ebullient of Apple's stories offers in its remarkably compressed and light-hearted fashion a postmodern commentary on no less than the entire Western tradition and its habitual privileging of mind over matter. The central conceit of the work is a revolt of the body's organs (the brains and eyes, those instruments of rationality and order, excepted) against the comically average "Max Apple": "All important decisions are tested on nobodies," his spleen tells him, adding shortly, "Now it's the body's turn to step into the twentieth century" (pp. 104, 105). Its central event is a hilarious trial, the upshot of which is a definitive reversal of the Cartesian cogito. Initiated by a suspensiveness that recognizes and surrenders to what can be neither explained nor controlled ("I am paralyzed, bereft of mind and body, yet in the midst of this crisis a strange indifferent calm overcomes me" [p. 113]); engineered with the help of memory, "the memory of fleeting sensuality" (p. 113), and by an acceptance of himself ("'I am what I am,' I whisper" [p. 113]), the movement is consummated by an existential turn and return to the world: "I shift gears. I rise. I walk. I spit. I think" (p. 114). Despite (or, more likely, because of) the fact that, as his brain reminds him, "Nothing is settled" (p. 114)—the jury, it eventuates, is hung but "Apple"'s organs voluntarily return to him—the narrator passes easily beyond confinement and restraint, himself the story's principal free agent: a potential loser who, in a still more triumphant replay of "Inside Norman Mailer"'s situation, wins the world.

To be sure, not all of the stories in *Free Agents* that suggest *The Oranging of America* propose so capacious and elastic a sense of the self; and one might, still pursuing our supposititious rearrangement, construct of these others a subset of the first, a less illusioned but still fundamentally affirmative series of variations on the concerns that dominate the earlier volume. "The Eighth Day," for example, a wonderfully funny and high-spirited story, at once plausible and bizarre (like so much of midfiction),[15] recalls in its concern with "knowing" the thematics of "Vegetable Love." Prodded by Joan, his lover, who "had devoted her adult life to knowing herself" (p. 44), the narrator submits himself to primal therapy, only to find that "circumcision and its pain seemed to have replaced in my consciousness the birth trauma. No matter how much I tried, I couldn't get back any earlier than the eighth day" (p. 44). It will be sufficient here to note that the story's ingenious and hilarious complications lead the narrator, Joan always attendant and urging, to the rediscovery of Rabbi Berkowitz, performer of the original operation, and result in the two men's agreement to participate in a therapeutic mock-"recircumcision." Berkowitz's inability to carry out the symbolic reenactment and the narrator's grateful relief constitute the story's anticlimactic climax. And also its point, which like "Vegetable Love"'s endorses the lesson that there are limits to theory. In brief, not everything can be known: there are things that can't be done, mysteries that can't be penetrated. But unlike Ferguson, the narrator of "The Eighth Day" neither foregoes his almost equally theoretical Joan (indeed it is she who is given Ferguson's line: "We tried" [p. 53]) nor discovers another pliable Kathleen. Instead, he settles for a more limited human definition and for a more circumscribed (circumcised?) fate. "I cruise the turnpike," he says near the end of the story, "not sure of whether I'm a failure at knowing myself. . . . I wake Joan. Fitfully, imperfectly, we know each other." And as if in confirmation of both that act and its imperfection, he adds, echoing Reb Berkowitz: "'A man,' I whisper, 'is not a chicken.' On the eighth day I did learn something" (p. 53).

"Vegetable Love," as we saw earlier, replaces absolutism (Annette's) with acceptance (Ferguson's) but to some degree controverts its suspensiveness with a vision of life opening onto an illimitable future. "The Eighth Day" draws from experience a more chastened lesson. And so too do two other stories in *Free Agents*. "Walt and Will" (titled when first published "Disneyad" and perhaps retitled to stress the fact that Will—in actuality Disney's brother was named Roy—*is* Walt's will, the efficacy and potency that he himself so conspicuously lacks) replays "Gas Stations"' opposition of the dreamer and the entrepreneur, but more ambiguously, with an intentional blurring of the characters' outlines and consequently of our sympathies. To be sure, in the classic contrast Walt's is the creative imagination, Will's merely the power of implementation; but faced with his brother's robust imperialism (Will, the self-proclaimed Columbus of Disney World, shares none of the Big Boss's melancholy, none of his bleakness about the future), Walt shrinks and pales, allowing Will to vulgarize his fascination with "random motion," allowing himself to be hoisted aloft "queasy-stomached over Orlando" (p. 7). Heroic only in his continuously betrayed allegiance to "constant movement and sound" (p. 2), but heroic in that, a failed Quixote powerless even to tilt against the empire Will has raised on the foundation of his originating idea, Walt is given the story's last word or, rather, its final gesture. Bowling with Will and "powerless as usual before the brilliant energy of his brother," Walt nevertheless "roll[s] one effortlessly down the middle" (p. 15): his protest, pathetic but genuine, against Will's materialist version of immortality (Howard Johnsonism without its benignity) and, more importantly, against his own hapless surrender of his will. It is not much, but it is something—a slight, fragile righting of the balance and, for the reader, a ratification of the idea, if no promise of its success.

Walt Disney has the unhappy feeling that for him there have been since his early days "no 'adventures,' no risks of his talent, no taste of the world" (p. 7). Slim Inudo, the protagonist of "Small Island Republics," is in his own way as imaginative and ingenious as Walt, but like Will he is also all energy and enterprise: a wheeler and a dealer; a Japanese-American Adam pushing the now exhausted frontier across the Pacific to Taiwan. In other words, Inudo resembles Howard Johnson far more, in his combination of usually opposing forces, than he does either Walt or Will; but it is also true that the ironies that play around Slim are, if not more profound, then more destabilizing, more alert (even as they delight in Inudo's brash triumph) to the incongruities and contradictions of power. Having already discussed "Small Island Republics" in chapter two, I don't want to repeat my analysis here. And there is no need to. By now it's clear that at least a quarter of the stories in *Free Agents* bear a strong family resemblance to those collected in *The Oranging of America*; and though several of them seem, in their moderated expectations or their "fertile unclarity," to be more kith than kin, still the connection can be seen to hold.

As it manifestly does not in the case of the "realistic" stories that exist at the other end of this still conjectural spectrum. The term realistic, it must be evident by now, needs always to be conjured with extreme circumspection; and the caution is nowhere more necessary than when it is intruded into a discussion of Apple, who has at various times rejected the word as a description of his own work. In his interview with McCaffery and Gregory, for example, Apple talks of his boredom with "that kind of fiction" (*IMA*, p. 23), a phrase that covers both the techniques and the assumptions of the writers who practice it. To the circumstantiality and verisimilitude of "description-centered realism" (*IMA*, p. 24) he opposes his own ideals of "speed" and "density" (*IMA*, pp. 23, 24); and against the lingering belief in the rationality and predictability of human beings and their world he sets *One Hundred Years of Solitude*: "Most people," he remarks, "don't see that the world around them is just as mysterious as Macondo" (*IMA*, p. 24). Now it is certainly the case that Apple's stories reject description-centered realism and, equally, that their aim is to make the seemingly incredible credible, the apparently improbable probable. What, then, does it mean to describe stories like "Momma's Boy," "Business Talk," "Help," and perhaps "Kitty Partners" as realistic? Simply that all of them are, like the realistic works discussed in the last chapter, stories of limits, which, in accepting limits, subvert the midfictional impulses of *The Oranging of America*, and, equally, of works like "Free Agents" and "The Eighth Day."

To say this is not to deny the range of these stories. Reminiscent of Ann Beattie's fiction, "Business Talk" reveals in the ordinary not the extraordinary but the quotidian. "I'm bored, restless, and in late afternoon always depressed," the narrator announces at the beginning of her account, and goes on to complain to her husband: "Every day is driving me crazy . . . I don't want to fall victim to the malaise of the times" (p. 126). But that is exactly what she does, notwithstanding her attempt to relieve life's tedium by opening a specialty shop featuring frozen yogurt (shades of Vasirin Kefirovsky!). "I get the lubricant," the story ends, "he the prophylactics. Sometimes we're old-fashioned people doing the best we can" (p. 134). Often funny but a bit too facile in its pervasive worldliness, "Business Talk" exudes a whiff of cynicism, for whatever the ironies it intends at the expense of its narrator, it is, like the not dissimilar "Help," a story of accommodation, an anti-epic of making do.

"Momma's Boy," on the other hand, adopts a very different register. Summoning up by way of comparison not Beattie but Carver, Apple's tale of a totally average, ordinary man explodes into violence as Gil Stein, following the dissolution of his dreary marriage, begins, to no one's surprise more than his own, to beat his mother, only, as the story ends, to be punched by her in turn. But for all its unwonted emphasis on physical outrage, "Momma's Boy" sits comfortably beside "Business Talk" and "Help," in all of which (and in "Kitty Partners" too) the keynote is frustration, a kind of Barthelmean anomie that, whether repressed into bleak acquiescence or unleashed in mindless fury, resolves nothing and promises less. That Apple's ironies play over the lives of his characters in these stories but leave neither them nor his readers with the suggestion of alternative possibilities is the crucial matter here—and something to be reckoned with in one's response to the boundaries that shape and determine his work. Next to "Free Agents"'s "ready for everything" one needs to place now the motto of Joyce Carol in "Post-Modernism": "Everything is the way it is" (p. 139).

*   *   *

So much, then, for the conditional, hypothetical, tentative restructuring of Apple's collection—for its sortings of *Free Agents*' stories into like and unlike and its attempt to account for their differences (or their progression) in terms of death's savaging presence in the book. Obviously, my argument has all along aimed at its own denial, and for good reason, since it is possible to demonstrate concretely the fallacy that underlies its assumption of inevitable growth, change, and development. By way of example, "Business Talk" dates from the same year (1977) as "Walt and Will" and "Free Agents"; "Help" is contemporary with "Small Island Republics" (1979), "Carbo-Loading" with "Kitty Partners" (1979 or 1980 in both cases); and "The Eighth Day" was completed later than all of these (1982).[16] In other words, a simple chronological arrangement would itself have made clear the disjunctiveness of the collection, and its difference from the kind of rationalized scheme I've been deliberately pursuing. But not clear enough, apparently, to suit Apple's intentions, which strive deliberately to maximize randomness, to set side by side, to mix and mingle grimness and hope, cynicism and whimsy, fantasy and realism.

Nevertheless, *Free Agents* is, almost despite itself, an entity, integral not in the sameness of the stories that compose it but in the incongruity that comprehends and welcomes their differences. The book, in short, is more than the sum of its parts; and what needs to be defined are the ways in which, willy-nilly, we configure the awareness the book forces on us that life is less consequential, less predictable than we like to imagine. As we pass from assertions of the limitless to revelations of the limited, and back again, taking in along the way any number of intermediate positions, we begin to comprehend the fact of the self's discontinuities and also, at the risk of compounding paradoxes, of its continuity—its continuity *as* discontinuousness and dispersion: its openness to a kaleidoscopic range of moods and attitudes that acts to enlarge our sense of the self's circumstantial freedom, and also of its circumstantial boundaries.

Given these boundaries, manifest in the exultation of "Free Agents" and in "Business Talk"'s quiet despair, are we entitled to seek out between these extremes some middle ground, some region of more measured and tempered response, and to endow it with the explanatory force of the typical, the characteristic, the central—any or all of those terms relegated by poststructuralist critics to the ash heap of outworn concepts? Granted, on one level the book floats the irreconcilable diversity and divergency of its options, which accounts for the series of small (and sometimes not so small) shocks we undergo as we read it. But surely it requires more than the forbearance of negative capability not to detect in the book, indeed in any book whatever, an inescapable modality by which, at another level, we grasp it in its entirety. Can anyone doubt that, for all the variousness and frequent vividness of Apple's palette in *Free Agents*, the book is more muted than its predecessor? Is it possible, after *The Oranging of America*'s triumphant songs of innocence, not to recognize everywhere in *Free*

Agents the stigmata of experience? *The Oranging of America* bespeaks a different time and another country: its America gives way in *Free Agents* to a place where "there is no safety" ("The American Bakery," p. 90). In the absence of the vaguely salvational future that the earlier volume regularly assumes, Apple's response is a redefinition of what is adequate, of what will suffice.

But where, if no single story can be said to sum up *Free Agents* or to constitute its center, are we to seek out this redefinition? In fact, "Eskimo Love" does in some sense represent the collection in miniature, *not* because it resolves the volume's tensions or mutes its polarities but because the irresolutions and conflicts of the whole are reduplicated, their coexistence ratified, in what is certainly its most accomplished story. Like "Vegetable Love," the tale embodies a dream of inhuman perfection, but perhaps because that dream is in this case the narrator's, and certainly because the narrator is at least partly a projection of his creator, it yields up complexities of tone and meaning that are absent from Annette Grim's self-assured pronouncements about her "spot." Naturally enough, the strategies of the later story are different as well, and "Eskimo Love," one comes to recognize, depends not on the kind of revelation "Vegetable Love" offers—Ferguson's and the reader's gradual understanding of Annette's devitalizing rigidity—but on a more fluid and irregular unfolding, an exfoliation, of what is in a sense given from the beginning. Thus in the opening paragraph, where the speaker first mentions his Eskimo love (she is in fact the subject of a *National Geographic* photograph), we are made aware of the connection between him and the bleak northern desolation that in one way or another almost continuously engrosses his attention: "Her eyes, accustomed to long stretches of barren waste, have no trouble reaching me from the glossy page" (p. 140). The call of like to like is the story's enabling perception; and although, as it soon emerges, the narrator's winter of the spirit follows inevitably on the death of his wife, it is by no means the case that his reactions to the loss, painful as they are, exhaust the significance of the frozen landscapes, real and imagined, that dominate the story.

Indeed, "Eskimo Love," despite the fact that this loss supplies its proximate cause or motive, is in the final analysis about life, not death—or, perhaps more accurately, about different ways of coping with the specific but also general reality of death. The point is made early on during an ice fishing expedition to Lake Michigan, at the end of which the narrator snags not the expected fish but, in a moment of surreal recognition, his dead wife: "She was in the area, she got entangled in the line. Not a bite, an accident. I see her frozen lips, her fish eyes. I cut her loose. We have already had our last words. Some deaths are final" (p. 144). The encounter speaks to the intensity, the ultimacy, of his despair. That much is painfully clear. But as the gesture of cutting loose intimates, something more is at stake, namely, an acknowledgment, even a willful acceptance, of death's irrevocability. On the other hand, in spite of the narrator's anger and frustration, it's just as clear that his acceptance is at this point meager, minimal—acquiescent but no more. Paralyzed by his despair, the narrator remains locked in his visions, as comforting as they are bleak, of ice and snow; and it is left to his friend Oscar to set forth what is at a certain level the story's counter-assertion of possibility, muted and ironic though it is: "Why don't you stop pretending you're an Eskimo or a hermit; why not rejoin mankind? You're a smart person. You can probably come up with a hundred ways to make yourself unhappy. . . . Just stop all the brooding. . . . Believe me, being happy is the toughest job of all" (p. 149).

But Oscar, goodheartedly, simplifies. To speak of Vicki's death and then of the narrator's retreat into fantasies of Eskimo love, to suggest a process of compensation or sublimation, is to describe a temporal sequence that is plausible but partial—and even, at a deeper level, false. For the fact is that the narrator's obsession with Eskimos predates not only the death of his wife but his first meeting with her. "I searched the crowd for Eskimos" (p. 141), he says as he describes that meeting, where, it also emerges, Vicki came "looking for remnants of the Ottoman Empire—Turks, Bedouins, hill and desert people with a grudge against history" (p. 141). "We found each other" (p. 141), he adds; and the ensuing marriage suggests, among other things, the meshing of complementary fantasies. It doesn't, however, any more than Vicki's death, explain the narrator's fascination. In fact, like *Free Agents* as a whole, the story seems intent on evading genetic or etiological explanations, which may help in turn to account for the phantasmagoric quality that envelops its deceptively simple narrative and also for its flexible handling of chronology. Smoothly embedding within one another different layers or stages of consciousness and recollection, "Eskimo Love" unobtrusively complicates and undermines its forward movement, forcing our attention away from its ostensible subject (the aftermath of the death) and onto its increasingly mysterious narrator.

Mysterious because, appearances to the contrary—what, after all, could be more intimate than the story he tells?—he withholds more than he reveals. And because, as we finally come to understand, his identification with and his attraction to all things Eskimo are in the first instance a function not of his predicament but of his character. In other words, if "Eskimo Love" addresses itself to a specific event, a determinate loss, it encompasses a good deal besides. And since that additional dimension is precisely *not* temporally specific and determinate, since it hovers, as it were, above or athwart the narrative, the temptation is strong to read the more into the less general: to find in the reaction to Vicki's death the token of a deeper and more habitual estrangement; to observe in the marriage the joining of fellow outsiders; to uncover in Oscar's affectionate urgings and reproaches ("Come, Narcissus of the North . . ." [p. 143]) an intuition that responds to a more complex, if not a more painful, emotional state than what arises from the grief of the moment. If all of this is true, it follows that the story's conclusion supplies an answer to the more comprehensive, as well as to the more immediate, problem it explores and that, in so doing, it reveals something profound about the intentional structure of the volume as a whole.

What that answer is emerges in the final scene, which, after the wintriness of everything that has preceded, is set significantly in the fall. We are prepared, that is, for a change, but hardly for the kind of transformation that "Vegetable Love" promises as Ferguson and Kathleen head "south" into what we assume to be a land of eternal spring or summer. One member of an eccentric foursome camping at Lake Saginaw, the narrator continues to brood about Vicki and Eskimos, but the atmosphere is notably more social. Oscar and his artist-friend Madelyn, whose current "project [is] the color brown" (p. 145)—thus their autumnal trip—have conscripted as his partner Sue, "a healthy outdoor girl" (p. 146) who has (it is her major credential) lately lived in Alaska. To be sure, there is no suggestion of grand harmonies and reconciliations: the women dislike one another, Sue can't stand either Madelyn or Oscar, Oscar claims not to like Madelyn; and the narrator confirms through his puns and jokes ("Sue, queen-to-be of my igloo" [p. 146]) his status as outsider, spectator of the life that goes on around him. Nevertheless, thanks partly to Oscar's exhortations, partly to Sue's debunking of his Eskimo dreams, but mostly to Sue herself, a psychic rearrangement does take place. "She is not my Eskimo," he admits, "but she is strong and young and honest" (p. 151). The willingness to make the distinction is the first step; the second, since something passive or resistant clings to the narrator, is initiated by Sue and leads to the story's richly ambiguous climax:

She takes my hand and pulls me into the creek. The water is no higher than my knees and surprisingly warm—warmer even than the air. The noise of our splashing doesn't bother a soul. I chase Sue through the creek. Stumbling on rocks we fall onto one another, laughing. There is no fish, no ice, no ghost underfoot, no Eskimo—just water—just camping with friends on a warm night in the middle of my life. It's enough.   (p. 152)

What most needs to be recognized here is that this conclusion—if by that word we mean the total harmonizing of conflict, the superseding of psychic disunity, in short, *resolution*—is, deliberately, no conclusion at all. But this is not, on the other hand, to deny the movement and change that its various elements signify. The regenerative force of the water imagery that dominates the passage; the atmosphere of laughter, warmth, and play; the exorcism that apparently frees the narrator from the obsessiveness of his past—all combine to suggest that he has begun, in Oscar's words, to "rejoin mankind." Yet something more and different is at work. Increasingly, the rhetoric of the passage—the repeated no's and just's that accumulate toward the end—plays off against the activity and joy that are its ostensible subject; and the final, summary remark, low-keyed, reflective, self-conscious as it is, still more definitively moderates, even skews, the general effect of spontaneity and liberation. In short, there is little reason to feel that the story's tensions do not, will not, persist. Nothing promises the eradication of the past or the beginning of new love. Sue, it's clear, is a momentary, though significant, diversion, while Vicki's death is, just as clearly, no less real or painful. As the reference to Dante indicates, the narrator's journey has at this point no more than begun.

Furthermore, despite Apple's determination to make the stories in *Free Agents* independent of one another, it is almost impossible not to bring to bear on "Eskimo Love" insights and attitudes that surface elsewhere in the volume. "Bridging," for example, which takes place eight months after Vicki's death, engages once again the problem of how to participate in a world that is "upside down" (p. 25). Wry and poignant, the story ostensibly focuses on the narrator's daughter and on her resistance to the process of development, change, and maturation that the title points to; but as we soon come to see, it implicates him as fully as it does her. "Jessica is going to have to learn to trust the world again," her psychiatrist tells him. "It would help if you could do it too" (p. 20). But like "Eskimo Love," the story is more about a direction than a destination; and the ending offers not the certainty of achievement but, at best, the paradox of an uncertain gain that ensures for the narrator yet another loss: "I promise to take you everywhere, my lovely child, and then to leave you. I'm learning to be a leader" (p. 26).

Loss is the key to "Pizza Time" as well, but here the attitude, for all the story's humor, is angry, resentful, and increasingly hostile as the narrator takes the measure of the new world of technology that threatens his children's ability *"to become reasonably sane, decent, compassionate, capable adults"* (p. 92). Less immediately moving than "Bridging," "Pizza Time" is nevertheless a more revealing story: a frantic confrontation between different beliefs, different interests, different Americas, whose concrete embodiments prove, on closer examination, less antithetical than they initially appear to be. Pitting himself in the story's climactic fantasy encounter against the electronic games that symbolize Jessica's and Sam's separation from him, the narrator, taking on the role of "avenging parent" (p. 99), announces: "I want some old-fashioned values or I destroy the place" (p. 100). Those values (sanity, decency, and so on) are spelled out but left general; and the question the story poses is how or where or in what soil they are to be grounded. This is not to say that the values dramatized everywhere in *The Oranging of America* are more specific. But sustained as they are by the spirit of that volume—by its assurance and gusto and confident openness to the future—they pass largely uncontested by the reader, even if Apple himself creates ambiguities that play around figures like Howard Johnson and Jack Spenser.

In the case of "Pizza Time," however, precisely because the story adopts a more beleaguered perspective, because the innocence that in *The Oranging of America* swept all before it has itself been swept away, we are inclined to seek out the norms that make its somewhat frenetic satire possible and to ask how substantial they are. Indeed, it may well be that the story is itself asking that very question. When, for example, the narrator says, "Listen, kids, how about a little less immediacy. How about a childhood more like mine, with three-D comic books, the Korean war, and one-car families" (p. 98), one assumes that the major irony is at his own expense—at the expense, that is, of ideals and dreams neither more admirable nor more solid than those that engross his children. If the assumption is correct, then what we hear in "Pizza Time" are, first and foremost, the suspect accents of middle age confirming its own past, setting against the Siren's song of "the technological future" (p. 100) "McDonald's and Kentucky Fried Chicken and the interstate highway system and all the antique Huts and Inns of my youth" (p. 97); and what Apple presumably means to expose in the process is a difference that is at most one of degree, not of kind. In other words, "Pizza Time" seems to make explicit the inexorable logic of development that turns "Gas Stations"' Big Boss from visionary into cynic, and does so without counterposing to such cynicism the stubborn optimism of that story's narrator (or does so only to undermine it). Not that the narrator of "Pizza Time" is any less determined to overcome what he sees as the chaos of contemporary life, but the frenzy of his mock-heroic battle with Pac-Man (battle rather than flight, significantly) suggests an understanding not only of what is at stake in the electronic age but, more importantly—if I'm right in attributing so radical an irony to the story—of how little the past, the venturesome, pioneering spirit of *The Oranging of America*, now has to offer him by way of consolation or support.

My aim is not, I should say, to extrapolate from "Pizza Time" to the volume as a whole a state of general and generalized disillusion. (As we've seen, the title story, for one, yields to none of its predecessors in its exuberance.) What *has* changed is something more important. The distinctive feature of Apple's second collection is that its characters are all—whether or not they recognize and accept their condition, and however they react to it—free agents, dependent on their own acts to define their situations and, in the absence of the fairy-tale promises that the America of the earlier volume still sustains, to shape their futures as best they can.

That last phrase brings me back to "Eskimo Love" and to the problem of exactly how we are to construe its final sentence. The words, needless to say, derive their meaning from the context the story supplies, but we will make better sense of their significance if we contrast them with Apple's earlier and more elaborate treatment in his novel *Zip* of what it means "to be enough." The episode in question comes early in the book when Ira, its protagonist, who is at this point "an almost complete male virgin,"[17] makes love to—or is made love to by—Debby, a forerunner of sorts of "Eskimo Love"'s Vicki. "When you kiss me," he writes, "do you know what I am thinking, I am thinking 'enough, this is enough.' There is a Hebrew song, 'Dayanu,' recounting in a folksy way all sorts of miracles and the chorus sings out after each one, 'Dayanu' ('It would have been enough')" (p. 38). Enough not only and not primarily because, given a happiness so exquisite, a little suffices (that is Ira's conscious thought) but because for him, as for the chorus, the miracle at hand is also "a gesture, a promise" (p. 38): a pledge of further or larger miracles to come. The chorus, Ira says in his gloss of the song, "would settle for" (p. 38) any single evidence of God's handiwork, but the notion of settling hardly does justice to a belief that finds in the experience of the part the salvatory possibility or probability of the whole. In other words, the forbearance of the song—"the Hebrew ditty of modesty" (p. 39), Ira calls it—derives less from acquiescence in the inscrutable ways of Providence than from the presumption that the universe is at once harmonious, predictable, and benign. Secularized, the belief is Ira's as well. "My mind is singing 'dy-dy-anu, dy-dy-anu,'" he writes as his lovemaking with Debby proceeds, ". . . [but] my eager hands are dancing to a wilder rhythm" (p. 39). Predictably, for him too "a small miracle happens" (pp. 39–40).

Ira, however, is not our concern. My point is simply that in this episode of *Zip* (as in the fairy-tale endings of *The Oranging of America*) the premise of sufficiency constitutes again the promise of the limitless and the unbounded. In "Eskimo Love," on the other hand, the needs and requirements of Apple's protagonist are of a different order. "It's enough" can be read as the recognition of a miracle, but one that is altogether more tempered and temporary. Modest in its scope, circumscribed in its effect, it speaks of chance and contingency, of a recovery no less random and haphazard than the loss it partly (but only partly) mitigates; for what is miraculous here is not the impingement of the extraordinary on the ordinary, which is what "Dayanu" implies and assumes, but the fact that, for a moment, the ordinary becomes extraordinary—becomes, in a reciprocal solicitation of self and world, the generative site of a new humanistic and existential ethic and of the form or forms that serve to express it.

Although no story or group of stories can claim to exhaust the diversity of *Free Agents*, "Eskimo Love," because of its own remarkable compass, manages to do justice to the collection's extremes (as well as to everything between) and thereby establishes not a median response but what is more important: the conditions that determine and predetermine the limits of all possible responses. At the end even of "Free Agents" "nothing is settled," and no more is it in the volume as a whole. While Ferguson and Kathleen are able to take off confidently for parts unspecified and unknown, the narrator of "Eskimo Love" reenters a world whose boundaries are both recognized and accepted—though only in the "realistic" stories are they seen as absolute. Jessica won't "bridge," a new elec-

tronic era impends, possibility has shrunk to less ample dimensions. But, arguably, to more convincing ones. Embedded in the ordinary, the details that cluster
in the final paragraph of "Eskimo Love" are not so much symbols as emblems:
emblems of a new relationship to being that stretches, but leaves intact, the
fabric of a world it is impossible fully to understand or to control but which,
now with a more chastened and profound sense of what life has to offer, Apple
chooses to find enough.

Does this mean that, its title notwithstanding, Apple's second collection of stories narrows and restricts the definition his work offers of what it means to be
free? Without question the volume presents a generally darker and more tensive,
as well as a more various, view of human capability. The change, however, lies
not in Apple's intentional grasp of the world but in certain aspects of the world
itself. Abstract and virtual in *The Oranging of America*, death has become in
Free Agents a stubbornly concrete fact that inevitably reconfigures the nature of
Apple's responses without altering their fundamental structure. But what, then,
is that structure? And what justifies the claim I've been making throughout this
chapter that, however significant the differences between the two books and
however great the resistance of *Free Agents* itself to the readerly desire for coherence and order, there is evident in both cases an unmistakable continuity of
perception and apprehension?

To begin with, the self, if I may rely upon one of Kierkegaard's particularly
helpful insights, "is just as possible as it is necessary; for though it is itself, it has
to become itself. Inasmuch as it is itself, it is the necessary, and inasmuch as it
has to become itself, it is a possibility."[18] The necessary in this context suggests
not an immutable essence but the existential limits of the self: the bedrock of a
process whereby the self affirms or denies in act what in some sense it already is.
The possible, on the other hand, describes the horizon of the necessary: the
realization of its processive activity or, since the possible is by definition contingent, the blocking or thwarting of that activity. To apply Kierkegaard's paradox to
Apple is to recognize first of all that *Free Agents*, because of its diversity, represents not the attainment of the possible (if, indeed, the possible is ever, in existential terms, finally and demonstrably attainable), but the somewhat frantic and
inchoate attempt at once to avoid self-definition and to position the self along
the lines of its own necessity. The problem, then, is to discover what those lines
are. In fact, Kierkegaard's sinuous formulation further invites the critic to distinguish within the category of the necessary between the authentic and the accidental: to discover which patterns declare themselves through their repetition
and persistence, not (to insist on this point) as some abstract and ineluctable

property of the self, its radial and radiant center, but as the visible trajectory of its specific movement through time.

In Apple's case, the patterns one comes gradually to detect have less to do with answers or solutions than with questions, and less to do with either than with a particular stance, a characteristic way of encountering the world. The questions concern what I've been calling the ethics of sufficiency: over and again, the stories, and *Zip* as well, turn on the attempt to stipulate how much is enough—to bridge the gap between the constancy of desire and its variously conceived satisfactions. But more is at stake. It might plausibly be argued that the mere asking of these questions, however obliquely or covertly, constitutes an admission of *dis*satisfaction, which betrays in turn a lurking, pervasive self-consciousness that, more and more, offers itself as the most radically defining feature of Apple's work.

To be sure, self-consciousness doesn't preclude a thematics of directness and involvement (or a valorization of them) any more than it necessarily implies a modernist, Prufrockian sense of helplessness and stasis. The issue is the way in which the self relates to the world, and in Apple's fiction—whether in expansive and spirited stories like "The Oranging of America" and "Vegetable Love," in the more grimly realistic studies of *Free Agents*, or in the complexly hesitant "Eskimo Love"—that relationship is always and invariably askew. Like E. M. Forster, Apple is "a master of *angle*";[19] and it is the angle that accounts both for the seemingly ingenuous "pop" vision of America that informs his first collection and for what McCaffery in his interview calls "the perspective of the perpetual outsider" (*IMA*, p. 11). Apple himself has denied that this perspective constitutes "a conscious strategy" (*IMA*, p. 11). "I'm just surprised," he told McCaffery, "that other people aren't as amazed as I am by daily life" (*IMA*, p. 11). Earlier in the interview Apple speaks about his reaction as he grew up to "all those strange cultural things that I am still amazed at" and he goes on:

My family was always fascinated by what the goyim did. . . . For me they're all absolutely marvelous creatures, not just seven-foot basketball players but all goyim. In some ways, all people. . . . Partly because of her [his grandmother], I've never taken the other, goyim, side of life for granted. I'm constantly amazed by the things I see around me: the motels, the supermarkets, the daily behavior of regular people, who are wondrous creatures to me.   (*IMA*, pp. 10–11)

In light of these remarks, it would obviously be a mistake to underestimate the effect on Apple of his Jewishness and, more, of his orthodoxy. "I am," he writes in "Stranger at the Table," "the minority of the minority" (*FA*, p. 67); and as the essay develops, the observance of Kosher rules, which is its subject, swells into "the heart and soul of being an outsider, the schizophrenia of social life"

(p. 70), and also into "a way of ordering the world" (p. 74). The last quotation is particularly telling, suggesting as it does the disorder of the personal life to which *Free Agents* so often and so eloquently speaks. Similarly, in "The American Bakery," a meditation on Apple's "love affair with English," he writes: "There is no safety. . . . Yet I wish for the security of exact words" (FA, p. 90). Although the essay again invokes Apple's experience of growing up as a Jew among gentiles, the feeling to which it testifies seems to resonate beyond that specific, if powerful, occasion: to reach out to a more general sense of what makes his world so clearly "other" and turns him into its bemused, often reluctant, spectator. *Free Agents* is, after all, a book about many ways of being an outsider, both in the more or less autobiographical pieces, where Apple appears not only as Jew but as widower and single parent, and in those stories that transpose alienation into less immediately personal and familiar shapes. In short, Apple's Judaism, however large and influential its role in creating the self's necessity, constitutes neither its equivalent nor its definition. His outsiderhood, his angle, patently exceeds cultural and even biographical determinations. To be a stranger at the world's table (in Apple's specific and restricted application of that phrase) is thus to acknowledge as well, and in a more complex way, an estrangement from it (and perhaps from one's own body)—to proclaim oneself an ironist, "standing," as he says of his grandmother, "in wonder before America."[20]

The sense of wonder and the sense of distance—complemented by a more covert dialectical sense of the pure and the defiled, the licit and the forbidden—accompany one another throughout Apple's fiction, and if the balance tips differently at different times, that is not to deny how mutually enabling and reinforcing the two are. *The Oranging of America* highlights the wonder, of course, and it's only by hindsight that one recognizes how fully the zestful endings of the stories confirm the evasiveness of most of their heroes: their determination to find the solace of perfection in other, more welcoming worlds. In *Zip*, on the other hand, where Debby accuses Ira of not acting and taking responsibility— "You poor Hamlet," she calls him (p. 125)—and where Ira himself feels "as if between me and the world there is a sheet of Saran Wrap" (p. 12), the question of distance, now directly thematized, takes center stage. As for *Free Agents*, we are, as we've seen repeatedly, witnesses in that book to a multiplicity of responses whose range resolutely confounds any desire to find in it some unequivocal statement of Apple's position—or, alternatively, constrains us to recognize, here and elsewhere, the instability, at least the flexibility, of that position. Walt Disney's minimal gesture of dissent jostles "Max Apple"'s luxurious assent (in the title story) to "everything"; and if one is tempted to take as crucial "Eskimo Love"'s injunction to "rejoin mankind," there is no assurance that its narrator has, in any final and absolute way, shaken off the apartness of which he stands accused by his friend Oscar.[21] Apartness, after all, if it is the ironist's burden, is also his way of coming to terms with the world's obdurate uncertainties—of stabilizing, though not necessarily resolving, them. No doubt, Apple will continue to answer variously the question of what is enough, but to assert this is only to recognize that the reiterated question both conceals and reveals a more fundamental necessity in his career—and, perhaps, in the nature of irony itself. In fact, for the ironist the quest for sufficiency, which is also an attempt to realize Kierkegaard's goal of the possible, describes ultimately, and impossibly, a quest for *self*-sufficiency, for a means by which the world can be both encountered and held at bay—or, encountered *because* held at bay.

This said, some discriminations are in order. Despite Apple's repeated stress on "rhythm, voice, finally style itself" as "a truth more profound to me than meaning" (FA, p. 90), his connections are not to be found with his metafictional contemporaries. Nor, despite his talk of "the sadness that turns us finally back to the words and the comfort of the next sentence,"[22] does his work replicate modernism's concern with the solaces of art—though, like other midfictionists, he probably shares more with the latter group than with the former, or than he does with more conventionally realistic writers. Apple's ironic imagination is neither heterocosmic nor reflexive, and his special relation to the world requires neither its aestheticizing nor its denial. It's true enough that the defining feature of Apple's "angle" is stylistic and that it manifests itself most particularly in the always off-beat, unexpected, but never merely bizarre or outré images that punctuate his work. From "Gas Stations," where Ted Johnson is said to have "sponged windshields" "the way Abraham must have washed the feet of angels" (OA, p. 99) to *Zip*, where the redoubtable "Solomon's four telephones ring blood" (p. 18) to "Walt and Will," where we come upon "the brothers Disney, all their lives close as testicles" (FA, p. 4); and on to "Eskimo Love," with its glimpse of Vicki as fish, its comically ingenuous response to Sue ("They have found me a Paul Bunyan" [FA, p. 146]), and its fantasticated description of what it means to be an Eskimo ("The Eskimo invented silence. His microbes are the size of thumbs, his viruses carry Swiss army knives. . . . Two Eskimos constitute a minyan" [p. 140])—in all these cases, and in dozens upon dozens of others, Apple's imagery serves at once to defamiliarize the ordinary and to confirm it: to jar us out of our complacency (art, as he says in "On Persisting as a Writer," is "the risk of an open destiny" [p. 23]), but not so far out as to lose contact with the world that has been reimagined for us.

In sum, the elements that compose Apple's fiction are constant, however variable and diverse their manifestations may be. But their constancy, as I began by saying, derives not from their coherence but from their continuity, just as their continuity inheres not in their resolution but in their tension. The world, whether the object of appropriative, if wishful, desire or, more recently, an emblem of all that is uncertain, unsafe, and upside down, remains real, though problematic: the necessary site of the activity through which the self realizes or fails to realize, what (again *in posse* rather than in essence) it is. But less easily than this formulation suggests. The potential of self and world alike is constrained, as well as defined, by their relationship; and that, as we've seen, roots itself in Apple's irony and in the concomitant pursuit of self-sufficiency, which, at its extreme, turns the "other" neither into partner, as in much of Barthelme's writing, nor, as in Berger's, into antagonist, but, less dynamically, into spectacle. Yet the bulk of Apple's work nevertheless resists the traditional dichotomies of Western thought as "Free Agents" does most explicitly and defiantly. For one thing, Apple, like other postmodern ironists, situates himself very much within the world he observes, but it is more significantly the case that for him, as for most midfictional ironists, the temptations of observation are themselves undermined by a countering attraction to, an impulse to be part of, the world's facticity, the dense particularity and diversity of its human but mysterious surface.

What impels Apple to blur the conventional lines between viewer and viewed is not, however, some mystical reverence for Being but an eschatological urgency that subtends the apparent (and real) geniality of his fiction. To speak, then, only of self and world as determinants of Apple's shifting responses is to miss the triangulate structure of the forces that underlie his work—and at whose apex stands, from the beginning, the chafing presence of death. It's tempting at this point to quote the famous Forsterian epigram, "Death destroys a man; the idea of Death saves him,"[23] for although Forster's words resonate somewhat differently in context, their relevance to Apple's writing is manifest. Theoretical in *The Oranging of America*, death declares itself in *Free Agents*; but in both it is, in its own incontrovertible sufficiency, at once the source of Apple's distanced and distancing perspective and the subversive agent that submits his perspective to continuous interrogation. More than most of his contemporaries, even in this quizzical age, Apple (to elaborate a point made earlier) offers the reader of his work not answers or solutions but the emphatic, thematized display of the tension that follows from their absence.[24] The title of Apple's latest collection finally represents then, it would seem, both a recognition of the unsystematic and unsystematized ethics his fiction expresses and the willingness to accept, along with the euphoria of freedom such an ethical position sometimes entails, the contingency and vagarious instability to which it also points. It follows that to be enough is no more and no less than to be sufficient, only and always, to the occasion—to the concrete specificity of whatever occasion life offers and death permits. In the uncertainty of the one and the certainty of the other, Apple increasingly undertakes the acts of negotiation that are at once the necessity of his writing and, in a more profound way, its possibility: the horizon of the self's hesitant, provisional, always renewed or renewable assent.

Notes

1. Apple's remarks were made in conversation with me.

2. Larry McCaffery and Sinda Gregory, "An Interview with Max Apple," *The Mississippi Review*, 13 (Fall 1984), 17–18. The interview will be referred to hereafter as *IMA*. I'm grateful to Professor McCaffery for supplying me with a copy of the typescript before it was published.

3. Cleanth Brooks, *The Well Wrought Urn: Studies in the Structure of Poetry* (New York: Harcourt, Brace-Harvest Books, 1947), p. 195.

4. Leo Bersani, *A Future for Astyanax: Character and Desire in Literature* (Boston and Toronto: Little, Brown, 1976), pp. 312 and 312–13.

5. See chapter three, above, for a fuller discussion of the problem of the author in contemporary criticism.

6. Roland Barthes, "The Death of the Author," *Image-Music-Text*, ed. and trans. Stephen Heath (New York: Hill & Wang, 1977), p. 147.

7. Maurice Merleau-Ponty, *Sense and Non-Sense*, trans. Hubert L. Dreyfus and Patricia Allen Dreyfus (Evanston, Ill.: Northwestern University Press, 1964), p. 20.

8. All six quotations come from *The Oranging of America and Other Stories* (New York: Grossman Publishers-Viking Press, 1976). Subsequent references to the volume will be given parenthetically in the text, accompanied, when necessary, by the abbreviation *OA*.

9. I've discussed (sometimes in more detail, sometimes from different angles) several of the stories in *The Oranging of America*, including this one, as well as a few from *Free Agents*, in *Horizons of Assent: Modernism, Postmodernism, and the Ironic Imagination* (1981; pbk. ed. Philadelphia: University of Pennsylvania Press, 1987), pp. 49, 132–33, 161–65.

10. See Patrick D. Hundley's "Triggering the Imagination: An Interview with Max Apple," *Southwest Review*, 64 (Summer 1979), p. 237.

11. Dennis Vannatta, in an essay called "Satiric Gestures in Max Apple's *The Oranging of America*," *Studies in Contemporary Satire*, 7 (Spring 1980), 1–7, reaches somewhat the same conclusion.

12. To choose one example from among many: in the McCaffery-Gregory Interview, Apple, speaking of "Small Island Republics," says: "I wasn't conscious of these things as I was doing the story. It's important to me *not* to be conscious of this kind of thing when I write. . . . I try to get away from the critical processes when I'm working best because I want to allow my intuition to lead me to places that the critic in me wouldn't allow" (*IMA*, p. 32).

13. In the McCaffery-Gregory Interview, Apple says: "It's that enlightenment I achieve at the end that's important . . . I felt I had become a seer in my relationship to Mailer and also in relationship to my own writing" (*IMA*, p. 22).

14. This and the following quotation are from *Free Agents* (New York: Harper & Row, 1984). Subsequent references will be given parenthetically in the text, accompanied, when necessary, by the abbreviation *FA*.

15. Although, as will become clear when I discuss *Free Agents'* realistic stories, not every piece in the volume can be claimed for midfiction, the term suits the book as a whole.

16. I'm grateful to Max Apple for supplying me with these dates.

17. Max Apple, *Zip: A Novel of the Left and the Right* (New York: Viking Press, 1978), p. 37. Subsequent references will be given parenthetically in the text.

18. Søren Kierkegaard, *The Sickness Unto Death*, in *Fear and Trembling and The Sickness Unto Death*, trans. Walter Lowrie (Garden City, N.Y.: Doubleday & Co., 1954), p. 168.

19. P. N. Furbank uses the phrase to describe Forster in "The Personality of E. M. Forster," *Encounter*, 35 (November 1970), 67.

20. Martin Levine, "A Storyteller's Grandson," *New York Times Book Review*, 17 June 1984, p. 11. In the McCaffery-Gregory Interview, Apple speaks revealingly of his ambivalence toward the body: "I always understood that the mind was everything. I was constantly angry—and I still am—that the body holds us up. And yet I also love the body" (*IMA*, p. 15).

21. To be sure, the narrator of "Bridging" experiences for a moment the feeling that he is "not watching and keeping score and admiring from the distance but [is] a participant, a player" (p. 25), but the recognition signals no lasting change in him or in the other characters of *Free Agents* who resemble him.

22. Max Apple, "On Persisting as A Writer," *Michigan Quarterly Review*, 21 (Winter 1982), 25.

23. E. M. Forster, *Howards End*, ed. Oliver Stallybrass (London: Edward Arnold, 1973), p. 236. In fact, the words are those of Forster's character, Helen Schlegel, but they unquestionably represent his own views.

24. When, on occasion, the tension slackens, as it does in "The National Debt" or "The Four Apples," the stories threaten to turn whimsical and arch.

four

on knowing (and not-knowing) the world

8

Barthelme his garden

Q: Are you bored with the question-and-answer form?

A: I am bored with it but I realize that it permits many valuable omissions: what kind of day it is, what I'm wearing, what I'm thinking. That's a very considerable advantage, I would say.

Q: I believe in it.

Donald Barthelme, "The Explanation"

Otherwise unnamed, Q and A, the interlocutors of "Basil from Her Garden," appear elsewhere in Barthelme's work (most notably, in "Kierkegaard Unfair to Schlegel"); and they will serve, in all their alphabetic purity, as convenient emblems of what that body of work intends.[1] To begin with, Barthelme, like one of the characters in "The Leap," is "a double-minded man. H[as] always been a double-minded man,"[2] which no doubt explains the attraction for him of various dialogic forms—forms that, by their structure alone, tend to suggest doubt or division and that invite a dialectical, ongoing apprehension of both self and world.[3] The recurrence of such stories is interesting enough in itself.[4] More significant, however, if also more problematic, is Barthelme's attitude toward the comedy or frustration of double-mindedness that he enacts in many of these dialogues. Thus, one of the speakers in "The Leap" responds to the statement that "purity of heart is to will one thing," by asserting his own, apparently more Barthelmean credo: "No. Here I differ with Kierkegaard. Purity of heart is, rather, to will several things, and not know which is the better, truer thing, and to worry about this, forever" (p. 384). No doubt, there are dangers in assuming that this character—or any character, for that matter—speaks for Barthelme, but in this case there are compelling reasons for the identification. In a recent essay (actually, a talk), Barthelme set forth his own eminently postmodern belief that "problems are a comfort. Wittgenstein said of philosophers that some of them suffer from 'loss of problems,' a development in which everything seems quite simple to them, and what they write becomes (I'm quoting) 'immeasurably shallow and trivial.' The same can be said of writers."[5]

And of the character in "The Leap" whom I've twice cited. What is at issue in both that story and the essay is a willingness to live with and in the untidiness of existence: to abide, even to welcome, the problematic; to see it, indeed, as "a comfort," if also—possibly a distinction without a difference—as a source of fertile worry. In any case, the contrast between the desire for "one thing" and the acceptance of "many things" is central to the dialectic of Barthelme's work and, arguably, nowhere more so than in "Basil from Her Garden," where Q and A sinuously and ironically explore the possibilities that define the world in which his characters live, act, and talk. I say "ironically" because, despite what appears to be a psychiatric encounter, it is A, the "patient," who emerges not only as the more resilient and independent but, finally, as the comforter of his interlocutor. (On the other hand, in "Kierkegaard Unfair to Schlegel" an earlier avatar of Q, speaking from within a similar situation, reminds A that "I'm not your doctor."[6]) At any rate, whatever the precise roles we are meant to attribute to the two, it is clear that Q's movement is from heuristic prompter to worried and aggravated participant in the dialogue, while A's is from generally willing and sometimes expansive respondent to increasingly assured and confident affirmer of the ordinary.

The effect, needless to say, is to destroy the *apparent* modality of the question-and-answer situation, to make it, in every possible way, ironic. But that is to get ahead of Barthelme and his story. Anterior to our awareness of how his characters reposition themselves in the course of their exchange is the more fundamental recognition that "Basil from Her Garden," like "The Leap," bases itself on the clash of two opposing cosmologies, each of which has, at one time or another, its attractions for the speakers. The first, represented by the jumpy, disjunctive, paratactic structure of the story, by its distractable, associative characters, and, perhaps, more graphically, by the clouds of "little black bugs flying around here"[7] that A irrelevantly notices at one point, suggests the irredeemable messiness and contingency of the (postmodern) world. The second, opposing view reveals itself in a sense of something lost and regretted, something *other* than the world Q and A inhabit—a prelapsarian Garden of coherence, order, and wholeness, as it might appropriately be called—whose emblems include flying, dreams, the "limitless," "never-ending" ocean (p. 38), religion, and, of course, as the ultimate source of them all, God. This longing for an alternative, if merely imaginable, elsewhere is, as stories like "A Shower of Gold," "The President," "Paraguay," and, especially, "Florence Green is 81" demonstrate, nothing new in Barthelme's fiction; and in A's ruminations on the possibility of "starting completely over in something completely new, changing the very sort of person I am" (p. 36) one hears echoes of Florence Green's wish "to go to some *other* place . . . Somewhere where *everything is different*"—a remark the narrator of that story glosses as follows: "A simple, perfect idea. The old babe demands nothing less than total otherness."[8]

Familiar too, as the cause of the desire for the entirely different, are the feelings that A, continually prompted by Q, acknowledges in his meditations on adultery, the central, or at least the most obsessive, concern of the dialogue:

A—There's a certain amount of guilt attached [to adultery]. But I feel guilty even without adultery. I exist in a morass of guilt. There's maybe a little additional wallop of guilt but I already feel so guilty that I hardly notice it. . . .

Q—You haven't answered me. This general guilt—

A—Yes, that's the interesting thing. I hazard that it is not guilt so much as it is inadequacy. I feel that everything is being nibbled away, because I can't *get it right*—

Q—Would you like to be able to fly?

A—It's crossed my mind.   (p. 37)

But, as I've already intimated, A does eventually *get it right*, manages, that is, to accommodate his guilt and inadequacy and to forego the temptation of flying; and it is at that point that the differences, not only between the story's cosmological choices, but between Q and A assert themselves unmistakably.

And yet, to phrase things in this way may suggest too dramatic a series of changes in "Basil from Her Garden." The fact is that throughout the story we come increasingly to recognize a real, if unsteady, modulation in A's responses and, equally, to question Q's role as Socratic facilitator and guide—to see mirrored in the relative strengthening of one ego the commensurate disintegration of the other. Thus, even before we reach the final section, we become aware that, of the two, it is Q, the ostensible cicerone, who is the more depressed ("only a bit depressed, only a bit" [p. 38]), the more naive and unsure, and, above all, the more theoretical and utopian in his hopes and aspirations. Or, as he puts it himself: "A new arrangement of ideas, based upon the best thinking, would produce a more humane moral order, which we need" (p. 38). Nevertheless, it is only in the tenth and closing scene of the story that the full dimensions of what has transpired become clear. "I sometimes imagine that I am in Pest Control" (p. 39), Q tells A and proceeds to relate a cheerful fantasy of himself as the agent of domestic order, a fantasy that ends as the young wife of the house "pins a silver medal on my chest and kisses me on both cheeks" (p. 39). Two things signify in Q's tale: first, that the emphasis falls on Control and not on the unseen Pests (though it is tempting to recall the contingent "little black bugs" of an earlier section) and, second, that rehearsing the conceit does nothing whatever to allay his worries about "last things" (p. 37).

Indeed, as "Basil from Her Garden" comes to its end and as A contemplates what he has already called "ordinary things" (p. 36), Q continues to fret about the unsatisfactoriness of life with a self-protective humor that reveals more than it conceals ("Does the radish worry about itself in this way? Yet the radish is a living thing. Until it's cooked" [p. 39]) and that finally protects nothing, as the lines that close the story make abundantly clear:

Q—Transcendence is possible.
A—Yes.
Q—Is it possible?
A—Not out of the question.
Q—Is it really possible?
A—Yes. Believe me.   (p. 39)

The easiest way to read these lines is to see in them Q's almost despairing need for reassurance and A's willingness to console and cajole. But it is more productive to recognize that the key word of the exchange means very different things to the two speakers—that for Q transcendence implies an ordering of the world (as well as a removal from it), a ridding it, as in the tale of the Pest Controller, of everything that makes life uneven, unpredictable, and recalcitrant, whereas for A it is a matter of coming to terms with guilt, anxiety, and thoughts of inadequacy *in the world*, as it is and as it offers itself to consciousness. Like Mad Moll of "The Emerald," with her "memories of God who held me up and sustained me until I fell from His hands,"[9] A (and Barthelme, on this reading) accept what follows from inhabiting a postlapsarian world; or, as A puts it in response to Q's Pest Control story: "It's finally a matter, perhaps, of fit. Appropriateness. Fit in a stately or sometimes hectic dance with nonfit" (p. 39). The orderly and harmonious suggestions of a dance are qualified, appropriately, by "hectic," as well as by the double-minded adverb "perhaps," and, most of all, by the acknowledgment of the "nonfit," that is, whatever stubbornly refuses Q's dreams and parables of order. Which is to say too that the story's apparent closure, its emphatic "Yes. Believe me," is anything but final, is, instead, a momentary halt in what must be a continuing dialogue with the world.

Up to this point, it might be argued, I've deliberately ignored, even contravened, Barthelme's contention that "the paraphrasable content of art is rather slight";[10] and it might further be said that I've been of Q's party in imposing on the story an orderliness that the story itself expressly aims to frustrate. Let me admit, then, that much of "Basil from Her Garden" remains, at least in the discursive context I've so far established for reading it, puzzling in the extreme and that, again in these specific terms, it is almost impossible to account for much that goes on in it. Which is, no doubt, why so many critics have been anxious to claim Barthelme as a metafictionist, to define his concerns as, exclusively, language and play. To be sure, some of the stories, earlier ones like "Sentence" especially, seem to fit naturally into this category. And, given the loosely assorted, willfully inconsequent, episodic structure of "Basil from Her Garden"; given the "many valuable omissions" to which an earlier A refers in the epigraph I've used;[11] and given, finally, the fact that most of its sections end, as often as not, with a sense of the apparently irrelevant or mysterious, it would be less than surprising to find this story swept into the metafictional bin as well. Furthermore, Barthelme has on occasion helped to promote such readings of his work by speaking, through his characters or in propria persona, of the "objecthood" of the work of art, as in "Kierkegaard Unfair to Schlegel," where yet another A objects "that Kierkegaard fastens upon Schlegel's novel [*Lucinde*] in its prescriptive aspect—in which it presents itself as a text telling us how to live—and neglects other aspects, its objecthood for one" (*KS*, p. 165).[12] On the other hand, Barthelme has recently offered an ambiguous and partial recantation of that position in "Not-Knowing": "Twenty years ago I was much more convinced of the autonomy of the literary objects than I am now, and even wrote a rather persuasive defense of the proposition that I have just rejected, that the object is itself world. . . . The proposition's still attractive. What's the right answer? Bless Babel" (p. 49). But it hardly required such a statement to make the point once more that many of his best stories, not to mention *The Dead Father*, are, whatever their playfulness, nothing if not moral: studies in smallness and risk that endorse an ethic of tentative, provisional pleasures against a background of daily life that frequently remains as frustrating as it is drab.

Which brings us back to "Basil from Her Garden." Ludic or moral? I would happily agree with those who, rejecting the choice as an unreal one, see the story as both, and would agree still more readily with those for whom the story is both and, in addition, something different still. The fact is that, to do justice to the variety of Barthelme's work, one needs to add to this raggedly taxonomic scheme yet another kind of fiction; and to describe it no one comes more snugly to hand than Susanne Langer. Langer's famous description of "the forms of feeling" in *Philosophy in a New Key* has more to do, of course, with music, ritual, and myth than with fiction. Its applicability to the last of these should, however, be apparent; and the notion of literature that resists discursive paraphrase but that conveys knowledge nevertheless (knowledge, precisely, of the morphology of feeling) helps at once to make sense of a story like "Basil from Her Garden" and to distinguish it from those of other writers who march under the reflexive, nonreferential banner of poststructuralist theory and who arrogate to themselves too exclusively the designation of postmodern.

My point is that we would do well to read various of the episodes in "Basil from Her Garden" (A's soliloquy on the ocean, Q's fantasy of Pest Control, to mention only two) neither as conventionally symbolic nor as allegorical but as emblematic: to seek in them such information about the forms of feeling as we require to make sense of what Barthelme is telling us about human beings living in a puzzling and quandarous world. If all of this sounds as if, by denying his metafictional status, I'm obliquely trying to rescue Barthelme for realism, it is not what I intend. As I've said so often in this study, the time has come to recognize that contemporary fiction does not lend itself to the kinds of binary oppositions that are the subject of Thomas Pynchon's anathematizations and that, in mapping the literary present, all too easily divide the field between the realistic and the metafictional. What has been excluded in this division of spoils is a middle ground where many of today's best writers, Barthelme among them, position themselves. Neither taking the world for granted nor regarding it as so impenetrable as to place it, effectively, *hors de combat*, midfiction, as we've seen, carves out for itself a more equivocal but also a more various space in which to bring the world into being.

That Barthelme is not a realist, no one, I think, will deny. As for his putative reflexiveness, a statement made in the latest interview with him—"I don't have any great enthusiasm for fiction-about-fiction"[13]—says all that probably needs to be said about Barthelme's aims and interests. My suggestion, then, is that, thematically, stylistically, and structurally, Barthelme's work, or much of the best of it, belongs with the tertium quid of midfiction; and although the terms I've been using are mine, not his, he has recently acknowledged as much in "Not-Knowing," the spirited and vivid essay from which I've been quoting. As playful and serious as "Basil from Her Garden," as associative in its logic, the essay can be viewed as a companion piece to the story, and, because of the light it sheds on its fictional brother, I want briefly to examine what it has to say about literature and its relation to the world it has traditionally been thought to represent.

The thesis of the essay, as its title suggests, is that "writing is a process of dealing with not-knowing, a forcing of what and how" (p. 38) and, further, that "the not-knowing is crucial to art, is what permits art to be made. Without the scanning process engendered by not-knowing, without the possibility of having the mind move in unanticipated directions, there would be no invention" (p. 38). Invention is the key word here, although in its older sense of "finding" rather than in the more usual (and metafictional) sense of "making up." What is being invented or found, as well as how, becomes clear later on, but first Barthelme deals with the various pressures of language (and of attitudes toward language) on literature during the last hundred years or so. Citing the growing complexity in "the effort toward mimesis" (p. 42), "the political and social contamination of language" (p. 41), and "a loss of reference . . . a world of reference to which all possible readers in this country can respond" (p. 43), Barthelme offers a still stronger assertion of the belief I've already noted, namely, that "problems, in part, define the kind of work the writer chooses to do, *and are not avoided but embraced*" (p. 44; my italics).

This assent to the complexities of writing (and of much else) leads, in turn, to the essay's central question: "In what sense is the work 'about' the world" (p. 46). The two related answers that Barthelme provides are, first, that "the world enters the work as it enters our ordinary lives, not as a world-view or system but in sharp particularity" (p. 47) and, second, "that art is always a meditation upon external reality rather than a representation of external reality" (p. 49). These propositions are fleshed out in a wonderfully inventive anecdote that is worth quoting at some length:

> Let us suppose that I am the toughest banjulele player in town and that I have contracted to play "Melancholy Baby" for six hours before an audience that will include the four next-toughest banjulele players in town. . . . There is one thing of which you may be sure: I am not going to play "Melancholy Baby" as written. Rather I will play something that is parallel, in some sense, to "Melancholy Baby," based upon the chords of "Melancholy Baby," made out of "Melancholy Baby," having to do with "Melancholy Baby"—commentary, exegesis, elaboration, contradiction.   (p. 49)

The passage does not end quite yet, and I will return in a moment to its close; but already certain things are clear. Despite the fact that what we have here may seem to be a meditation on intertextuality, on art's (the banjulele player's) response to, and only to, art ("Melancholy Baby"), the opposite—or nearly the opposite—is true. For, as Barthelme argues elsewhere in the essay, "the prior history of words [and I take it that, in Langer's sense, music and words equally express that prior history] is one of the aspects of language the world uses to smuggle itself into the work" (p. 48). "Melancholy Baby" functions, in other words, not only as an aesthetic limit but, more broadly, as any "reality" that exists outside us. It follows that, although Barthelme doesn't broach directly the question that haunts the poststructuralist imagination—whether we can in any way know the world or, to phrase it alternatively, whether we are irretrievably caught, and caught up, in a web of language—the tale of the banjulele player nonetheless implies both that the world (in a manner of speaking) leans on us and that we, in our turn, reciprocate the pressure: commenting, elaborating, contradicting, in short, *referring* to whatever that world is or may be. More succinctly, as Pierre Thévenaz writes, "the world gives itself to consciousness which confers on it its meaning."[14]

My invocation at this point of a phenomenological philosopher is altogether deliberate. Barthelme has, at various times in his career, acknowledged a debt of sorts to phenomenology. Thus, for example, in his interview with Klin-kowitz, he says: "As to 'deeper cultural sources' [Klinkowitz's phrase], I have taken a certain degree of nourishment (or stolen a lot) from the phenomenolo-gists: Sartre, Erwin Straus, etc." (*TNF*, p. 52); while in "Not-Knowing," he writes, in confirmation of the views I've been attributing to him:

Art is a true account of the activity of mind. Because consciousness, in Husserl's formu-lation, is always consciousness *of* something, art thinks ever of the world, cannot not think of the world, could not turn its back on the world even if it wished to. This does not mean that it's going to be honest as a mailman; it's more likely to appear as a drag queen.   (p. 50)[15]

But sources, even deeper sources, are not the issue here. At stake is the fact that Thévenaz's account of consciousness as a locus of both reception and "inven-tion" coincides so neatly with Barthelme's own sense of art's limits and possibil-ities: "The interest of my construction, if any," he notes in concluding his story of the banjulele player, "is to be located in the space between the new entity I have constructed and the 'real' 'Melancholy Baby,' which remains in the mind as the horizon that bounds my efforts" (p. 49). As emblem of the world, "Mel-ancholy Baby" suggests the "reality" that constrains the artist who imagines or invents it into significative existence; and as the prototypically phenomenologi-cal word "horizon" intimates, not-knowing depends as much upon the fluid boundaries of consciousness (what "bounds my efforts") as upon consciousness itself, so that Barthelme's space or gap becomes precisely the middle ground I spoke of earlier, where the world, neither steady and immutable nor opaque and irrelevant, offers itself to interrogation rather than re-presentation, even as it asserts (above all, to the artist as drag queen) its equivocal but undeniable pres-ence.

If I appear to have digressed, it has only been so as to circle back, now with theoretical provisions, to a reconsideration of what Barthelme is about in his unsettling and problematic story. What, then, can we now say about "Basil from Her Garden" in the light of Barthelme's apologia? To begin with, the fiction is obviously, richly, and precisely concerned with the "ordinary things" A speaks of—bow-hunting, haircuts, television, cancer, adultery, not to mention the con-tents of A's wallet: "Credit cards, pictures of the children, driver's license, forty dollars in cash, Amex receipts—" (p. 39). More to the point, it is concerned with how these things, the world, seep into or impinge on consciousness "in sharp particularity." No doubt, the world in question is, from Q's psychiatric interpretation of the dream with which the story opens to A's ruminations about

God's intentions, to a large degree a cultural and linguistic construct, a matter, as poststructuralists would argue, of codes that interpose themselves between us and what we naively persist in regarding as reality. But, as Barthelme argues in "Not-Knowing": "If words can be contaminated by the world they can also carry with them into the work trace elements of world which can be used in a positive sense" (p. 48). Furthermore, the story is not only about the specific, linguistically-determined systems that cause A's guilt and anxiety. There is, too, the object of A's covetousness, Althea: the solicitation of a world that is, whatever else we say about it, palpably there.

This is not, however, to suggest that either adultery in general or Althea in particular embodies the answer to A's dilemma. On the contrary, the tensions that make Althea at once desirable and forbidden remain to the end; and the question, perhaps, is more nearly one of defining what attitudes A (and, by extension, human beings) need to adopt in order to deal with life's inevitable contradictions, the "hectic dance [of fit] with nonfit," as they appear to "poor lapsarian futiles whose preen glands are all out of kilter" (*TL*, p. 384). The choices that the story offers are, it seems to me, three. There is, first of all, the residual sense of the genuinely extraordinary that leads Q down the dangerous and impossible path of a perfect and irrefrangible order. But as A argues throughout and as even Q acknowledges ("He critiques us, we critique Him" [p. 39]), God's commandments are no longer gospel. In the second place, the story offers the consequences of acquiescence in life's dailiness, a possibility that Barthelme has mooted from time to time, and nowhere more effectively than in "City Life," which ends with Ramona's comically dreary and defeated words: "I accepted. What was the alternative?"[16] In "Basil from Her Garden," A's thoughts are equally occupied with the quotidian, as, intermittently, he contemplates his wife, Grete:

It's an architectural problem, marriage. If we could live in separate houses, and visit each other when we felt particularly gay— It would be expensive, yes. But as it is she has to endure me in all my worst manifestations, early in the morning and late at night and in the nutsy obsessed noontimes. When I wake up from my nap you don't *get* the laughing cavalier, you get a rank pigfooted belching blunderer.   (p. 38)

But A's self-awareness is something different from Ramona's resignation, less monolithic, more elastic; and in the story as a whole, A both confronts and contests the sources of his predecessor's weariness, accepting her version of dailiness but moving beyond it as well.

The clue to this third and final attitude, which seems to me Barthelme's too, is embedded in the story's title or, rather, in the episode to which it refers. Q has asked him about coveting his neighbor's wife, and A's answer brings us to the unobtrusive center of the fiction:

I like Rachel but I don't covet her, she's covetable, quite lovely and spirited, but in point of fact our relationship is that of neighborliness. I jump-start her car when her battery is dead, she gives me basil from her garden, she's got acres of basil, not literally acres but—   (p. 38)

Nothing, in fact, is changed by this description—not the architecture of marriage, nor the guilt of adultery, and still less A's felt inadequacy in the face of life. But in Rachel and her basil, and in A's neighborly relationship with her, there is imaged another, postlapsarian garden that celebrates—amidst all the angst and tension, in the face of Q's desirous reaching for transcendence—the *ordinary*. More than the daily (but incorporating it), Barthelme's garden is populated by characters who are, as he described them in one of his interviews, "knitting lively lives—perhaps in subdued tones" (*ACH*, p. 40).

Double-minded though it is, Barthelme's witty assertion nevertheless contrives to stress the liveliness and activity of his characters and, in so doing, designates the traits that mark his own fictional grasp of the world, his intentionality, as well. Thus, to have A say of Rachel that "she's got acres of basil, not literally acres but—" is to open up to us unimaginable (or only imaginable) visions of abundance, even though he and Barthelme, inevitably, pinch back this figurative excess and, it is implied, settle for the perceptible and the finite. But what matters is that we are given the movement of the imagination *before* it is vaguely and regretfully cut to size (forms of feeling indeed!), which is also to say that, as much as his conception of *la vie quotidienne*, this movement continues to inform his sense of what "ordinary" life has to offer. As does his choice of spice. Functional and unexotic, adding flavor and delight nonetheless to the world's otherwise insipid stew, basil, itself part of that world, figures the exact purpose and rewards of a garden, that enclave of nature and cultivation, which, like Candide's and like Barthelme's own writing, borrows the world to find and *make* pleasure in it. In short, the ordinary, here and elsewhere in Barthelme's work, is the ground, the middle ground, of whatever possibilities A's uneven progress evokes: a garden of earthly anxieties and delights, where one lives not, as in *The Waste Land*, between memory and desire but in an acceptance (more vigorous, riskier, than Ramona's passive response) of all the contradictions, the "problems," that inhabiting a fallen and imperfect world entails.

It is perhaps worth insisting that Rachel's garden promises no easy answers, no solutions or resolutions (as I suggested earlier, the story's ending ironically contests its own closural gestures), nothing extraordinary except the ordinary itself. If, nevertheless, this reading seems unduly moral and extravagant in its claims for the referential function of Barthelme's literary enterprise, it may be best to give the last word to Barthelme himself, who ends "Not-Knowing" in the following way:

It's our good fortune to be able to imagine alternative realities, other possibilities. We can quarrel with the world constructively. . . . "Belief in progress," says Baudelaire, "is a doctrine of idlers and Belgians." Perhaps. But if I have anything unorthodox to say, it's that I think art's project is fundamentally meliorative. The aim of meditating about the world is finally to change the world. It is this meliorative aspect of literature that provides its ethical dimension. We are all Upton Sinclairs, even that Hamlet, Stéphane Mallarmé.   (p. 50)

One final note: it's unlikely that anyone will confuse Barthelme with Upton Sinclair; it may be time, however, to recognize just how different he is from either Hamlet or Mallarmé—or, indeed, from the metafictional standard-bearer he is, even now, too often taken to be.

Notes

1. I've dealt more comprehensively with Barthelme's fiction in *Horizons of Assent: Modernism, Postmodernism, and the Ironic Imagination* (1981; pbk. ed. Philadelphia: University of Pennsylvania Press, 1987). See pp. 45–47, 141–42, 149–50, and, especially, chapter six.

2. Donald Barthelme, "The Leap," *Sixty Stories* (New York: G. P. Putnam's Sons, 1981), p. 379. Subsequent references to this story, designated as *TL* (and to other works after their first citation), will be given parenthetically in the text.

3. This is true even, or especially, of the question-and-answer stories, which might, on the face of it (that is, because of their formulaic quality), seem to inhibit genuine dialogue. Barthelme's use of the form plays against and disrupts the notion of speakers fixed in static, unchanging roles.

4. They are clustered most thickly in *Great Days* but there are dialogues in *Sadness, City Life,* and the "previously uncollected" section of *Sixty Stories,* as well as in *The Dead Father.*

5. Donald Barthelme, "Not-Knowing," in *Voicelust,* ed. Allen Wier and Don Hendrie Jr. (Lincoln and London: University of Nebraska Press, 1985), pp. 40–41.

6. Donald Barthelme, "Kierkegaard Unfair to Schlegel," *Sixty Stories,* p. 167. The story will be referred to hereafter as *KS.*

7. Donald Barthelme, "Basil from Her Garden," *The New Yorker,* 21 October 1985, p. 36. Broken into parts and rearranged, the story, or most of it, reappears in Barthelme's latest novel, *Paradise* (New York: G. P. Putnam's Sons, 1986).

8. Donald Barthelme, "Florence Green is 81," *Come Back, Dr. Caligari* (Boston: Little, Brown, 1964), pp. 14–15.

9. Donald Barthelme, "The Emerald," *Sixty Stories,* p. 410.

10. The statement appears in an interview with J. D. O'Hara, "Donald Barthelme: The Art of Fiction LXVI," *The Paris Review,* 80 (Summer 1979), 199.

11. Donald Barthelme, "The Explanation," *City Life* (1970; rpt. New York: Bantam Books, 1971), p. 80.

12. See too, Barthelme's comment in an interview with Jerome Klinkowitz in *The New Fiction: Interviews with Innovative American Writers,* ed. Joe David Bellamy (Urbana: University of Illinois Press, 1974), p. 52: "This new reality [he is speaking of collage], in the best case, may be or imply a comment on the other reality from which it came, and may be also much else. It's an *itself,* if it's successful." The interview will be referred to hereafter as *TNF.*

13. The statement appears in an interview conducted by Larry McCaffery and included in *Anything Can Happen: Interviews with Contemporary American Novelists*, ed. Tom LeClair and Larry McCaffery (Urbana: University of Illinois Press, 1983), p. 38. The interview will be referred to hereafter as *ACH*.

14. Pierre Thévenaz, *What is Phenomenology? and Other Essays*, ed. James M. Edie (Chicago: Quadrangle Books, 1962), p. 50.

15. See too "The Catechist," a quasi-dialogic story, in *Sadness* (1972; rpt. New York: Bantam Books, 1974), with its reference to "the works of Scheler, who holds that love is an aspect of phenomenological knowledge" (p. 121).

16. Donald Barthelme, "City Life," *Sixty Stories*, p. 159.

9

Grace Paley's world-inventing words

People require strengthening before the acts of life.

Grace Paley, "Living"

I digressed and was free.

Grace Paley, "Faith in a Tree"

"When I was a little girl, I was a boy,"[1] Grace Paley told the audience of a recent symposium, a remark that ironically pays tribute to the power critics with a good many different axes to grind have come to find in the so-called "discourse of the Father."[2] Insidiously formative (Paley went on to suggest), it shaped "a lot of little girls who like to get into things and want to be where the action is, which is up the corner someplace, where the boys are. And I understand this very well, because that was what really interested me a lot. I could hardly wait to continue being a boy so that I could go to war and do all the other exciting boys' things" (*PWW*, p. 247). The point of the reminiscence, which is central to Paley's feminist ethic, is made elsewhere and more obliquely in the opening section of "Ruthy and Edie," where the two characters enact different but congruous responses to "the real world of boys"[3]—a phrase sardonically intended to suggest the prevailing ideological atmosphere of the girls' working- and middle-class Bronx neighborhood. Ruthy, recalling the young Paley, dreams of war and bravery, of fighting for her country, of joining the boys who "ran around the block a lot, had races, and played war on the corner" (p. 115), while Edie, more passive and "feminine," clings to her vision of "that nice family life" (p. 117) she derives from her reading of books like *The Bobbsey Twins*. The ironic turn of the episode comes when both girls panic at the approach of "an ordinary middle-sized dog" (p. 117) and, more dramatically still, when Ruthy, fleeter of foot or quicker of mind, runs into her apartment house, holding the door shut not only against the dog but against the terrified Edie. So much, then, for Ruthy's all too theoretical notions of chivalry, as she betrays both her friend and herself. But we read partially at best if we stop there. Paley means to imply not that either Ruthy's fear or her reaction is implausible but, rather, that reading about Roland's Horn at Roncevaux has hardly prepared her to face the more commonplace dangers of her ordinary life. Consequently, if the irony is partly at Ruthy's expense, it is aimed far more directly at the ideas she has ingested in her emulation of "the real world of boys," the shadow and precursor, as the remainder of the story makes clear, of the equally false and more pernicious world of men.

I'll come back to "Ruthy and Edie" shortly, but it will be useful first to pursue some of the larger implications, literary as well as political, of its brief prolegomenon. To begin with, and as virtually all of Paley's critics have noted in their obligatory discussions of her best-known story, "A Conversation with My Father," patriarchal discourse complacently assumes a number of fundamental and determinative values—those, for example, in Joyce Meier's words, of "abstraction, linearity, possession, cause-and-effect progression."[4] In short, the paternal world—encoded in the father's request that his daughter compose "a simple story . . . Just recognizable people and then write down what happened to them next"[5]—bases itself on unexamined and peremptory powers of discernment and identification. Defensively but still smugly, it prescribes an impossibly "simple," stable, and objective mirror to reflect what it takes to be the inevitable, sequential trajectory of life's beginnings, middles, and ends. Paley's own discourse, as critics have also recognized, is predicated instead on the belief that, as the narrator of "A Conversation" puts it (she is commenting on "plot, the absolute line between two points which I've always despised. Not for literary reasons, but because it takes all hope away"): "Everyone, real or invented, deserves the open destiny of life" (p. 167).

The possibility of change, which the story-telling daughter confers on her character in defiance of the father's cynical insistence (understandable given his life and times) that she recognize "Tragedy! Plain tragedy! Historical tragedy! No hope. The end" (p. 173), relates, in turn, to Paley's belief that art's beginnings, like its endings, rest on what is not already known. Thus, in "Of Poetry and Women and the World," Paley, echoing Barthelme's formulation, speaks, though in terms of her own interests and career, of not knowing and, by extension, of learning to know the world:

When I came to really thinking as a writer, it was because I began to live among women. Now the great thing is that I didn't know them, I didn't know who they were. Which I should have known, since I had all these aunts, right? But I didn't know them, and that, I think, is really where lots of literature, in a sense, comes from. It really comes, not from knowing so much, but from not knowing. It comes from what you're curious about. It comes from what obsesses you. It comes from what you want to know.   (p. 249)[6]

The passage underlies what Paley has several times said, that her aim as an artist is to provide "the illumination of what isn't known, the lighting up of what is under a rock, of what has been hidden" (*PWW*, p. 250).[7] To a degree, however, the credo, as expressed here, threatens to mislead. Paley's stories make abundantly clear that the issue is not one of discovering or revealing what is already there, available to the scrutiny of anyone and everyone willing to turn the rock over, but, rather and as in Barthelme's case, that it has to do with "inventing."

To be sure, one needs, just as when dealing with Barthelme's "Not-Knowing," to be gingerly in establishing the meaning of a word currently so overdetermined, especially since it is a good deal more common in Paley's work and, I will argue, central to an understanding of her aesthetic. Briefly, it can be said for now that in reading Paley we are dealing with invention as a function not of the free-floating, unanchored imagination—what Larry McCaffery refers to when he says that metafictionists "insist that the reader accept the work as an invented, purely made-up entity"[8]—but of imagination inextricably entangled with a world that, at the very least, provides the foundation for whatever it is that invention intends and accomplishes. In short, imagination of the metafictional kind is, for Paley, closer to "fantasy" (*PWW*, p. 251), whereas writers like her, she says, "write about things, not just words, about a certain subject matter."[9]

On the other hand, it is just as clear that the world, according to Paley, is variously perceived and construed, that, partly because of temperament and partly because of historical circumstance, human beings inevitably grasp their common world differently.[10] Thus, the narrator of "The Immigrant Story," insists to her old friend Jack: "I believe I see the world as clearly as you do . . . Rosiness is not a worse windowpane than gloomy gray when viewing the world";[11] while Paley herself, commenting on her characters in "A Conversation with My Father," says of them that "they were really speaking from their own latitude and longitude, and from their own time in history."[12] Obviously, the suggestion is that at least to some degree our modes of seeing are, and must be, perspectival; and if there is, from story to story, some variation in the degree of determination Paley attributes to her characters' responses, there is no question but that she asserts, everywhere and always, the individual, subjective basis of experience.

That insistence constitutes, one might argue, the most persuasive reason for excluding Paley from the ranks of realistic writers: those who, to invoke J. P.

Stern's definition one last time, "take reality for granted." I've indicated already that for Paley perception is limited, partial, and, in phenomenological terms, "situated." But there is more to it than that. In "Faith in a Tree," Paley attributes to her protagonist what is obviously in some sense her belief as well: "Despite no education," Faith says, "Mrs. Finn always is more in charge of word meanings than I am. She is especially in charge of Good and Bad. My language limitations here are real. My vocabulary is adequate for writing notes and keeping journals but absolutely useless for an active moral life."[13] Of course Paley's stories are precisely about "an active moral life," but the subject is approached over and again by way of fluid interrogation rather than definitive statement: like Alexandra in "Enormous Changes at the Last Minute," Paley is "an enemy of generalization."[14]

And an enemy, too, of the kind of circumstantial detail that Apple calls "description-centered realism." It is worth stressing—since in this respect, as in others, she is paradigmatic of other writers discussed in this book—that, for all her concern with the ordinary, the everyday, the commonplace, Paley is not given to highly sensuous textures. The things of the world matter, certainly, but they are not the primary object of her attention; and it is therefore hardly surprising that Paley's descriptions tend to be vivid but sketchy. We hear, for example, of "the most admirable mountain or . . . the handsomest forest or hay-blown field," of "the tan deserts and the blue Van Allen belt and the green mountains of New England," or of a "sunny front room that was full of the light and shadow of windy courtyard trees."[15] Like Selena in "Friends," who is described as speaking "very matter-of-factly—just offering a few informative sentences" (p. 76), Paley favors the laconic. But only up to a point. In some ways a remarkably conceptual writer, she offers us images and conceits ("Living as I do on a turnpike of discouragement"; "my lumpen time and my bourgeois feelings"[16]) that are as witty and unexpected as Barthelme's, as eccentric as Apple's. And even that does not tell the whole story, for the tropological aspects of her storytelling are, like Barthelme's in "Basil from Her Garden," deployed so as to render the forms of feeling. The weight of Paley's stories is, above all, the weight of intersubjective acts and encounters; their density, partly the result of the repeated presence of children, friends, lovers, and husbands and, still more importantly, of the ways in which these people impinge on one another through their feelings and ideas, their needs and desires. In short, it is not the empirical world that is rendered in the universe of Paley's fiction—not first and foremost, at any rate—but the feelings that derive from being in the world and from the need, somehow, to make sense of what is not transparent to either heart or mind.

Given the fact that by now most of Paley's critics are in agreement that she is not a realist, it may seem supererogatory to labor the point. Nevertheless, old habits die hard, not to say old labels; and it is revealing that some of her most perceptive commentators, even as they reject the idea of realism, sneak it in by the back door. Kathleen Hulley, for example, having asserted that Paley's "style is neither realistic nor naturalistic," later on in her essay describes one of the "tracks" her stories run along as, precisely, "realistic."[17] Marianne DeKoven, for her part, argues that "Paley reconciles the demands of avant-garde or postmodern form for structural openness and the primacy of the surface with the seemingly incompatible demands of traditional realist material for orchestrated meaning and cathartic emotion."[18] And, most revealingly of all, Jerome Klinkowitz maintains that Paley "practices her own storytelling art with a more experimental sense of realism."[19]

My intention, however, is not to catch Paley's critics in contradictions but to confront the far more dubious and, as it seems to me, misleading assumption that, if Paley is not a realist, she is therefore, and as a result, not only a postmodernist but a metafictionist. Of those who make this argument, probably the most thoroughgoing—although he never actually uses the word metafiction—is Nicholas Peter Humy, who, in a discussion of "A Conversation with My Father," contends that the protagonist wants her father "to see the process of storytelling anew, to see how, in the telling, the story becomes defamiliarized, becomes, not what it is about, but what it *is*. And what it is is a form which, according to Shklovsky, reveals the experience of its making."[20] Humy is right, of course, that the story "reveals the experience of its making." It does not follow, however, that that is all it is "about." In fact, "A Conversation" is preeminently about different ways of apprehending life and art, and what the story denies is not the world but the world's transparency and self-evidence before language. As I indicated earlier, what *is* in doubt is our ability to grasp the world objectively, to apprehend it in a way that is not at once mediated and contingent. But for Paley, at least, contingency is a two-way street, an emblem of dependence on what we perceive as much as on the categories through which we perceive. To say, therefore, as another critic does, that "the voice of Paley's fiction . . . assumes its freedom to create its own laws and logic through play"[21] is to exaggerate the autonomy Paley claims for herself and her work and to confuse the always partly determined possibilities of midfictional invention with the theoretically absolute freedom (linguistic, at least) of poststructuralist *jeu* and *jouissance*.

Klinkowitz in his brief essay does neither of these things, but it is worth attending to his argument nevertheless. "For Grace Paley," he writes, "metafiction . . . is a peculiarly social matter, filled with the stuff of realism other metafictionists have discarded. . . . Only Grace Paley finds them [realistic conventions] to be the materials of metafiction itself."[22] But precisely because this argument is ostensibly more subtle and persuasive, it makes clear how inadequate to our understanding of contemporary literature is the draconian choice of either realism or metafiction—or, as with Klinkowitz's "experimental realism," of some combination of the two. No doubt, and to his credit, Klinkowitz senses something operative in Paley's fiction that cannot be subsumed to the notion of metafiction. But, unable to find a name and an identity for such work, he and other critics I've cited choose instead to pursue and, more, to reify what, for them, continues to be its constituent and still separable elements. It needs to be emphasized, therefore, that, by modifying and adulterating the idea of realism, by failing to take adequate account of those ontological and ideological features that must enter into its definition, these critics effectively undermine their arguments, just as they also, and more importantly, fail to recognize the integrity of what is in fact another form and vision altogether, one that is not *part* realism and *part* metafiction but uniquely and indivisibly itself. As I've been contending throughout this book, and as Paley demonstrates perhaps more than anyone else discussed in it, the binaryism of our current categories betrays the very diversity that gives to postmodern fiction in particular its vitality and richness. Which is also to argue, once again, that in order to do justice to Paley, as to the writers already considered, we require a descriptive middle ground capable of encompassing assumptions and strategies that give primacy to neither language nor the world but that seek—in ways and with means that are entirely their own—to recognize and negotiate the claims of each and both.

At issue, then, is the artist, in this case Paley, as the site where invention and receptivity join, and, by way of confronting head-on the claims of metafictionally disposed critics, it will be useful to focus on two of her more deliberately reflexive stories. What needs to be determined, most of all, is whether reflexivity implies only (and merely) a story's concern with its own fictional processes—a concern which is, furthermore, generally taken to imply a disbelief in literature's referential function—or whether, in Robert Alter's words, what we witness as we read is "the dialectic between fiction and 'reality' . . . a play of competing ontologies."[23] The remaining and longer section of "Ruthy and Edie," to which I want to return now, begins, at least, to make clear that for Paley reflexivity is to be seen not as the antithesis of referentiality but as its complement.[24]

First, however, what always matters more to Paley than such generalizations: the particulars of individual lives. Gathered together to celebrate Ruthy's fiftieth birthday, the women in the story wander among their memories and their concerns (as usual, very little "happens" by way of traditional action or plot); and it is not long before the reader recognizes as the background of these the continuity between, indeed the identity of, "the real world of boys" and the equally "real" world of men. The women find themselves, as much as when they were girls, the unwilling victims not only of specific situations and problems (international relations, war, urban blight, capitalism[25]) but more importantly, of a series of mind sets, categories, and received ideas seen, by men at any rate, as essential and eternal truths. Their task, then, is to set against this bogus essentialism an ever-renewing, existential awareness of the world, which is, as it happens, more in accord with their feelings and which is the unstated, perhaps not fully recognized agenda of their discursive talk.

This is not to suggest that Ruthy, Edie, Faith, and Ann speak with one voice or form a kind of seamlessly unified feminist collective. Edie, for example, manifestly an adult version of her younger self, is in some sense the odd woman out, the not fully awakened woman. ("Sometimes," Faith says, "I think you're half asleep" [RE, p. 123]). Tearful and intermittently hopeless, for all her idealism, Edie tells the others: "You know you three lead such adversarial lives. I hate it. What good does it do?" (p. 123). Yet, as the narrator comments, "They were all, even Edie, ideologically, spiritually, and on puritanical principle against despair" (p. 123), and it is Edie who, though "softly," says "bravo" to Ann's birthday resolution: "Let us go forth with fear and courage and rage to save the world" (p. 124). In a larger sense, therefore, the friends *are* at one, united, not necessarily in their advocacy of this or that issue, nor yet in their special ways of responding, but in their women's way of seeing, which is, most fundamentally, their impulse to save the world from the assumptions of boys and men, and from their mirroring shape: the relentless, forward-moving, sequential prison of time.

We are back, in other words, to the kinds of problems broached by Paley in "A Conversation with My Father," and it is, in fact, at this more general, almost parabolic, level that "Ruthy and Edie" operates, even as it continues to root itself in the concrete and specific: Ruth's joyous and doting response to the arrival of her young grandchild, Letty, which is shadowed by the unexplained absence of another of her daughters. As that absence betrays its effect in Ruthy's repeated hugging of Letty, the story ends:

Letty began to squirm out of Ruth's arms. Mommy, she called, Gramma is squeezing. But it seemed to Ruth that she'd better hold her even closer, because, though no one else seemed to notice—Letty, rosy and soft-cheeked as ever, was falling, already falling, falling out of her brand-new hammock of world-inventing words onto the hard floor of man-made time.   (p. 126)

The metaphor of the fall as used here is neither theological nor, except incidentally, Wordsworthian. Whereas one cannot avoid altogether an awareness of "shades of the prison-house" closing upon Letty, the narrator's phrase is intended to focus on time not as an emblem of some general human condition but as something molded specifically in the image of Man, or, more accurately, of men. Consequently, Letty's soft "world-inventing words" sum up more than the child's way of coming to terms with what surrounds her; they are Paley's and her characters' weapon against the mediations of those man-made categories that present themselves as adequate, necessary, and self-evident representations of reality itself.

But if this celebration of creativity, of "the open destiny of life" is central to "Ruthy and Edie," it is not all that the story has to say on the subject. Earlier, Ruth, meditating on Letty's movement from a "present full of milk and looking" (p. 121) to her first experiments with language, concludes: "In this simple way the lifelong past is invented, which, as we know, thickens the present and gives all kinds of advice to the future" (p. 121). No doubt the passage, like the one that closes the story, privileges the freedom of invention, but, as the context it provides makes clear, that freedom depends upon an altogether concrete and irreducible experience of the world language brings into being—but does not, as in some metafictional and poststructuralist models, simply "make up." As John R. Boly argues in a recent critique of Derrida, "no human mind can ever totally escape a perspective field with its horizon of enabling limits";[26] and if part of what Paley is after is a revelation of how paternal discourse coerces, or attempts to coerce, perception according to its own unacknowledged preconceptions, it is no less her aim to demonstrate the extent to which consciousness is anchored in the world it invents. Surely that is the burden of the narrator's comment in "A Conversation with My Father," when, arguing for the possibility of change in the character she has created, she says of her: "She's my knowledge and my invention" (p. 173). Denying the claims that either phrase, taken by itself, would seem to make—in the first case, for realism; in the second, for metafiction—the two together acknowledge as twin sources of the narrator's (and, it seems fair to say, of Paley's) inspiration: consciousness *and* the world. The phenomenological axiom according to which "the world gives itself to consciousness which confers on it its meaning" comes to hand here again. But one might as well give the last word to Paley herself. "When I was writing stories," she said in her interview with Joan Lidoff, "it was really me getting the world to speak to me."[27] In short, if "the hard floor of man-made time" awaits those who fail to keep vital the generative impulses of "world-inventing words," something more barren still attends those others for whom invention, endlessly mirroring the self-enclosed universe of poststructuralist language, floats free of the world, and of reference, altogether.

In the course of "Friends," Faith Darwin, Paley's most ubiquitous character and the narrator of the story, expresses her irritation over an allusion to the dead daughter of Selena (one of the four women to whom the title refers) as "the kid." "I didn't like to hear 'the kid,'" Faith says to herself. "I wanted to say 'Abby' the way I've said 'Selena'—so those names can take thickness and strength and fall back into the world with their weight" (*Fr*, p. 79). Thickness and strength are what characterize Paley's best work as well, and nowhere more so than in "Friends," which, of all the stories in *Later the Same Day*, most fully and skillfully realizes the possibilities, strategic and axiological, defended in "A Conversation with My Father." My emphasis on the facticity, the affective weight, of Paley's enterprise, is not, however, meant to indicate that either her conception of reality or the techniques she uses to render it assume the consistency, still less the "readability," of the world, the text, or, as some would have it, the world as text. On the contrary, and as Faith's remark makes clear, all of these are implicated in a creative, reciprocal, and ongoing relation with consciousness. "The fact of the world" (*Fr*, p. 88), as Faith later calls it, is no more (but also no less) than the fluid and unstable boundary of perception, the horizon of signification as act.

Given all this, it is hardly surprising that Paley's stories are, at their most successful, amazingly free-form. One might, for example, note that "Friends" focuses first on the visit that Faith, along with Susan and Ann, pays to the dying Selena and then on the visitors' return trip to New York. One might add too that both occasions spark memories, discussions, disagreements, revaluations, all of which disrupt and subvert the linear movement of Faith's account. But this summary hardly conveys what is most striking about "Friends," namely, the fact that its structure is so radically, if unobtrusively, associative and discursive. "Plot," Paley has said, "is only movement in time . . . but that doesn't mean it moves dead ahead in time,"[28] a remark that Virginia Woolf would have endorsed, and for similar reasons. For what both women share is the belief that the writer's obligation is not to re-present a fixed and stable reality but to suggest the ways in which an elusive "otherness" modifies, even as it is modified by, the constitutive activity of consciousness. Thus, although "Friends" is in some sense about death and dying (and, as we shall see, about their opposites), it is more immediately, or at least more fundamentally, attentive to the problem of coming to terms with experience, of sorting out perceptions and feelings that are not as simple or single as they are for, say, the characters of Carver and Beattie. In other words, like Barthelme—although her work is generally without the calculated extravagance and playfulness of fictions like "Overnight to Many Distant Cities" or "Basil from Her Garden"—Paley presents a world that is a more supple, sinuous, and mysterious place than it is for the realists; and to the degree that past and present, memory and interpretation, self and other, intermingle in the narrative to-and-fro of "Friends," what the story registers is precisely the difficulty of knowing the world, along with the still more urgent need to know it.

As the difficulty manifests itself in the fabric of the storytelling, in the low-keyed and subtle ways "Friends" keeps the reader off-balance, so the urgency makes itself felt in the affirmations the story wrests from the jumble of recollected encounters and events that Faith relives in the process of narrating them. For if, according to both Paley and Barthelme, knowledge, far from being merely a passive reception of the world's pre-existing being, is instead a response elicited by the pressures of the not-known, then it follows that knowledge is to be found only in and through the activity involved in generating it. Or, as Faith puts it, more concretely: "Though the world cannot be changed by talking to one child at a time, it may at least be known" (*Fr*, p. 78). In fact, a good deal of value-laden knowledge is generated and affirmed in "Friends," though, as its technique dictates, always hesitantly, tentatively, and, as its subject requires, with due consideration of the story's background of egoism, death, and loss.

Even without Faith's confirming remark, it is easy enough to conclude that the story dwells repeatedly on the value of act and effort. Moreover, like many other midfictional works, it does so in a way that is characteristically modest and tempered. Speaking, for example, of "our coming eviction, first from liveliness, then from life" (p. 83), Faith comments:

Luckily, I learned recently how to get out of that deep well of melancholy. Anyone can do it. You grab at roots of the littlest future, sometimes just stubs of conversation. Though some believe you miss a great deal of depth by not sinking down down down. (pp. 83–84)

Recalling Virginia Woolf again ("I want to sink deeper and deeper, away from the surface, with its hard separate facts"[29]), this time, however, by way of contrast, the passage orients itself toward the open or uncharted and, accepting life's inevitable disunities, it opts for a distinctively human rather than a quasi-metaphysical depth. The same ethos informs the story's midfictional confirmations of the ordinary and the daily as mysterious and extraordinary[30]—most notably in its treatment of the relationships, however flawed or difficult, to which the title refers. More generally, it ratifies the world as the necessary site and foundation of whatever creative gestures both "the little disturbances" and the genuine sorrows of women and men allow.

"Creative" is the key word here and becomes, if anything, still more central as "Friends" draws to its close, since in its final paragraphs the story turns reflexively on itself and reveals that, whatever else it may be, it is a meditation on art, both as a specifically literary enterprise and as an emblem of all human responses to "the fact of the world." Reacting to her son's solicitude for her, his irritation at what he takes to be her unwarranted hopefulness, and his own inconsistent vitality and gloom, Faith sums up the digressive tale she has told about herself and her friends as follows:

Meanwhile, Anthony's world—poor, dense, defenseless thing—rolls round and round. Living and dying are fastened to its surface and stuffed into its softer parts.

He was right to call my attention to its suffering and danger. He was right to harass my responsible nature. But I was right to invent for my friends and our children a report on these private deaths and the condition of our lifelong attachments.   (p. 89)

Again, the crucial concept has to do with the idea of invention, and, by way of bringing together the various threads of my argument, it may be useful one last time to explore how exactly, in its use of the term, Paley's aesthetic compares with other twentieth-century beliefs about the autotelic, mimetic, tautological, or mediative functions and powers of art. Obviously, her position is at once less magical than the modernists' and more interrogative than the realists'. Art, that is, presents itself for Paley neither as a self-sufficient counterpoint to the unsat-isfactoriness of life (art being only one value among many) nor as an instrument that simply records and comments upon a shared and common world (the world being more plastic and interpretable than this view suggests). Which is not, however, as some of her critics would have it and as Raymond Federman insists, to maintain "that reality *as such* does not exist."[31] To be sure, Paley's work, including the passage just quoted, acknowledges the ambiguities both of con-sciousness and the world; but it needs to be emphasized that art represents for her, as it does not for the metafictionists, a way of reaching out to the world, of doing justice to it by calling into question the very substantiality it also affirms.

For Paley, then, invention is a way of being in the world, the self's means of conferring significative value on what inchoately solicits and surrounds it. And it is also, in "Friends," the middle ground on which she stages the contest between living and dying and urges, in the face of rampant mortality, the claims of friendship and love. To put matters this way is, I recognize, to risk making Paley sound sentimental, but the effect of the story is neither to resolve nor to transcend, as sentimental literature does, life's fractures and disjunctions. The "report" that Faith "invents" encompasses "private deaths" as well as "lifelong attachments," so that what is at issue is not an effort to ignore or mitigate the fact of death but the attempt to accept it and, through that acceptance, to make possible the raggedly continuing activities of life. Nor is it, one must add, only the story's ending that justifies its suspensiveness and its assent. Throughout, it is the narrator's voice to which we attend, as it threads its way among the bits and pieces of past and present, giving to them a consistency that is, at best, only potentially theirs. Often defensive, at once concealing and defending its vulner-ability, sometimes even a bit hard in its jokiness, generally understated but ready, as in the description of "Anthony's world," to move into other registers, the story's various but ultimately compassionate voice is what earns "Friends" the right to its final affirmation.

Words like "compassionate" and "affirmation" threaten once again to rattle the bones of sentimentality; and so it is probably worth insisting that not only

"Friends" but Paley's work as a whole articulates what can most accurately be called an economy of gain *and* loss. "All of life is tragic," she has said, sounding for the moment very much like the father in "A Conversation." "Sorrow is just natural."[32] And indeed, as it defines itself in her three volumes of stories, life is often disappointing and frustrating, the cause, for women especially, of considerable desperation and bitterness. Displaying from the beginning signs of "man's inhumanity,"[33] it is filled, in her most recent and gloomiest collection particularly, with the certain and unmistakable odor of mortality. But although all of this is true enough, it represents only part of what Paley has to say. Against (but never in place of) the experience of inevitable and not so inevitable disillusionments and defeats she sets a sense of hope and possibility, embodied in characters who, like Aunt Rose in "Goodbye and Good Luck," consider life more their creation than their fate or who, like Virginia in another story, conclude that "all that is really necessary for survival of the fittest, it seems, is an interest in life, good, bad, or peculiar."[34] Paley's survivors exhibit, above all, pluck and determination, a capacity to enjoy what they can and to distinguish the little disturbances of man from the "catastrophes of God."[35] When all is said and done, and whatever may be urged to the contrary, it continues to be for Paley "the interesting world,"[36] as open and unpredictable as the digressive techniques she characteristically uses to express it.

Her stories, then, as compared, for example, with Beattie's more limited and lapidary efforts, aim not for a state of grace, stylistic or otherwise, but for the riskier, more human condition of world-invention: the continual and continually imperiled creation of the self in act and in time. In this sense, as in her privileging of the ordinary, Paley, for all the uniqueness of her talent, recalls the other writers discussed in this book, who would, I think, agree with the spirit of one of her recent remarks: "When I'm asked—Is she a heroine?—I'm not really interested in that, I'm not interested in that extraordinary person to that extent, except to the degree that all those people are extraordinary to *me*."[37] We are, in other words, dealing once again with the extraordinariness of the ordinary. This focus—as well as its attendant belief that change, in the nature of things, is as partial as it is slow—may, I recognize, seem in its deliberately un- or antiheroic stance to impugn the capacity of human beings definitively to shape their world and their fates. It can only be said therefore that the need for heroism of this kind, *la recherche de l'absolu*, is something less than self-evident in an age when literary, no less than political, rhetoric, whether of the right or the left, has become increasingly missionary, strident, and self-assured.

Or, perhaps, what we witness as we follow the fortunes of midfictional characters like Mad Moll, Oedipa Maas, or Faith Darwin, to choose radically different incarnations of the same impulse, is a redefinition of what it means to be heroic. Along with Paley, the novelists and short-story writers I've concentrated on seek neither, like the modernists, to substitute for the disorder of life the less assailable order of art nor, like the metafictionists in their own radically world-denying maneuvers, to gambol on the playing fields of language. To be sure, though less absolute in their hopes and beliefs, they acknowledge, along with the world's indeterminacies and imperfections, a more personal sense of loss: in Apple's case, the loss of an earlier and simpler America; in Barthelme's, of a perhaps mythic single-mindedness; in Pynchon's, of a time before men and the depredations of consciousness; in Elkin's, of the integrated self; and in Berger's, of the natural and normal, the prelapsarian ease of being in the world. Obviously, such unrealizable dreams have their effect in shaping the works of these writers, but final, all-resolving unities are not, in fact, what they are after. On the other hand, they reject as well the limits and constraints assumed by realists: the assumption of a world at once immutable and independent of creative intervention. Instead, and with a more chastened sense of the heroic, midfiction presumes, in small and modest ways, to bring about change in a world it knows it cannot ever fully control or understand. Barthelme's "wine of possibility," Elkin's manic celebration of energy, Mooney's confirmation of the human, Apple's notions of sufficiency and assent, Berger's acts of definition, Paley's "open destiny," and, most especially, Pynchon's hectic, labyrinthine pursuit of diversity, all speak to this attempt.

But in different ways. As I've been arguing from the beginning of this study, contemporary fiction has fallen victim to a too partial and exclusive sense of what it proposes, not to say, achieves. If the concept of midfiction can be seen to provide an alternative to the mutually exclusive choices of realism and metafiction, it needs itself to be thought of not as one more monolithic category but as a capacious middle ground on which broadly like-minded writers raise the most varied and heterogeneous structures. Nevertheless, even terms like midfiction and middle grounds project their own borders and boundaries, and so as to keep these as flexible as possible, it is probably wise to end by minimizing rather than stressing the constitutive powers such taxonomic categories possess. At the last, there is something to be said for focusing not only on what such works represent collectively (whether in formal or in ideological terms) but on what each of them specifically and distinctively intends.[38] In short, what joins the writers studied in this book is also, paradoxically, what distinguishes them from one another: the still lively (but no longer imperial) humanistic impulse that seeks to do justice to the world's irreducible particularity by inventing it into always unique and individual being. To what end? Partly, no doubt, to defend and confirm in acts of creation the validity of the now thoroughly beleaguered self, but also, as another of Paley's reflexive narrators says, conceding her "debts" to the immediate world around her, "in order, you might say, to save a few lives."[39]

Notes

1. Grace Paley, "Of Poetry and Women and the World," *TriQuarterly*, 65 (Winter 1986), 247. The essay will be referred to hereafter as *PWW*. The symposium, sponsored by *TriQuarterly*, was called "The Writer in Our World."

2. Joyce Meier, "The Subversion of the Father in the Tales of Grace Paley," *Delta*, 14 (1982), 122.

3. Grace Paley, "Ruthy and Edie," *Later the Same Day* (New York: Farrar, Straus & Giroux, 1985), p. 115. The story will be referred to hereafter as *RE*.

4. Meier, p. 122. See also Nicholas Peter Humy, "A Different Responsibility: Form and Technique in Grace Paley's 'A Conversation with [My] Father,'" *Delta*, 14 (1982), 87–95. For Humy, the father's conception of literature and life is basically Aristotelian.

5. Grace Paley, "A Conversation with My Father," *Enormous Changes at the Last Minute* (1974; rpt. New York: Dell Publishing Co., 1975), p. 167. The story will be referred to hereafter as *CF*.

6. On Paley's friendship with Barthelme, see Kathleen Hulley, "Interview with Grace Paley," *Delta*, 14 (1982), 38–39. On the back cover of *Enormous Changes*, Barthelme is quoted as saying: "There's no writer in our country whose work exceeds in beauty and truth that of Grace Paley." And on the back of the other two collections he describes her as "a wonderful writer and troublemaker. We are fortunate to have her in our country."

7. See Paley's remark in her interview with Hulley: "Writing does not help me deal with anything! . . . I mean if I wrote a poem, it doesn't help me to *deal with* it, [it] helps me to *think about it*" (p. 38). And see also, Joan Lidoff, "Clearing Her Throat: An Interview with Grace Paley," *Shenandoah*, 32, 3 (1981), 23.

8. Larry McCaffery, *The Metafictional Muse: The Works of Robert Coover, Donald Barthelme, and William H. Gass* (Pittsburgh: University of Pittsburgh Press, 1982), p. 5. For such a metafictional approach to invention, see Coover's "The Magic Poker," *Pricksongs & Descants* (1969; rpt. New York: New American Library, 1970). The story opens: "I wander the island, inventing it" (p. 20), and the word recurs throughout, most notably on p. 33: "At times, I forget that this arrangement is my own invention. I begin to think of the island as somehow real, its objects solid and intractable, its condition of ruin not so much *an aesthetic design* as an historical denouement" (my italics).

9. The remark appears in an interview with Nina Darnton, "Taking Risks: The Writer as Effective Teacher," *New York Times* ("Education Life," Section 12), 13 April 1986, p. 66.

10. None of which, however, rules out for Paley the possibility of change. See, for example, the poem that ends "Of Poetry and Women and the World" (pp. 252–53), which makes as clear as anything she has written her personal, social, political, and feminist agenda.

11. Grace Paley, "The Immigrant Story," *Enormous Changes at the Last Minute*, p. 180.

12. Lidoff, p. 19.

13. Grace Paley, "Faith in a Tree," *Enormous Changes at the Last Minute*, p. 91.

14. Grace Paley, "Enormous Changes at the Last Minute," *Enormous Changes at the Last Minute*, p. 130.

15. The quotations come from three different stories by Paley: "Midrash on Happiness," *TriQuarterly*, 65 (Winter 1986), 151; "Faith in a Tree," p. 95; "Friends," *Later the Same Day*, p. 85. "Friends" will be referred to hereafter as *Fr*.

16. The first quotation is from "A Woman, Young and Old," *The Little Disturbances of Man* (1959; rpt. New York: New American Library, 1973), p. 40, the second from "Faith in a Tree," p. 86. On Paley's imagery, see Marianne DeKoven's fine essay,

"Mrs. Hegel-Shtein's Tears," *Partisan Review*, 48, 2 (1981), 217–23. DeKoven speaks, rightly, of Paley's "startling, comic-bizarre language and imagery" (p. 221).

17. Kathleen Hulley, "Grace Paley's Resistant Form," *Delta*, 14 (1982), 3, 4.

18. DeKoven, p. 217.

19. Jerome Klinkowitz, "Grace Paley: The Sociology of Metafiction," *Delta*, 14 (1982), 82. Klinkowitz develops his notion of "experimental realism" in *The Self-Apparent Word: Fiction as Language / Language as Fiction* (Carbondale and Edwardsville: Southern Illinois University Press, 1984), chapter 6.

20. Humy, p. 90.

21. Diane Cousineau, "The Desires of Women, the Presence of Men," *Delta*, 14 (1982), 64.

22. Klinkowitz, p. 81.

23. Robert Alter, *Partial Magic: The Novel as a Self-Conscious Genre* (1975; rpt. Berkeley and Los Angeles: University of California Press, 1978), p. 182.

24. McCaffery, in *The Metafictional Muse*, distinguishes between two kinds of metafiction. The first, he writes, "either directly examines its own construction as it proceeds or . . . comments or speculates about the forms and language of previous fictions" (p. 16). The second seeks "to examine how *all* fictional systems operate, their methodology, the sources of their appeal, and the dangers of their being dogmatized" (p. 17). This useful distinction will serve to discriminate between different sorts of non-metafictional but still reflexive stories as well; and, as will become apparent, "Ruthy and Edie" especially belongs in the second of these groups.

25. In "Of Poetry and Women and the World," Paley asserts that "war is man-made. It's made by men. It's their thing, it's their world, and they're terribly injured in it. They suffer terribly in it, but it's made by men" (p. 247).

26. John R. Boly, "Nihilism Aside: Derrida's Debate over Intentional Models," *Philosophy and Literature*, 9 (October 1985), 163.

27. Lidoff, p. 7.

28. Lidoff, p. 18.

29. Virginia Woolf, "The Mark on the Wall," *A Haunted House and Other Stories* (New York: Harcourt, Brace & World, 1949), p. 39.

30. In her interview with Hulley, Paley said: "I'm anti-mystic too. . . . What I think is mysterious is life. What I'm trying to do is to show how mysterious ordinary life is" (p. 35).

31. Raymond Federman, "Fiction Today or the Pursuit of Non-Knowledge," *Humanities in Society*, 1 (Spring 1978), 122.

32. Hulley, "Interview," p. 30.

33. Grace Paley, "In Time Which Made a Monkey of Us All," *The Little Disturbances of Man*, p. 149.

34. Grace Paley, "An Interest in Life," *The Little Disturbances of Man*, p. 98.

35. Grace Paley, "An Interest in Life," p. 99.

36. Grace Paley, "Faith in a Tree," p. 89.

37. Lidoff, pp. 12–13.

38. By "each of them" I mean to suggest both an individual story or novel and, more comprehensively, the body of a particular author's work.

39. Grace Paley, "Debts," *Enormous Changes at the Last Minute*, p. 18.

Index

Abrams, M. H., 9

Acceptance, 27, 29, 36, 59–61, 64, 68, 94, 113, 121, 123, 127, 130n33, 132, 137, 139, 142, 146, 147, 156, 162, 170, 183

Adams, Henry, 14n14

Affirmation, 27, 183; in Max Apple, 29, 39n21, 134, 142; in Barthelme, 37, 121–123, 127–128; in Berger, 68; of diversity in Pynchon, 10; in Elkin, 39n21; in Forster, 10; and midfiction, 22; in Paley, 183; of parable, 27; of referential function of contemporary literature, 6; of self, 152. *See also* Acceptance; Assent; Suspensiveness

Alter, Robert, 20, 23n7, 178, 187n23

Althusser, Louis, 14n14

Altieri, Charles, 13n9, 105–107, 110, 128n5

Anderson, Wilda C., 14n21

Antihumanism, Antihumanists, 11; and American criticism, 8; and defense of difference, 10–11; and Merleau-Ponty, 108; and metafictionists, 108, 124; and postmodern writing, 6; and poststructuralist theory, 6, 108; and Pynchon, 9; restrictiveness of, 9; and Spanos, 8–9; and surfictionists, 108. *See also* Humanism, Humanists

Apple, Max, 3, 4, 7, 12, 28–30, 37, 131–156, 157n1, 157n12, 157n13, 157n16; acceptance in, 29, 132, 137, 139, 142, 146–147, 156; affirmation in, 29, 39n21, 134, 142; assent in, 156, 185; and death, 135–136, 139–141, 145–147, 152, 156; and diversity, 12, 132, 152; as experimental but not self-referential, 18; existential ethic in, 6, 151; and the extraordinary, 6, 141, 144, 151; and humanism, 6, 12, 151; "incoherence" in, 133, 140; intentional structures in, 148; as ironist, 28–29, 136, 154–156; and Kierkegaard, 152; language in, 33; and limits, 141, 144, 151–152; loss in, 185; and metafiction, 155; middle grounds in, 4, 137, 145; and midfiction, 140, 142, 144, 157n15; and midfictionists, 94, 155, 185; and modernism, 29–30, 36, 132, 136, 155; morality of, 29–30, 136–137; and New Criticism, 132–134; and openness of form in, 29, 136; and the ordinary, 6, 141, 144, 151–152, 155; and parable, 140–141; and possibility, 37, 134, 137, 141, 147, 151, 156; and postmodernism, 132–133, 141, 156; and Paley, 176; and Pynchon, 94; and realism, 28, 38–39n8, 141, 143–144, 151, 153, 155, 157n15, 176; as satirist, 136, 157n11; and self, 137, 142, 152–154, 156; and self-consciousness, 153; and self-sufficiency, 155–156; and smallness, 28–29; and stories as fairy tales, 134–136, 141, 150–151; and style, 155; subversion of midfictional impulses in, 144; sufficiency in, 140, 151, 153, 155, 185; suspensiveness in, 29, 37, 137, 139–142; values in, 134, 139 —— works: "The American Bakery," 39n10,

189

Apple, Max (*cont.*)
146, 154; "Bridging," 140, 149, 151, 158n21;
"Business Talk," 144–145; "Carbo-Loading,"
141, 145, 157n14; "Disneyad" (*see* "Walt and
Will"); "The Eighth Day," 142, 144–145;
"Eskimo Love," 140, 146–155; "The Four
Apples," 158n24; "Free Agents," 37, 141,
144–145, 151, 156, 157n14; *Free Agents*,
39n10, 131–133, 140–156, 157n9, 157n14,
157n15, 158n21; "Gas Stations," 134–135,
137, 142, 150, 155; "Help," 144–145; "In-
side Norman Mailer," 134, 137, 142; "Kitty
Partners," 144–145; "Momma's Boy," 144;
"My Real Estate," 134–135, 137; "The Na-
tional Debt," 158n24; "Noon," 135, 137;
"On Persisting as a Writer," 155, 158n22;
"On Realism," 39n8; "The Oranging of
America," 28–29, 134–135, 137–138, 153,
157n9; *The Oranging of America*, 37, 131,
133–146, 149–154, 156, 157n8; "Patty-
Cake, Patty-Cake . . . a Memoir," 137;
"Pizza Time," 149–150; "Post-Modernism,"
144; "Selling Out," 134, 136; "Small Island
Republics," 28–30, 33–36, 39n9, 143, 145,
157n12; "Stranger at the Table," 153–154;
"Understanding Alvarado," 132, 137; "Vegetable Love," 134, 138–140, 142, 146, 148,
153; "Walt and Will," 142–143, 145, 154–
155; "The Yogurt of Vasirin Kefirovsky," 136;
Zip, 132, 150–151, 153–155, 157n17
Arnold, Matthew, 9, 11, 14n14, 71n7
Assent, 22, 36–37, 68, 113, 121–123, 130n33,
156, 167, 183, 185. *See also* Acceptance; Affirmation
Auden, W. H., 38n5
Auerbach, Erich, 9, 21
Author, theories of the, 46–47, 51–52; attack
against traditional, in Barthes, 44, 46,
54n12; in Baudry, 44; and Berger, 43–44,
46, 53; in Bersani, 132; in Derrida, 44; in
Federman, 44; in Foucault, 44; in contemporary criticism, 44, 132–133, 157n5; and
location of the author, 51–52; and midfiction, 45; and Merleau-Ponty, 47, 51;
phenomenological, 46–47, 51–53, 132;
postmodern, 44, 132–133, 157n5

Babbitt, Irving, 9
Bailey, Peter, J., 39n12
Bakhtin, M. M., 80, 101n12
Banks, Russell, 7
Barth, John, 18, 45
Barthes, Roland, 6, 19, 23n5, 44, 46, 54n12,

105–106, 109, 128n4, 157n6
Barthelme, Donald, 6, 105–106, 156, 161–
171, 171n1, 171n12, 181; acceptance of the
world in, 36, 121, 123, 162, 170; affirmation
in, 37, 121–123, 127–128; assent in, 36–37,
121–123, 167; and Carver, 118; and consciousness, 167–168; and dialogic form, 35,
161–164, 171n3, 171n4; and diversity, 37;
excluded from reflexivists, 18; and experimental literature, 12n1, 124; and the extraordinary, 36–37, 123–125, 170; "father" as
emblem of humanism in, 106; and "forms of
feeling," 165–166, 176; and homosexuality,
86; and humanism, 10, 104–106; and intention, 122; intentionality in, 170; and interrogation of meaning, 121; and invention, 6–7,
166, 175; ironic affirmation in, 128; and
irony, 123, 162; and knowledge, 182; and
language, 35, 165–166; and limits, 120–121;
and loss, 185; and metafiction, 6–7, 34–35,
75, 121–122, 130n32, 165–166, 171; and
middle grounds, 4, 166, 168, 170; and
middles, 75; as midfictionist, 34–35, 37, 94,
121–124, 128, 166, 185; and mimesis, 166;
and modernism, 36–37, 100; and moral criticism and fiction, 4, 34–35, 37–38, 120,
122–123, 165, 170; and the ordinary, 35–37,
122–123, 128, 162, 168, 170; and organic
criticism, 133; and Paley, 174–176, 181,
186n6; and parable, 128n1; and parody, 45,
133; and phenomenology, 167–168; and play,
165; and possibility, 34, 128, 168, 185; and
postmodernism, 162, 165; and poststructuralist theory, 165, 168–169; and Pynchon, 86,
94, 100; and randomness 121; and realism,
120–121, 166; and reality, 121; and reference, 166–167; and referential nature of his
fiction, 35, 39n22, 121, 170; and reflexiveness, 34, 165–166; and rejection of depth,
121; and skepticism, 122; and smallness, 12,
104, 117, 165; and suspensiveness, 36, 121
—— works: "The Abduction from the Seraglio," 130n39; "Basil from Her Garden," 121,
161–166, 168–170, 171n7, 176, 181; "The
Catechist," 172n15; "City Life," 35, 169,
172n16; *City Life*, 171n4, 171n11; *Come
Back, Dr. Caligari*, 130n37, 171n8; *The
Dead Father*, 12, 14n22, 35, 38, 40n26,
54n19, 100, 104–105, 108, 117, 120,
128n1, 165, 171n4; "The Death of Edward
Lear," 35; "The Dolt," 100n1; "The Emerald," 34–38, 39–40n23, 123, 130n36, 164,
171n9; "Engineer-Private Paul Klee," 35,

Kaelin, Eugene, F., 47, 51–52, 54n11, 54n15, 54n20
Kakutani, Michiko, 129n23
Kant, Immanuel, 20
Kierkegaard, Søren, 152–153, 155, 157n18, 161, 165,
Klee, Paul, 54n19
Klinkowitz, Jerome, 23n4, 168, 171n12, 177–178, 187n19, 187n22

Langer, Susanne, 165–167
Lawall, Sarah, 54n11
Lawrence, D. H., 32, 85
Leavis, F. R., 9
LeClair, Thomas, 39n12, 39n13, 39n15, 39n18
Leverenz, David, 101n17, 102n22
Levine, George, 90, 102n31, 109–110, 129n13, 129n17
Levine, Martin, 158n20
Lévi-Strauss, Claude, 67
Lidoff, Joan, 180, 186n7, 186n12, 187n27, 187n28, 187n37
Lodge, David, 17, 23n9

McCaffery, Larry, 12n1, 33–34, 38n1, 39n16, 39n18, 45, 53n6, 103n43, 121–122, 130n32, 172n13, 175, 186n8, 187n24
McCaffery, Larry and Sinda Gregory, 14n23, 143–144, 153, 157n2, 157n12, 157n13, 158n20
McFague, Sallie, 25–27, 34, 37, 38n2, 38n3
MacNeice, Louis, 38n5
Macquarrie, John, 107, 129n10
Magliola, Robert R., 52, 54n11, 54n14, 54n21, 54n22,
Mailer, Norman, 157n13
Mallarmé, Stéphane, 171
Marin, Louis, 25, 38n4
Marxism, 11
Meier, Joyce, 174, 186n2, 186n4
Mendelson, Edward, 98, 100–101n3, 101n9, 103n40, 103n41
Merleau-Ponty, Maurice, 46–48, 50–53, 53–54n9, 54n18, 54n19, 124, 133; and antihumanists, 108; and authorial self, 46, 52; and concept of the "intentional arc," 63; and consciousness, 47, 55; and contingency, 50, 107; and definition of modern humanism, 107–108; vs. empiricism, 47; and existential cast of ideas, 47; and existential criticism, 52; fissures and lacunae in, 53; and humanism, 107–108, 129n11; vs. idealism, 47; inten-

tionality in, 47, 50; and midfiction, 50–51, 124; vs. mimesis, 47; vs. nonreferentiality, 47; and perception, 47–48, 50–52; and phenomenological consciousness, 133; and phenomenological theories of authorship, 46–48, 51–52; and postmodernism, 50–51; and poststructuralism, 50. See also Intentionality; Phenomenology
——— works: Phenomenology of Perception, 47–48, 54n9, 63, 70n5; The Primacy of Perception and Other Essays, 47, 50, 53–54n9; The Prose of the World, 47–48, 54n9; Signs, 47–48, 50–52, 54n9, 129n11; Sense and Non-Sense, 46, 50, 54n9, 157n7
Metafiction, Metafictionists, 3, 4, 19, 24, 27, 103n43, 110, 121, 130n32, 185; antihumanism of, 108, 124; antimimetic bias of, 22, 55; and Apple, 155; authorial intention in, 44–45; authorial voice in, 133; and Barthelme, 6–7, 34–35, 75, 121–122, 130n32, 165–166, 171; denial of limits in, 124; equated with experimentalism, 3; fabulation and, 38n1; Federman as exponent of, 4; and "fictional" status of the author, 45; identified with reflexivity, 18–19, 22; and the imagination, 7, 130n32; and the inflexibility of modernism, 51; and invention, 175; and language, 185; and midfiction, 7, 38, 124, 130n32, 184–185; and Paley, 7, 175, 177–178, 180, 183–185; and parable, 25–26; and Pynchon, 94, 103n43; and realism, 22, 34, 49, 110, 121, 177–178; referential nature of, 22, 121; and reflexiveness, 18–19, 22, 24, 44–45, 133; skepticism of, 10–11; Sukenick as exponent of, 4; supposed decline of, 18; and the word, 124. See also Federman; Reflexiveness; Sukenick; Surfiction
Middle grounds, 3–6, 22–23, 166, 178, 185; in Apple, 4, 137, 145; in Barthleme, 4, 166, 168, 170; in Elkin, 4; boundaries of, 185; and humanism, 108; interrogation in, 22; in midfiction, 22–24, 39n20, 185; in Paley, 178, 183; in Phenomenology, 5; in Pynchon, 6, 77, 80, 82, 85, 88–90, 92–93, 95, 97, 100. See also Midfiction
Middles, 3, 5, 12, 17–23, 75–100. See also Middle grounds; Midfiction; Pynchon
Midfiction, 5, 7–8, 11–12, 24, 26, 34, 39n20, 45, 50, 77, 108, 113, 124, 127–128, 130n32, 142, 166, 184–185; and affirmation, 22; as alternative to realism and metafiction, 185; and Apple, 94, 140, 142, 144, 155, 157n15, 185; and assent, 22; and the

author, 45; and Bartheleme, 34–35, 37, 94, 121–124, 128, 166, 185; and Berger, 45–46, 64–65, 94, 185; and catatonic realists, 122, 124; consciousness in, 46, 124; creation of existential definition in, 11, 124; creation of self in, 11, 108, 185; and contemporary realism, 124; and contingency in, 27; definition of, 34, 39n20; and Didion, 113–114; and diversity, 8; and Elkin, 32–33, 185; as it eschews the extremes of realism and metafiction, 34, 124, 184–185; and experimentalism, 23; and the extraordinary, 27, 34, 124, 182; humanism as a challenge to, 108; and humanism, 108, 123–124, 127–128, 185; invention in, 6; and irony, 128, 156; and language, 33; and loss, 184–185; meaning in 34, 37; and metafiction, 7, 38, 124, 130n32, 184–185; and Merleau-Ponty, 50–51, 124; and middle grounds, 22–24, 39n20, 185; and modernism, 34, 50–51, 184–185; and Mooney, 124–127, 185; and New Criticism, 34; and the ordinary, 27, 34, 114, 124, 128, 182; and Paley, 177, 182, 184–185; vs. parable, 25–27, 34, 37–38; and parody, 45, 53n3, 125; and possibility, 27, 127–128; vs. postmodern forms, 34, 124; and Pynchon, 5, 77, 94, 98–100, 185; and questioning of the author, 45; and reality, 124; and recognition of limits, 127; referential nature of, 45; and rejection of metafiction's reflexiveness, 24, 124; and rejection of realism's belief in mimesis, 24; and rejection of surfictionists, 124; representational function of, 45; as response to realism, 7, 23–24, 26, 34, 38, 108, 120–121, 185; secularism of, 26; and self, 11, 108, 185; smallness as aim of, 12, 108, 124, 128; suspensiveness of 27, 29; testing limits of, 124; values in, 127; and the word, 124. *See also* Suspensiveness; Reflexiveness

Miller, J. Hillis, 52, 54n11

Modernism, 6, 19–20, 27, 51, 68, 121, 128, 129n16, 133, 185; and Apple, 29–30, 36, 132, 136, 155; and Barthelme, 36–37, 100; and Berger, 56, 68; and closure, 129n16; and Elkin, 30–32, 36, 100; and Federman, 19; and form, 52; and midfiction, 34, 50–51, 184–185; and Paley, 183–185; and parable, 25–27; and postmodernism, 19, 27, 50–51, 110; primitivism of, 31, 99; and Pynchon, 94–95, 99–100; and realism, 109–110, 129n16; and significant form, 19–20; slogans of attack in, 44; structures of recurrence in, 53; and Sukenick, 19; unity in, 133

Molesworth, Charles, 53n4, 121, 130n32

Mooney, Ted, 3, 124–128; *Easy Travel to Other Planets*, 124–128, 130n38; and consciousness, 126; and the extraordinary, 124–125; as ideological alternative to realists and metafictionists, 6; irony in, 126, 128; and midfiction, 124–127, 185; and the ordinary, 128; and parody, 125

Moral Criticism and moral fiction, 4–5, 105; in Apple, 30, 136–137; in Barthelme, 4, 34–35, 37–38, 120, 122–123, 165, 170; in Berger, 43, 65; in Elkin, 37–38; impasse of in literature, 8; and middle grounds, 4; and midfiction, 34, 38; in Paley, 176; and parable, 26

More, Paul Elmer, 9

Morrison, Toni, 7

New Criticism, 9, 34, 81, 132–133

Nietzsche, Friedrich, 44

Nochlin, Linda, 17, 23n2

Nohrnberg, James, 102–103n40

Norris, Christopher, 48, 54n16

O'Donnell, Patrick, 12n1

O'Hara, Daniel T., 13n6, 13n9

O'Hara, J. D., 121–123, 130n31, 130n32, 171n10

Olderman, Raymond, 39n18

Olson, Charles, 105, 107

Ordinary, the, 5, 184. *See also* Apple; Barthelme; Berger; Didion; Elkin; Extraordinary, the; Humanism; Midfiction; Mooney; Paley; Parable; Pynchon

Orwell, George, 38n5, 63

Oxenhandler, Neal, 53n8

Ozier, Lance W., 90–91, 101n18, 102n33, 102n35, 102n36, 102n37

Paley, Grace, 173–185; aesthetic of, 183; acceptance in, 183; affirmation in, 183; assent in, 183; and Apple, 176; and Barthelme, 174–176, 181, 186n6; and Beattie, 184; and consciousness, 180–181, 183; and diversity of postmodern fiction, 178; and the extraordinary, 182, 184; feminist ethic of, 173, 179, 186n10; "forms of feeling" in, 176; and imagination, 175; and invention, 175, 178, 180, 183–184; irony in, 174; and knowledge, 182; language in, 178, 180; and loss, 184–185; and metafiction, 7, 175, 177–178, 180, 183–184; middle grounds in, 178, 183; and midfiction, 177, 182, 184–185; and modern-

Paley, Grace (*cont.*)
    ists, 183–185; and morality, 176; and "open
    destiny," 185; and the ordinary, 176, 182,
    184, 187n30; and otherness, 181; and par-
    able, 179; and phenomenology, 176, 180;
    and plot, 181; as postmodernist, 177–178;
    and poststructuralism, 177, 180; and realism,
    176–178, 180; and realists, 175–177, 181,
    183; and reality, 178–181, 183; referentiality
    in, 178, 180; reflexiveness of, 178, 182; and
    self, 181, 183–184; and suspensiveness, 183;
    value of act and effort in, 182; and world as
    text, 181
    ———— works: "A Conversation with My Fa-
    ther," 174–175, 177, 179–181, 184, 186n5;
    "Debts," 187n39; "Enormous Changes at the
    Last Minute," 176, 186n14; *Enormous
    Changes at the Last Minute*, 176, 184,
    186n5, 186n11, 186n13, 186n14, 187n39;
    "Faith in a Tree," 173, 176, 186n13,
    186n15, 186n16, 187n36; "Friends," 180–
    184, 186n15; "Goodbye and Good Luck,"
    184; "The Immigrant Story," 175, 186n11;
    "In Time Which Made a Monkey of Us All,"
    187n33; "An Interest in Life," 187n34,
    187n35; *Later the Same Day*, 181, 184,
    186n3, 186n15; *The Little Disturbances of
    Man*, 184, 186n16, 187n33, 187n34; "Liv-
    ing," 173; "Midrash on Happiness," 186n15;
    "Of Poetry and Women and the World,"
    173–175, 186n1, 186n10, 187n25; "Ruthy
    and Edie," 173–174, 178–180, 186n3,
    187n24; "A Woman, Young and Old,"
    186n16
Parable, 25–27, 29–30; affirmation of, 27; in
    Bartheleme, 128n1; in Beattie, 116; in Ber-
    ger, 43, 56, 65; compared to midfiction, 25–
    27, 34, 37–38; continual alteration of, 25;
    distinguished from metafiction, 25–26; and
    Elkin, 34; and the extraordinary, 27; and
    modernism, 25–27; as moral fiction, 26;
    and the ordinary, 25, 27, 34; and Paley, 179;
    and postmodernism, 26–27; preference for
    open over closed form in, 25; and realism,
    25–26; and revisionary theology, 25–27, 34,
    38n2, 38n3
Parody, 5, 45, 53n3, 57, 66, 71n7, 80, 100,
    125, 133
Pearce, Richard, 102n38, 103n42
Pearlstein, Philip, 27
Phenomenological Criticism. *See* Phenome-
    nology
Phenomenology, 5, 7, 46, 52; and Barthelme,

167–168, 172n15; and Berger, 5, 46, 66, 68–
    69; combined with ethical criticism, 5; and
    congruence with postmodernism, 50–51; and
    consciousness, 21, 52, 133, 168, 180; and
    deconstruction, 48; defense of and Derrida,
    50; and existentialist criticism, 51–52; and
    hermeneutical studies, 4; and "incoherence"
    in contemporary fiction, 4; intentional struc-
    tures in, 5; intentionality of consciousness in,
    47, 50, 81; language as a challenge to, 50;
    and middle grounds, 5; and Paley, 176, 180;
    and phenomenological criticism, 46; as phi-
    losophy of presence, 48; postmodernism as
    challenge to, 50; postmodern and poststruc-
    turalist objections to, 48, 50; as practical crit-
    icism, 48; and psychology, 52; in Pynchon,
    5, 81–82; and reader-response criticism, 4;
    and reading, 48–49; reference and meaning
    in, 48; and self-effacing empathy of phenom-
    enological studies, 4–5; strengths and limita-
    tions of, 4; theories of authorship in, 46–47,
    51–53, 132. *See also* Intentionality; Merleau-
    Ponty
Poirier, Richard, 81, 101n16, 102n21
Pollitt, Katha, 115, 130n26
Pope, Alexander, 31
Popper, Karl, 20
Postmodernism, Postmodernists, 36, 51, 68,
    110, 121, 124, 129n16; acceptance in, 121,
    132; aims of, 27; antiformalism of, 52–53;
    antihumanism of, 6; in Apple, 132–133,
    141, 156; attacks against phenomenology in,
    48, 50; and the author, 44, 132–133, 157n5;
    and the authorial self, 45; and Barthelme,
    162, 165; and Berger, 56, 59, 64, 68; and
    centers, 54n23; conjoined with contemporary
    realism, 110; diminished scale of, 110; and
    humanism, 6, 104, 110; incoherence in, 4,
    133; and irony, 156; and limits, 124; and
    Merleau-Ponty's philosophy, 50–51; midfic-
    tion distinguished from, 34; midfiction and
    rejection of extremes of, 124; and modernist
    heritage, 19, 27, 50–51, 110; and order, 36;
    and Paley, 177–178; and parable, 26–27; and
    phenomenology, 48, 50; and Pynchon, 81,
    93–94, 99; randomness and contingency of
    world in, 110, 114; and realism, 121, 124,
    129n16; and referential function of contem-
    porary literature, 6; and reflexive writing, 19;
    and smallness, 29; and structures of recur-
    rence in, 53. *See also* Reflexiveness; Metafic-
    tion
Poststructuralism, Poststructuralists, 45, 133,

145, 169; aesthetics of the text in, 105; anti-humanism of, 6, 108; and attacks on humanism, 6, 8–11, 105–108; and attacks on phenomenology, 48, 50; and the author, 132–133, 157n5; and Barthesian sign-system, 19; and Barthelme, 165, 168–169; and Berger, 44, 56, 61; and death of the autonomous self, 44; and defense of difference, 10; dispersing thematic centers in, 56; and humanist heritage, 104; and language, 167; and Merleau-Ponty's philosophy, 50; and metacriticism, 19; and opposition to Marxism, 11; and Paley, 177, 180; and referential function of contemporary fiction, 6; and the self, 61, 95, 105; skepticism of, 10–11

Poulet, George, 132

Practical criticism, 48, 133

Primitivism, 31–33, 36, 56, 60, 69, 85, 90–91, 99

Pynchon, Thomas, 3, 7, 75–100, 101n4, 101n10; and acceptance, 94; and affirmation, 10; as antihumanist, 9; and Apple, 94; and Barthelme, 86, 94, 100; and Berger, 86, 94; and binaryism, 75, 79, 90–91, 93, 95, 97, 166; and the body, 85; and closure, 99; and Conrad, 80–82, 87–89, 91–92, 101n4, 101n15; consciousness in, 84–85, 99; diversity in, 10, 97, 100, 185; "double vision" in, 4, 75, 80, 90; and Elkin, 100; and entropy, 79–80, 86–87, 92; extraordinary resisted in, 93; and experimental literature, 12n1, 18; extremism of, 6, 77, 79–80, 84–85, 88–93, 96; and Forster, 10, 14n17; and homosexuality, 85–88; humanism in, 10, 80–81, 89, 92–93, 97, 99; idealistic tendency in, 95; as ideological alternative to realists and metafictionists, 6; intentionality in, 81–82, 93, 98; intentional structures in, 5, 75–76; intention in, 5, 75–76, 78, 81, 89; limits in, 6; loss in, 185; and metafiction, 94, 103n43; middle grounds in, 6, 77, 80, 82, 85, 88–90, 92–93, 95, 97, 100; middles (and exclusion of) in, 5, 75–77, 82, 91, 93, 97, 100; and midfiction, 5, 77, 94, 98–100, 185; and modernism, 94–95, 99–100; and New Critics, 81; and the ordinary, 93; and organic criticism, 133; and openendedness, 99; and order as meaning, 94; and parody, 5, 80, 100; and phenomenology, 5, 81–82; and possibility, 91–93, 98–99; and postmodernism, 81, 93–94, 99; and poststructuralist attack on self, 95; primitivism in, 90–91, 99; randomness and contingency in, 94; reflexivity in, 99; referentiality in, 100; religious imagery in, 94, 98; self in, 93–95, 100; and smallness, 108; and suspensiveness, 6, 98; and values, 77, 82–83, 89, 101n5

——— works: *Gravity's Rainbow*, 5–6, 75–94, 97–100, 100n2, 101n4, 101n15, 101n17, 102n22, 102n23, 102n29, 102n30, 102n32, 102n38, 103n40; *The Crying of Lot 49*, 5–6, 8, 10, 13n7, 14n16, 75–77, 92–100, 100n2, 100–101n3, 102–103n40, 103n42; "Mortality and Mercy in Vienna," 101n15; *Slow Learner*, 93, 102n39; *V.*, 5–6, 12n2, 75–82, 84, 86, 90–94, 97–99, 100n2, 101n5, 101n9, 101n11, 101n15, 102n38

Realism, 4, 18, 20, 22, 23n1, 23n9, 27, 109–110, 120, 127; in Apple, 28, 38–39n8, 141, 143–144, 151, 153, 155, 157n15, 176; ascendancy of, 18; and Barthelme, 120–121, 166; and Berger, 61, 64, 68; and Bellow, 4, 22; catatonic realism as a form of, 6, 112, 114–115, 117, 119–120, 122, 124; conjoined with postmodernism, 110; as a contemporary form, 3–4, 6–7, 17–18, 22, 108, 110–111, 115–117, 119, 121, 127; diminished scale of, 110; and experimentalism, 18; and humanism, 108, 110–111; and humanism as a challenge to, 108; and limits, 120; and metafiction, 22, 34, 49, 110, 121, 177–178; and middle grounds, 39n20; and midfiction, 7, 23, 26, 34, 38, 108, 120–121; midfiction as an alternative to, 24, 34, 185; and mimesis, 3, 21–22, 24, 109; and modernism, 109–110, 129n16; and parable, 25–26; and postmodernism, 121, 124, 129n16; and referential function of literature, 20; and self, 108; and smallness, 108, 117; and surfiction, 49; in Updike, 4, 22, 129n16. *See also* Beattie; Carver; Didion; Paley; Pynchon; Robison

Reference (Referential fiction), 4, 6, 20, 22, 24, 35, 39n22, 100, 121, 166–167, 170, 180

Reflexiveness (Reflexive fiction), 4, 18, 20, 22, 23n7, 27; and Barth, 18; and Barthelme, 18, 34, 165–166; and Berger, 55, 59; and Carver, 118; and Coover, 18; and current theory, 20, 55; and experimental writing, 18–19; and Federman, 18; and Gass, 18; and middle grounds of midfiction, 4, 39n20; midfiction as an alternative to, 24; and Paley, 178, 182; and postmodernism, 19; and reflexivity as experimentalism's far-left wing, 4, 18–19; and

Reflexiveness (*cont.*)
   Pynchon, 99; and Sukenick, 18. *See also* Experimentalism; Metafiction; Surfiction
Reid, Alastair, 37
Rhys, Jean, 109
Richard, Jean-Pierre, 132
Richards, I. A., 9
Rilke, Rainer Maria, 90
Robbe-Grillet, Alain, 105–106, 128n7
Robison, Mary, 4, 6, 108, 115, 119, 130n25; as catatonic realist, 115
Romanticism, 20, 31, 56
Rose, Margaret, 53n4

Said, Edward, 9
Sanders, Scott, 39n15, 39n19, 78–79, 84, 101n10, 102n32
Sartre, Jean-Paul, 168
Saussure, Ferdinand de, 56
Scarron, Paul, 49
Schaub, Thomas H., 102n25, 102n38, 103n43
Schmitz, Neil, 102n29
Scholes, Robert, 13n8, 23n4, 38n1
Seidel, Michael, 87, 102n27
Self, the, 20; as "absent," 133; in Apple, 137, 142, 152–154, 156; attacks against, 44–46; in Berger, 46, 61–62, 66, 69; and Carver, 112; concept of coherence of, 44; death of, 44; existential limits of, 152; fear of, 114–115; in Kierkegaard, 152–153; loss of, 44; in midfictional writers, 11, 108, 185; in Paley, 181, 183–184; and phenomenology, 46; and poststructuralism, 61, 95, 105; in Pynchon, 93–95, 100; and realism, 108; and significant form, 19–20
Shinn, Roger, 107, 129n10
Shklovsky, Victor, 177
Sinclair, Upton, 171
Sklar, Robert, 78, 101n8
Slade, Joseph, 75, 100n3, 101n15, 101n20
Smallness, 104–128; in Apple, 28–29; in Barthelme, 12, 104, 117, 165; in Beattie, 117, 119; in contemporary realism, 108; and humanism, 108, 128; in midfiction, 12, 108, 124, 128; in postmodernism, 29; in Pynchon, 108
Smith, Marcus and Khachig Tololyan, 102n30
Spanos, William V., 8–11, 13n9, 13n10, 13–14n11, 14n15, 105–108, 110, 128n6
Spitzer, Leo, 52, 54n22
Stern, J. P., 22, 23n1, 109–110, 129n12, 129n15, 175–176
Sterne, Laurence, 49

Stevick, Philip, 12n1
Stimpson, Catherine, 86, 102n24
Straus, Erwin, 168
Structuralism, 52, 56, 104–105, 132
Sukenick, Ronald, 4, 18–19; covert aestheticism of, 19; and experimentalism, 12n1; as metafictionist, 4; and modernism, 19; and postmodernism, 19; as reflexivist, 18; as surfictionist, 4. *See also* Metafiction; Surfiction
Surfiction, Surfictionists, 19–20, 22, 44–45, 126; antihumanism of, 108, 124; attempts to dissolve authorial intention in, 44; and consciousness, 19; Federman as exponent of, 4; and language, 124; and midfiction, 124; and modernism, 20; and Mooney, 126; and realism, 49; and reflexivity, 19–20, 44–45; and significant form, 19; Sukenick as exponent of, 4; and the word, 124
Suspensiveness, 27; and Apple, 29, 37, 137, 139–142; and Barthelme, 36, 121; and Berger, 60, 64–65, 68; and midfiction, 27, 29; and Paley, 183; and Pynchon, 6, 98
Swift, Jonathan, 60, 87

Tanner, Tony, 77, 100–101n3, 101n6, 101n7, 101n13, 101n15
Thale, Jerome, 89, 102n28
Thévenaz, Pierre, 21, 23n8, 167–168, 172n14
Todorov, Tzvetan, 8, 11, 13n8, 14n20
Tolstoy, Leo, 28
Trilling, Lionel, 9, 14n14

Undank, Jack, 14n21
Updike, John, 4, 22, 68, 129n16

Valéry, Paul, 107
Vannatta, Dennis, 157n11
Varo, Remedios, 95
Voltaire (François-Marie Arouet), 11
Vonnegut, Kurt, 26

Warner, Rex, 38n5
Waugh, Patricia, 38n1
Wilde, Alan, *Horizons of Assent*, 7, 12–13n5, 23n7, 38n7, 39n16, 39n21, 128n2, 130n33, 157n9, 171n1
Williams, Raymond, 14n14
Wittgenstein, Ludwig, 162
Wolcott, James, 116, 130n29
Wolfley, Lawrence, 102n23
Woolf, Virginia, 32, 94, 101n4, 109, 181–182, 187n29
Wordsworth, William, 179